Programming Wireless Devices with the Java™ 2 Platform, Micro Edition

The Java™ Series

Lisa Friendly, Series Editor
Tim Lindholm, Technical Editor
Ken Arnold, Technical Editor of The Jini™ Technology Series
Jim Inscore, Technical Editor of The Java™ Series, Enterprise Edition

Ken Arnold, James Gosling, David Holmes
The Java™ Programming Language, Third Edition

Joshua Bloch
Effective Java™ Programming Language Guide

Greg Bollella, James Gosling, Ben Brosgol, Peter Dibble,
Steve Furr, David Hardin, Mark Turnbull
The Real-Time Specification for Java™

Mary Campione, Kathy Walrath, Alison Huml
The Java™ Tutorial, Third Edition:
A Short Course on the Basics

Mary Campione, Kathy Walrath, Alison Huml,
Tutorial Team
The Java™ Tutorial Continued:
The Rest of the JDK™

Patrick Chan
The Java™ Developers Almanac 2000

Patrick Chan, Rosanna Lee
The Java™ Class Libraries, Second Edition, Volume 2:
java.applet, java.awt, java.beans

Patrick Chan, Rosanna Lee
The Java™ Class Libraries Poster, Sixth Edition, Part 1

Patrick Chan, Rosanna Lee
The Java™ Class Libraries Poster, Sixth Edition, Part 2

Patrick Chan, Rosanna Lee, Doug Kramer
The Java™ Class Libraries, Second Edition, Volume 1:
java.io, java.lang, java.math, java.net, java.text, java.util

Patrick Chan, Rosanna Lee, Doug Kramer
The Java™ Class Libraries, Second Edition, Volume 1:
Supplement for the Java™ 2 Platform,
Standard Edition, v1.2

Kirk Chen, Li Gong
Programming Open Service Gateways with Java™
Embedded Server

Zhiqun Chen
Java Card™ Technology for Smart Cards:
Architecture and Programmer's Guide

Li Gong
Inside Java™ 2 Platform Security:
Architecture, API Design, and Implementation

James Gosling, Bill Joy, Guy Steele, Gilad Bracha
The Java™ Language Specification, Second Edition

Jonni Kanerva
The Java™ FAQ

Doug Lea
Concurrent Programming in Java™, Second Edition:
Design Principles and Patterns

Rosanna Lee, Scott Seligman
JNDI API Tutorial and Reference:
Building Directory-Enabled Java™ Applications

Sheng Liang
The Java™ Native Interface:
Programmer's Guide and Specification

Tim Lindholm and Frank Yellin
The Java™ Virtual Machine Specification, Second Edition

Vlada Matena and Beth Stearns
Applying Enterprise JavaBeans™:
Component-Based Development for the J2EE™ Platform

Roger Riggs, Antero Taivalsaari, Mark VandenBrink
Programming Wireless Devices with the Java™ 2
Platform, Micro Edition

Henry Sowizral, Kevin Rushforth, and Michael Deering
The Java 3D™ API Specification, Second Edition

Kathy Walrath, Mary Campione
The JFC Swing Tutorial:
A Guide to Constructing GUIs

Seth White, Maydene Fisher, Rick Cattell,
  Graham Hamilton, and Mark Hapner
JDBC™ API Tutorial and Reference, Second Edition:
Universal Data Access for the Java™ 2 Platform

Steve Wilson, Jeff Kesselman
Java™ Platform Performance:
Strategies and Tactics

The Jini™ Technology Series

Eric Freeman, Susanne Hupfer, Ken Arnold
JavaSpaces™ Principles, Patterns, and Practice

Jim Waldo/Jini™ Technology Team
The Jini™ Specifications, Second Edition,
  edited by Ken Arnold

The Java™ Series, Enterprise Edition

Rick Cattell, Jim Inscore, Enterprise Partners
J2EE™ Technology in Practice:
Building Business Applications with the Java™ 2 Platform,
  Enterprise Edition

Patrick Chan, Rosanna Lee
The Java™ Class Libraries Poster, Enterprise Edition,
  version 1.2

Nicholas Kassem, Enterprise Team
Designing Enterprise Applications with the Java™ 2
  Platform, Enterprise Edition

Bill Shannon, Mark Hapner, Vlada Matena, James
  Davidson, Eduardo Pelegri-Llopart, Larry Cable,
  Enterprise Team
Java™ 2 Platform, Enterprise Edition:
Platform and Component Specifications

http://www.javaseries.com

Programming Wireless Devices with the Java™ 2 Platform, Micro Edition

J2ME™
Connected Limited Device Configuration (CLDC)
Mobile Information Device Profile (MIDP)

Roger Riggs

Antero Taivalsaari

Mark VandenBrink

Jim Holliday, Editor

ADDISON-WESLEY

Boston • San Francisco • New York • Toronto • Montreal
London • Munich • Paris • Madrid
Capetown • Sydney • Tokyo • Singapore • Mexico City

Library of Congress Cataloging-in-Publication Data is available.

The publisher offers discounts on this book when ordered in quantity for special
sales. For more information, please contact:

Pearson Education Corporate Sales Division
One Lake Street
Upper Saddle River, NJ 07458
(800) 382-3419
corpsales@pearsontechgroup.com

Visit AW on the Web: www.awl.com/cseng/

ISBN 0-201-74627-1
Text printed on recycled paper
1 2 3 4 5 6 7 8 9 10—CRS—0504030201
First printing, June 2001

"Computers in the future may weigh no more than 1.5 tons."
— Popular Mechanics, 1949

*"The greatest enemy of good software is the
dream of perfect software."*
— Based on a quote by Prussian General Karl von Clausewitz

*"Walking on water and developing software from a specification
are easy if both are frozen."*
— Ed Berard, Life-Cycle Approaches

"I hate quotations. Tell me what you know."
— Ralph Waldo Emerson

Contents

Figures

Foreword

With the delivery of the Java™ 2 Platform, Micro Edition (J2ME™), Java technology has come full circle. The Java technology we know today originally sprang from a project whose goal was to investigate the potential impact of digital technologies outside the mainstream of the computer industry. It was clear that this big expanse of interesting territory was the space close to everyday people. Consumer electronics, telephony and embedded systems were increasingly becoming a part of the fabric of everyday life.

Being a group with a very hands-on engineering background, we decided to build an artifact as a way to lead our understanding down into the details. We built a small (for its day!) handheld device, not unlike today's PDAs. As we considered the implications of this new world, we encountered serious issues with the underlying tools we were using to build the software:

- *Heterogeneity was a fact of life.* The consumer world has many different CPU and system architectures. In the desktop world, these differences ("WinTel" versus Macintosh) partition the market based on low level details that most people know little about. In the consumer/embedded world, there are many more architectures than the two of the desktop world. The fragmented chaos that would ensue would cause serious problems. Heterogeneity becomes an even more urgent issue when these devices are connected in a network and they start sharing software.

- *Reliability is a huge issue.* Non-technophiles have a justifiably low tolerance for systems that malfunction. There are a number of areas where low-level issues in the programming language design (memory integrity being one) have a large impact.

- *Security must be addressed.* There is no bigger threat to a network than a "teen-age guy" out to have fun. (I know, I was one!) Security is not something that can be painted on afterwards: it has to be built in from the beginning.

- *Consumer devices have a long life span.* They live within a world that evolves. This drives a lot of issues in system construction, versioning, and modularity.

- *These systems were becoming distributed and needed to run on more than one machine.* They needed to span many machines that would work together to provide a cohesive experience—from small systems like cell phones, at the edge of the network, to large systems like the switches that connect them.

These pressures came together and caused a problem. My job on the project was to tackle this and the result was the Java programming language. The early implementations were targeted at low end devices.

We released the language to the world in 1995 and it experienced phenomenal popularity. One of the side effects of that popularity was that it quickly moved upscale and was very heavily used in large industrial-strength applications. The smaller scale fringes of the network got left behind in the enthusiasm.

J2ME brings the technology back to its roots. Programming for these smaller devices can be much more challenging than for large scale systems because of the constraints in size and speed, but it is generally more rewarding because they have a more personal interaction with their users.

With this book you will learn how J2ME is applied in the wireless world. Wireless applications are a major milestone in making this technology accessible to a much wider community of software developers. The most important opportunities are those that are unexpected, that come from curious people experimenting.

Read. Enjoy. Join in the fun.

James Gosling, Mountain View, California
April 2001

Preface

In the past three years, Sun has collaborated with major consumer device manufacturers and other companies to create a highly portable, secure, small-footprint Java™ application development environment for resource-constrained, wireless consumer devices such as cellular telephones, two-way pagers and personal organizers. This work started with the development of a new, small-footprint Java virtual machine called the *K Virtual Machine* (KVM). Two Java Community Process (JCP) standardization efforts, *Connected, Limited Device Configuration* (CLDC) and *Mobile Information Device Profile* (MIDP), were then carried out to standardize the Java libraries and the associated Java language and virtual machine features across a wide variety of consumer devices. Twenty-four companies participated in these standardization efforts directly, and more than five hundred companies and individuals participated indirectly by sending feedback while the standardization efforts were in progress. Major consumer device companies such as Motorola, Nokia, NTT DoCoMo, Palm Computing, Research In Motion (RIM) and Siemens played a key role in these efforts.

This book intends to make the results of the standardization work in the wireless Java technology area available to the wider software development community. At the high level, this book combines two Java Community Process Specifications, JSR-30 (CLDC 1.0) and JSR-37 (MIDP 1.0), and presents them as a single monograph. We have added a general introduction to the Java 2 Platform, Micro Edition (J2ME™), provided more background material, and included a number of sample applications to illustrate the use of CLDC and MIDP in the real world. We also provide some guidelines and instructions for getting started with Java 2 Platform, Micro Edition.

A reference implementation of the software discussed in this book is available from Sun Microsystems under the Sun Community Source License (SCSL).

Intended Audience

This book is intended for software developers, content providers and other professionals who want to develop Java™ software for resource-constrained, connected devices. The book is also targeted to consumer device manufacturers who want to build small Java Powered™ devices and would like to integrate a compact Java application development platform in their products.

Objectives of This Book

This book intends to

- provide an overview of Java 2 Platform, Micro Edition (J2ME™),
- provide a general introduction to the application development platforms defined by the J2ME standardization efforts,
- explain the technical aspects of the J2ME Connected, Limited Device Configuration (CLDC),
- explain the technical aspects of the J2ME Mobile Information Device Profile (MIDP),
- provide sample programs to illustrate the use of CLDC and MIDP,
- help you write your own J2ME applications.

How This Book Is Organized

The topics in this book are organized as follows:

- **Chapter 1, "Introduction,"** provides a context for Java 2 Micro Edition and the CLDC and MIDP Specifications.
- **Chapter 2, "Overview of Java 2 Platform, Micro Edition (J2ME™),"** provides an overview of Java 2 Micro Edition, its configurations and profiles.
- **Chapter 3, "Goals, Requirements, and Scope,"** defines the goals, requirements and scope of the CLDC and MIDP standardization efforts.
- **Chapter 4, "High-Level Architecture and Security,"** presents the high-

level architecture of the CLDC and MIDP standards, as well as discusses the security features of these standards.

- **Chapter 5, "Connected Limited Device Configuration,"** introduces the CLDC standardization effort and summarizes the supported Java programming language and virtual machine features compared to the Java 2 Platform, Standard Edition.

- **Chapter 6, "CLDC Libraries,"** introduces the Java class libraries defined by the *CLDC Specification*.

- **Chapter 7, "Mobile Information Device Profile,"** introduces the MIDP standardization effort.

- **Chapter 8, "MIDP Application Model,"** introduces the *MIDlet* application model defined by the *MIDP Specification*.

- **Chapter 9, "MIDP User Interface Libraries,"** introduces the user interface libraries defined by the *MIDP Specification*.

- **Chapter 10, "MIDP Networking Libraries,"** introduces the networking libraries defined by the *MIDP Specification*.

- **Chapter 11, "MIDP Persistence Libraries,"** introduces the record management system (RMS) defined by the *MIDP Specification*.

- **Chapter 12, "Additional MIDP APIs,"** introduces some additional MIDP application programming interfaces (APIs) such as Timers.

- **Chapter 13, "Sample Applications,"** illustrates the use of CLDC and MIDP libraries through some sample applications.

- **Chapter 14, "Summary,"** provides a summary of the topics discussed in the book, as well as outlines some future directions.

- **Appendix A, "CLDC Application Programming Interface,"** contains the application programming interface documentation in Almanac format for the CLDC.

- **Appendix B, "MIDP Application Programming Interface,"** contains the application programming interface documentation in Almanac format for the MIDP.

Related Literature and Helpful Web Pages

The Java™ Language Specification, First Edition by James Gosling,
Bill Joy, and Guy L. Steele. Addison-Wesley, 1996,
ISBN 0-201-63451-1

The Java™ Language Specification, Second Edition by James Gosling,
Bill Joy, Guy L. Steele, and Gilad Bracha. Addison-Wesley, 2000,
ISBN 0-201-31008-2

The Java™ Virtual Machine Specification, Second Edition by Tim
Lindholm and Frank Yellin. Addison-Wesley, 1999,
ISBN 0-201-43294-3

Connected, Limited Device Configuration Specification
`http://java.sun.com/aboutJava/communityprocess/final/jsr030/`

Mobile Information Device Profile Specification
`http://java.sun.com/aboutJava/communityprocess/final/jsr037/`

Java 2 Micro Edition Product Web Page
`http://java.sun.com/products/j2me/`

K Virtual Machine (KVM) Product Web Page
`http://java.sun.com/products/kvm/`

Connected, Limited Device Configuration (CLDC) Product Web Page
`http://java.sun.com/products/cldc/`

Mobile Information Device Profile (MIDP) Product Web Page
`http://java.sun.com/products/midp/`

J2ME Wireless Toolkit Product Web Page
`http://java.sun.com/products/j2mewtoolkit/`

Acknowledgments

Like most books, this book represents the work of many people. In this case, however, an unusually large number of people around the world have worked to make the Java 2 Platform, Micro Edition—and hence this book—a reality. What started out as a two-person research project at Sun Labs grew rapidly into a highly collaborative product development and standardization effort involving hundreds of people in different companies. The summary below is an attempt to give a high-level glimpse into the different groups of people who participated in this journey. To these and many others too numerous to mention, we give our thanks and appreciation for what they did to make these ideas and this book possible. Attempting to name these people in no way diminishes the contributions of those who we also meant to name but in the press of time and the failure of memory somehow overlooked.

Many people read draft versions of this book, and sent us comments that improved the book substantially. The authors would like to thank David Baum, Bill Bush, Cristina Cifuentes, Greg Czajkowski, Steffen Grarup, Dean Hall, Tim Lindholm, Alex Kuzmin, Stuart Marks, Tasneem Sayeed, Nik Shaylor, Howard Thamm, Ravi Viswanathan and Frank Yellin for their willingness to send comments and constructive criticism on the various versions of the book and the sample MIDlets. As usual, any remaining errors are the sole responsibility of the authors. Special thanks to Mark Patel for contributing the animation code in Chapter 9.

The authors would also like to thank Lisa Friendly for allowing us to publish this book in Sun's Java book series and for lending us capable technical writing resources to finish this book. Jim Holliday, our technical writer and editor at Sun Microsystems, edited various versions of this book tirelessly. Without his expertise in the mysteries of desktop publishing, grammar and that pesky topic known as punctuation, this work would have been much worse for the wear.

Numerous companies have been involved in the standardization efforts related to the Java 2 Platform, Micro Edition. The following companies participated in the CLDC and MIDP standardization efforts discussed in this book: America Online, Bull, DDI, Ericsson, Espial Group, Fujitsu, Hitachi, J-Phone, Matsushita, Mitsubishi, Motorola, NEC, Nokia, NTT DoCoMo, Oracle, Palm Computing, Research In Motion (RIM), Samsung, Sharp, Siemens, Sony, Sun Microsystems, Symbian and Telcordia Technologies. We would like to thank all the CLDC and MIDP expert group members and other individuals from the aforementioned companies for their active participation and valuable contributions.

In addition to the companies listed above, hundreds of other companies and individuals sent us feedback while the CLDC and MIDP standardization efforts were in progress. The authors found it amazing how much of their time people were willing to contribute to ensure the progress of the Java technology in the wireless space.

From Sun, we would like to thank Bert Sutherland and Neil Wilhelm at Sun Labs for their initial support and encouragement to start the Spotless research project that led to the development of the K Virtual Machine (KVM) and the subsequent product development efforts. Bill Bush, Doug Simon and Bill Pittore played an essential role in the development of the Spotless system—the precursor of the KVM. Thanks to the continued efforts and support by Jon Kannegaard, Jim Mitchell, Bob Sproull, Mario Wolczko and many other people at Sun Labs, the active exchange of ideas and technology—and sometimes people—has continued even after the Spotless system had been successfully transferred into a product organization.

Like Bert Sutherland constantly used to remind people when he was the director of Sun Labs, technology transfer is a contact sport. Adam Abramski, Alan Brenner, Bill Bush, Mitch Butler, Mike Clary, Moshe Gotesman, Jim Mitchell, Patrice Peyret, Frank Yellin and many others had a central role in ensuring the successful transfer of the Spotless technology to the Java Software product organization. Alan Brenner, who subsequently became the director of the Java Consumer Software organization, nurtured the initial product teams and visited numerous companies to gain support for the proposed standardization efforts in this area.

Various product groups in Sun's Java Software division participated in the design and implementation of the CLDC and MIDP reference implementations. The authors would like to thank the KVM team, MIDP team and Wireless Toolkit team members who worked on the reference implementations of the standards and products discussed in this book. The TCK (Technology Compatibility Kit) and

Quality Assurance teams at Java Consumer Software also played a critical role in ensuring the quality and compatibility of the products. Special thanks go to Karen Hsiang for keeping all the teams coordinated, as well as to Alex Kuzmin for his relentless pursuit of quality and his willingness to go that extra mile (and spend those extra hours!) to make things happen on time.

From Motorola, we would like to thank Jim Van Peursem for co-representing Motorola in the MIDP expert group. Every project has its genesis, and the KVM project within Motorola had its start with the team of Bala Kumar, Matt Long, Jim Lynch, John Osman, Iris Plaxton, Paul Su and Ranjani Vaidyanathan—thanks guys for being there from the beginning and making CLDC and MIDP happen in Motorola.

Someone once said that hardware without software is a space heater. Similarly, without products, the CLDC and MIDP specifications are limited in their value. Thanks to Jyh-han Lin's Florida-based iDEN team for taking the earlier KVM efforts seriously, putting KVM in their product roadmaps, and shipping Motorola's first CLDC and MIDP compliant phone. In a similar vein, thanks to Michael Chu's Beijing-based "Tai Chi" team for their support. Finally, a big thanks to the Austin-based Wireless Software and Services (WSAS) team under Anne-Marie Larkin, in particular to Scott Osborne who managed the CLDC and MIDP engineering team, and to Jim Erwin who managed the CLDC and MIDP test team.

The preparation of this book has been a rather challenging endeavor itself. All the authors are located in different states and time zones, and because of the extensive amount of travel involved in standardization and product development work these days, a significant portion of the text in this book was written in airplanes, airports and hotels. Luckily, the advances in wireless technology have made it easier for people to stay in touch regardless of their physical location. Unfortunately, it also means that it is increasingly difficult to avoid those after 8 pm phone calls and urgent text messages and e-mails, especially from your co-authors and colleagues located in more Western time zones. The standards defined in this book, for better or worse, will probably only accelerate this trend.

And finally, but most importantly:

Roger would like to thank Cathy, Kimberly, Brian and Catie for their support and forbearance during this exciting and intensive endeavor.

Antero would like to thank Leena, Eva Maria, Eetu and Ella for their love, support and patience—because of the projects discussed in this book, our family ended up staying in Silicon Valley a lot longer than originally planned.

Mark would like to thank Joy, Zachary and Abby for their love, support, patience and understanding about those long trips and time away from home.

Roger Riggs, Burlington, Massachusetts
Antero Taivalsaari, Cupertino, California
Mark VandenBrink, Austin, Texas
April 2001

CHAPTER 1

Introduction

1.1 The Wireless Internet Revolution

The wireless communications industry has seen explosive growth over the past several years. This has made wireless communication one of the hottest and fastest growing technology areas in the world. The total number of cellular phone subscribers worldwide will exceed 600 million in 2001, and it is estimated that there will be over one billion wireless subscribers in the world by 2003. In contrast, the installed base of personal computers was around 311 million worldwide at the beginning of year 2000.

At the same time, the rapid emergence of the Internet has changed the landscape of modern computing. People have become more and more dependent on the information that is available on the Internet, and they will increasingly want access to the Internet, not only from their personal computers and office workstations but also from mobile, wireless devices. Consequently, the rapid and efficient deployment of new wireless data and mobile Internet services has become a high priority for communication equipment manufacturers and telecommunication operators.

The transition to wireless, mobile Internet devices will fundamentally alter the landscape and architecture of communication networks, devices and services. Unlike in the past, when wireless devices typically came from the factory with a hard-coded feature set, the devices will become more and more customizable. The possibility of downloading new applications and features over wireless networks will open up completely new possibilities for device manufacturers, network operators, service and content providers and device users themselves.

The wireless Internet revolution will be facilitated by another important technological advance: the introduction of third generation (3G) broadband wireless networks. While current wireless networks have limited data rates, allowing the users to transfer only up to a few tens of kilobits of data per second, third generation wireless networks will provide data rates ranging from hundreds of kilobits up to a few megabits per second. There will be enough bandwidth to transfer live video and high-quality audio, as well as to download significantly larger applications and services than today.

All these changes will happen relatively fast. Even though it will still take a few years before broadband wireless networks are in widespread use, it is safe to estimate that the majority of new wireless devices, especially cell phones, will have connectivity to the Internet one way or another in the next two to five years.

1.2   Why Java™ Technology for Wireless Devices?

The wireless Internet revolution will transform wireless devices from voice-oriented communication devices with relatively static, hard-coded functionality into extensible, Internet-enabled devices with advanced data and software support. These devices will need to support dynamic downloading of new software, and need to be capable of running software written not only by the device manufacturers themselves, but also software written by third-party software developers. This will make the devices much more dependent on software and will place a much higher emphasis on software interoperability, security, and reliability.

The Java™ programming language is ideally suited to become the standard application development language for wireless devices. After all, the Java platform provides the following benefits:

- *Dynamic delivery of content.* New applications, services and content can be downloaded dynamically over different kinds of networks.

- *Security.* Class file verification, well-defined application programming interfaces and security features ensure that third-party applications behave reliably and cannot harm the devices or the networks.

- *Cross-platform compatibility.* Standardized language features and libraries mean that applications and content can be transferred flexibly between different devices, within constraints of the supported J2ME™ configuration and profiles (see Section 2.3, "Key Concepts of the J2ME Architecture," for details).

- *Enhanced user experience and interactive content.* The standards defined for wireless Java technology support sophisticated user interaction and provide compelling graphics capabilities for small devices.

- *Offline access.* Applications can also be used without active network connection. This reduces transport costs and alleviates the impact of possible network failures.

- *The power of a modern object-oriented programming language.* The Java programming language has far better abstraction mechanisms and higher-level programming constructs than other languages and tools that are currently used for wireless software development, allowing applications to be developed more efficiently.

- *Large developer community.* It is estimated that there are more than 2.5 million Java software developers worldwide. The Java programming language is rapidly becoming the most popular programming language taught in schools and universities. The developer talent needed for Java software development already exists and is readily available.

Ultimately, Java technology will deliver far more compelling, entertaining and engaging capabilities to wireless devices. What is particularly important is that this can be accomplished *incrementally*, by complementing existing technologies and standards, rather than by competing with them. One of the key things we emphasize throughout this book is that we are *not* defining a new operating system or a complete system software stack for wireless devices. Rather, the goal of this work is to define and standardize a portable wireless *application development environment* that targets primarily third-party application developers and will open the devices for third-party software development. This environment can be added flexibly on top of the existing software and hardware solutions that the device manufacturers already have. Typically, the changes required to the existing system software are very small. For more information, see Section 3.1, "High-Level Goals."

1.3   A Bit of History

The Java programming language was initially targeted towards consumer devices, especially the interactive TV market. However, over time the Java platform evolved more and more towards the needs of desktop and enterprise computing. Enterprise applications generally require rich library functionality, and over time the Java libraries grew larger and more comprehensive to cater better to the needs of the enterprise market and large server-side applications. However, this evolution made the libraries too large and unsuitable for the majority of small, resource-constrained devices.

In January 1998, the *Spotless* project was started at Sun Microsystems Laboratories (Sun Labs) to investigate the use of the Java programming language in extremely resource-constrained devices. The research goal of the project was to build a Java runtime environment that would fit in less than one-tenth of the typical size. At the implementation level, the goal was to build a Java virtual machine with the following characteristics:

- *small size*

- *portability*

- *ease of use and readability of the source code*

Small size is important, since the majority of wireless, mobile devices (for example, cell phones) are still very resource-limited, and often have only a few tens or hundreds of kilobytes of memory available for applications. Portability, ease of use and the readability of the source code are equally important. Most embedded device manufacturers need to support dozens or even hundreds of different hardware configurations that run on several different hardware platforms, and it would be not only tedious but also very expensive to spend a lot of time porting and customizing the Java platform implementation to all those hardware configurations and platforms. Also, embedded device manufacturers cannot generally be expected to be experts on the Java programming language or virtual machine. Therefore, the easier the implementation is to understand and use, the faster the device manufacturers will deploy it across their devices.

Even though the Spotless effort was initially a research project, the project group established active contacts with external customers early on. External customers, especially Motorola, played a significant role in convincing Sun to turn the Spotless system from a research project into a commercial product. The product version of the Spotless virtual machine is nowadays known as the K Virtual Machine (KVM) or the *KJava Virtual Machine*. The Spotless system is documented in the Sun Labs technical report *The Spotless System: Implementing a Java system for the Palm Connected Organizer* (Sun Labs Technical Report SMLI TR-99-73).

1.4   J2ME™ Standardization Efforts

Once Motorola, Nokia, NTT DoCoMo, Palm Computing, RIM, Siemens, and other device manufacturers joined the KVM development effort, standardization was necessary in order to guarantee interoperability between the different kinds of Java

Powered™ devices from different manufacturers. Two Java Community Process (JCP) standardization efforts were launched in the fall of 1999.

The first of these standardization efforts, *Connected, Limited Device Configuration* (CLDC), was launched on October 1, 1999. The goal of this effort was to define the "lowest common denominator" Java platform for a wide variety of small, connected, resource-constrained devices. This specification defines the minimum required complement of Java technology components and libraries for small devices. Java programming language and virtual machine features, core libraries, input/output, networking, and security are the primary topics addressed by the *CLDC Specification*. The CLDC standard does not target any specific device category. Rather, it defines a general-purpose building block on top of which more device category specific *profiles* are defined. Eighteen companies participated in the CLDC standardization effort.

The second standardization effort, *Mobile Information Device Profile* (MIDP), was started in late November 1999. That effort was based on the platform defined by the CLDC standardization effort, adding features and APIs that focus specifically on two-way wireless communication devices such as cell phones and two-way pagers. Application model, user interface, networking and storage APIs are the primary focus areas of the *MIDP Specification*. Twenty-two companies participated in the MIDP expert group work.

The CLDC standardization effort is described in more detail in Chapter 5, "Connected Limited Device Configuration," and Chapter 6, "CLDC Libraries." The MIDP standardization effort is discussed in Chapter 7, "Mobile Information Device Profile" and subsequent chapters. The general framework for these, as well as other Java technology standardization efforts in the small device space, is known as *Java 2 Platform, Micro Edition* (J2ME) or simply *Java 2 Micro Edition*. An introduction to Java 2 Micro Edition is provided in the next chapter.

CHAPTER 2

Overview of Java 2 Platform, Micro Edition (J2ME™)

2.1   Java 2 Platform

Recognizing that one size does not fit all, Sun Microsystems has grouped Java technologies into three editions, each aimed at a specific area of today's vast computing industry:

- *Java 2 Platform, Enterprise Edition (J2EE™)* for enterprises needing to serve their customers, suppliers and employees with scalable server solutions.

- *Java 2 Platform, Standard Edition (J2SE™)* for the familiar and well-established desktop computer market.

- *Java 2 Platform, Micro Edition (J2ME™)* for the combined needs of:

  - consumer and embedded device manufacturers who build a diversity of information devices,

  - service providers who wish to deliver content to their customers over those devices,

  - content creators who want to make compelling content for small, resource-constrained devices.

Each Java platform edition defines a set of technologies that can be used with a particular product:

- Java virtual machines that fit inside a wide range of computing devices,

- libraries and APIs specialized for each kind of computing device,

- tools for deployment and device configuration.

Figure 2.1 illustrates the Java 2 Platform editions and their target markets, starting from the high-end platforms on the left and moving towards low-end platforms on the right. Basically, five target markets or broad device categories are identified. Servers and enterprise computers are supported by Java 2 Enterprise Edition, and desktop and personal computers by Java 2 Standard Edition. Java 2 Micro Edition is divided broadly into two categories that focus on high-end and low-end consumer devices. Java 2 Micro Edition is discussed in more detail later in this chapter. Finally, the Java Card™ standard focuses on the smart card market.

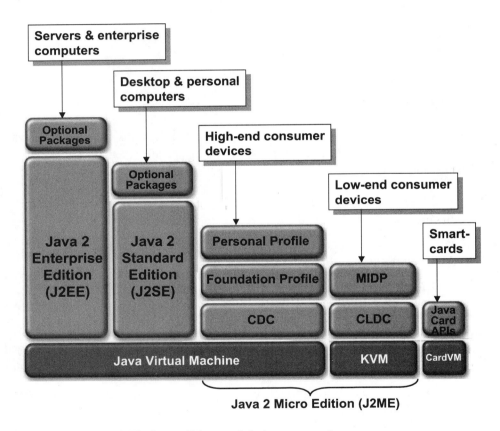

Figure 2.1   Java 2 Platform editions and their target markets

2.2   Java 2 Platform, Micro Edition (J2ME)

Java 2 Platform, Micro Edition (henceforth referred to as *Java 2 Micro Edition* or J2ME) specifically addresses the large, rapidly growing consumer space, which covers a range of devices from tiny commodities, such as pagers, all the way up to the TV set-top box, an appliance almost as powerful as a desktop computer. Like the larger Java editions, Java 2 Micro Edition aims to maintain the qualities that Java technology has become known for, including built-in consistency across products, portability of code, safe network delivery and upward scalability.

The high-level idea behind J2ME is to provide comprehensive application development platforms for creating dynamically extensible, networked devices and applications for the consumer and embedded market. J2ME enables device manufacturers, service providers and content creators to capitalize on new market opportunities by developing and deploying compelling new applications and services to their customers worldwide. Furthermore, J2ME allows device manufacturers to open up their devices for widespread third-party application development and dynamically downloaded content, without losing the security or the control of the underlying manufacturer-specific platform.

At a high level, J2ME is targeted at two broad categories of products:

- *High-end consumer devices*. In Figure 2.1, this category is represented by the grouping labeled *CDC* (Connected Device Configuration). Typical examples of devices in this category include TV set-top boxes, Internet TVs, Internet-enabled screenphones, high-end wireless communicators and automobile entertainment/navigation systems. These devices have a large range of user interface capabilities, total memory budgets starting from about two to four megabytes and persistent, high-bandwidth network connections, often using TCP/IP.

- *Low-end consumer devices*. In Figure 2.1, this category is represented by the grouping labeled *CLDC* (Connected, Limited Device Configuration). Cell phones, pagers, and personal organizers are examples of devices in this category. These devices have very simple user interfaces (compared to desktop computer systems), minimum memory budgets starting at about 128 kilobytes, and low bandwidth, intermittent network connections. In this category of products, network communication is often not based on the TCP/IP protocol suite. Most of these devices are usually battery-operated.

The line between these two categories is fuzzy and becoming more so every day. As a result of the ongoing technological convergence in the computer, telecommunication, consumer electronics, and entertainment industries, there will be less distinction between general-purpose computers, personal communication devices, consumer electronics devices, and entertainment devices. Also, future devices are more likely to use wireless connectivity instead of traditional fixed or wired networks. In practice, the line between the two categories is defined more by the memory budget, bandwidth considerations, battery power consumption and physical screen size of the device, rather than by its specific functionality or type of connectivity.

Because of strict manufacturing cost constraints, the majority of high-volume wireless devices today such as cell phones belong to the low-end consumer device category. Therefore, this book focuses only on the CLDC and MIDP standards that were specifically designed for that category of products.

2.3   Key Concepts of the J2ME Architecture

While connected consumer devices such as cell phones, pagers, personal organizers and TV set-top boxes have many things in common, they are also extremely diverse in form, function, and features. Information appliances tend to be special-purpose, limited-function devices. To address this diversity, an essential requirement for the J2ME architecture is not only small size but also modularity and customizability.

In general, serving the information appliance market calls for a large measure of flexibility in how computing technology and applications are deployed. This flexibility is required because of

- the large range of existing device types and hardware configurations,

- the different usage models employed by the devices (key operated, stylus operated, voice operated),

- constantly improving device technology,

- the diverse range of existing applications and features,

- the need for applications and capabilities to change and grow, often in unforeseen ways, in order to accommodate the future needs of the consumer.

The J2ME architecture is intended to be modular and scalable so that it can support the kinds of flexible deployment demanded by the consumer and embedded markets. To enable this, the J2ME environment provides a range of Java virtual machine technologies, each optimized for the different processor types and memory footprints commonly found in the consumer and embedded marketplace.

For low-end, resource-limited consumer products, the J2ME environment supports minimal configurations of the Java virtual machine and Java libraries that embody just the essential capabilities of each kind of device. As device manufacturers develop new features in their devices, or service providers develop new and exciting applications, these minimal configurations can be expanded with additional libraries that address the needs of a particular market segment. To support this kind of customizability and extensibility, two essential concepts are defined by the J2ME environment:

- *Configuration*. A J2ME configuration defines a minimum platform for a "*horizontal*" category or grouping of devices, each with similar requirements on total memory budget and processing power. A configuration defines the Java language and virtual machine features and minimum class libraries that a device manufacturer or a content provider can expect to be available on all devices of the same category.

- *Profile*. A J2ME profile is layered on top of (and thus extends) a configuration. A profile addresses the specific demands of a certain "*vertical*" market segment or device family. The main goal of a profile is to guarantee interoperability within a certain vertical device family or domain by defining a standard Java platform for that market. Profiles typically include class libraries that are far more domain-specific than the class libraries provided in a configuration. One device can support multiple configurations.

Configurations and profiles are discussed in more detail below. Both configurations and profiles use the capabilities of the Java virtual machine (JVM), which is considered to be part of the configuration. The virtual machine usually runs on top of a *host operating system* that is part of the system software of the target device. The high-level relationship between the different software layers—the JVM, configuration, profiles and the host operating system—is illustrated in Figure 2.2.

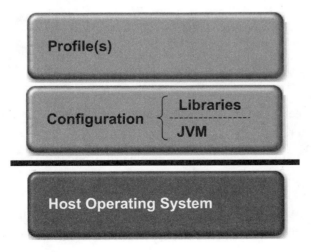

Figure 2.2   Software layers in a J2ME device

J2ME configurations and profiles are defined through the Java Community Process (JCP). For further information on the Java Community Process, refer to the Java Community Process web site.[1]

2.3.1   Profiles

Application portability is a key benefit of Java technology in the desktop and enterprise server markets. Portability is an equally critical element in the consumer device space. However, application portability requirements in the consumer space are very different from portability requirements demanded by the desktop and server markets. In most cases consumer devices differ substantially in memory size, networking and user interface capabilities, making it very difficult to support all devices with just one solution.

In general, the consumer device market is not so homogeneous that end users can expect or require universal application portability. Rather, in the consumer space, applications should ideally be fully portable within the same device family. For example, consider the following types of consumer devices:

- cellular telephones,

- washing machines,

- electronic toys.

It seems clear that each of these represents a different market segment, device family or application domain. As such, consumers would expect useful applications to be portable within a device family. For example:

- A discount broker's stock trading application is generally expected to work on different cell phones, even though the phones are from different manufacturers.

- It would be annoying if a highly useful grape-juice-stain-removing wash cycle application available on the Internet runs on an old brand-X washer, but not a new brand-Z washer.

- A child's birthday party could be less enjoyable if the new toy robot doesn't "talk to" or "play games with" the new electronic teddy bear.

On the other hand, consumers do not expect the stock trading application or an automobile service program to run on the washing machine or the toy robot. In

---

[1] http://java.sun.com/aboutJava/communityprocess

other words, application portability *across* different device categories is not necessarily very important or even meaningful in the consumer device space.

In addition, there are important economic reasons to keep these device families separate. Consumer devices compete heavily on cost and convenience, and these factors often translate directly into limitations on physical size and weight, processor power, memory size and power consumption (in battery-powered devices). Consumers' wallets will usually favor devices that perform the desired functions well, but that do not have added cost for unnecessary features.

Thus, the J2ME framework provides the concept of a *profile* to make it possible to define Java platforms for specific vertical markets. A profile defines a Java platform for a specific vertical market segment or device category. Profiles can serve two distinct portability requirements:

- A profile provides a complete toolkit for implementing applications for a particular kind of device, such as a pager, set-top box, cell phone, washing machine, or interactive electronic toy.

- A profile may also be created to support a significant, coherent group of applications that might be hosted on several categories of devices. For example, while the differences between set-top boxes, pagers, cell phones and washing machines are significant enough to justify creating a separate profile for each, it might be useful for certain kinds of personal information management or home banking applications to be portable to each of these devices. This could be accomplished by creating a separate profile for these kinds of applications and ensuring that this new profile can be easily and effectively supported on each of the target devices along with its "normal" more device-specific profile.

It is possible for a single device to support several profiles. Some of these profiles are very device-specific, while others are more application-specific. Applications are written "for" a specific profile and are required to use only the features defined by that profile. Manufacturers choose which profile(s) to support on each of their devices, but are required to implement all features of the chosen profile(s). The value proposition to the consumer is that any application written for a particular profile will run on any device that supports that profile.

In its simplest terms, a profile is a contract between an application and a vertical market segment. All the devices in the same market segment agree to implement all the features defined in the profile. And the application agrees to use only those features defined in the profile. Thus, portability is achieved between the applications and the devices served by that profile. New devices can take advantage of a large and familiar application base. Most importantly, new compelling applications (perhaps completely unforeseen by the original profile designers and device manufacturers) can be dynamically downloaded to existing devices.

At the implementation level, a profile is defined simply as a collection of class libraries that reside on top of a specified configuration and that provide the additional domain-specific capabilities for devices in a specific market segment.

In our example above, each of the three families of devices (cell phones, washing machines and intercommunicating toys) would be addressed by a separate J2ME profile. The only one of these profiles in existence at the current time is the MIDP, designed for cell phones and other two-way communication devices.

2.3.2   Configurations

In the J2ME environment, an application is written "for" a particular profile, and a profile is "based upon" or "extends" a particular configuration. Thus, all of the features of a configuration are automatically included in the profile and may be used by applications written for that profile.

A configuration defines a Java platform for a "horizontal" category or grouping of devices with similar requirements on total memory budget and other hardware capabilities. More specifically, a configuration:

- specifies the Java programming language features supported,

- specifies the Java virtual machine features supported,

- specifies the basic Java libraries and APIs supported.

The J2ME environment is designed so that it can be deployed in more than one configuration. Each configuration specifies the Java language and virtual machine features and a set of libraries that the profile implementer (and the applications using that profile) can safely assume to be present on all devices when shipped from the factory. Profile implementers must design their code to stay within the bounds of the features and libraries specified by that configuration.

In its simplest terms, a configuration defines a "lowest common denominator" platform or building block for device manufacturers and profile implementers. All the devices with approximately the same amount of memory and processing power agree to implement all the features defined in the configuration. And the profile implementers agree to use only those features defined in the configuration. Thus, portability is achieved between the profile and the devices served by that configuration.

In our example above, each of the three profiles (for cell phones, washing machines and electronic toys) would most likely be built upon the same configuration, the CLDC. This configuration provides all the basic functionality to serve the needs of each of these, and perhaps many more, profiles.

To avoid fragmentation, there are a very limited number of J2ME configurations. Currently, (see Figure 2.1) only two standard J2ME configurations are available:

- *Connected, Limited Device Configuration (CLDC)*. This configuration focuses on *low-end consumer devices*. Typical examples of CLDC target devices include personal, mobile, battery-operated, connected information devices such as cell phones, two-way pagers, and personal organizers. This configuration includes some new classes, not drawn from the J2SE APIs, designed specifically to fit the needs of small-footprint devices.

- *Connected Device Configuration (CDC)*. This configuration focuses on *high-end consumer devices*. Typical examples of CDC target devices include shared, connected information devices such as TV set-top boxes, Internet TVs, and high-end communicators. This configuration includes a much more comprehensive set of Java libraries and virtual machine features than CLDC.

Figure 2.3 illustrates the relationship between CLDC, CDC and Java 2 Standard Edition (J2SE). As shown in the figure, the majority of functionality in CLDC and CDC has been inherited from Java 2 Platform, Standard Edition (J2SE). Each class inherited from the J2SE environment must be precisely the same or a subset of the corresponding class in the J2SE environment. In addition, CLDC and CDC may introduce a number of features, not drawn from the J2SE, designed specifically to fit the needs of small-footprint devices.

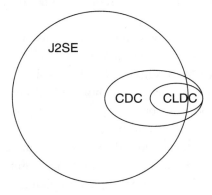

Figure 2.3   Relationship between J2ME configurations and Java 2 Standard Edition

The most important reason for the configuration layer in the J2ME environment is that core Java libraries needed across a wide variety of Java platform implementations are usually intimately tied with the implementation of a Java virtual machine. Small differences in the specification of a configuration can require a number of significant modifications to the internal design of a Java virtual machine, and can require a substantial amount of additional memory footprint. Such modifications would be very expensive and time-consuming to maintain. Having a small number of configurations means that a small number of virtual machine implementations can serve the needs of both a large number of profiles and a large number of different device hardware types. This economy of scale provided by the J2ME environment is very important to the success and cost-effectiveness of devices in the consumer and embedded industry.

2.4   The K Virtual Machine (KVM)

CLDC and MIDP commonly run on top of Sun's K Virtual Machine (KVM). KVM is a compact, portable Java virtual machine specifically designed for small, resource-constrained devices. The high-level design goal for KVM was to create a new Java virtual machine with the following characteristics:

- small, with a static memory footprint of the core of the virtual machine starting from about 60 kilobytes, depending on compilation options and the target platform,

- clean, well-commented and highly portable,

- modular and customizable,

- as complete and fast as possible without sacrificing the other design goals.

The "K" in KVM stands for "kilo." It was so named because its memory budget is measured in tens of kilobytes (whereas desktop systems are measured in megabytes or even gigabytes). KVM is suitable for 16/32-bit microprocessors with a total memory budget of no more than a few hundred kilobytes. This typically applies to digital cellular phones, pagers, personal organizers, portable audio/video devices and small retail payment terminals.

The minimum total memory budget required by a KVM implementation is about 128 kilobytes, including the virtual machine, minimal libraries and some heap space for running Java applications. A more typical implementation requires a total memory budget of 256 kilobytes, of which at least 32 kilobytes is used as runtime heap space for applications, 60 to 80 kilobytes is needed for the virtual machine itself, and the rest is reserved for class libraries. The ratio between volatile memory (*e.g.*, DRAM) and non-volatile memory (*e.g.*, ROM or Flash memory) in the total memory budget varies considerably depending on the implementation, the device, the configuration, and the supported profiles. A simple KVM implementation without system class preloading support needs more volatile memory than a KVM implementation with system classes (or even applications) preloaded into the device.

The actual role of KVM in the target devices can vary significantly. In some implementations, KVM is used on top of an existing native software stack to give the device the ability to download and run dynamic, interactive, secure Java content on the device. In other implementations, KVM is used at a lower level to also implement the lower-level system software and applications of the device in the Java programming language.

For further information on KVM, refer to the KVM product web site (`http://java.sun.com/products/kvm`).

CHAPTER 3

Goals, Requirements, and Scope

The CLDC and MIDP standards intend to bring the benefits of Java technology to resource-constrained wireless devices with limited Internet connectivity. This chapter reviews the goals, requirements, and scope of these standards.

3.1 High-Level Goals

The general goal of the J2ME standardization efforts discussed in this book is to define a *highly portable, secure, small-footprint application development environment* for resource-constrained, connected devices. We emphasize the term *application development environment*. The CLDC and MIDP standards are not intended to replace existing system software stacks or to serve as a complete operating system for small devices. Rather, the goal of these efforts is to define an environment that can be added flexibly on top of an existing system software stack to support third-party application development and secure, dynamic downloading of applications.

The CLDC and MIDP standardization efforts have slightly different but complementary goals. Connected, Limited Device Configuration is intended to serve as a generic, "lowest common denominator" platform that targets all kinds of small, connected devices—independently of any specific device category. Mobile Information Device Profile builds on top of CLDC and focuses on a specific category of devices: wireless, mobile, two-way communication devices such as cellular telephones and two-way pagers.

3.1.1   Dynamic delivery of Java applications and content

One of the greatest benefits of Java technology in the small device space is the dynamic, secure delivery of interactive services and applications over different kinds of networks. Unlike in the past, when small devices such as cell phones and pagers came from the manufacturer with a hard-coded feature set, device manufacturers are increasingly looking for solutions that allow them to build *extensible, customizable devices* that support rich, dynamic, interactive content from third-party content providers and developers. With the recent introduction of Internet-enabled cell phones, communicators and pagers, this transition is already underway. Several wireless device manufacturers are already offering cell phones that allow the users to download new applications such as interactive games, screen savers, banking and ticketing applications, wireless collaboration tools, and so on (Figure 3.1).

Note that such customizability is not necessarily limited to just communication devices such as cell phones or two-way pagers. For instance, it is quite realistic to imagine automobile engines to obtain new service programs and updates as they become available, washing machines to download new washing programs dynamically, electronic toys to automatically download updated game programs, and so on. The range of possible applications is virtually endless.

One of the main goals of both the Connected, Limited Device Configuration and Mobile Information Device Profile is to take this transition several steps further by allowing the use of the Java programming language as the standard platform for the secure delivery of dynamic content for these extensible next-generation devices.

3.1.2   Third-party application development

The focus on dynamically delivered applications means that CLDC and MIDP are intended not just for hardware manufacturers and their system programmers, but also for *third-party application developers*. In fact, we assume that once Java Powered™ small devices become commonplace, the vast majority of application developers for these devices will be third-party developers rather than device manufacturers.

This focus on third-party application development has some important implications for the features and libraries included in CLDC and MIDP standards. First, the CLDC and MIDP specifications include only high-level libraries that provide sufficient programming power for the third-party application developer. For instance, the networking APIs included in MIDP provide the programmer with meaningful high-level abstractions, such as the ability to transfer whole files or web pages at once, rather than require the programmer to know about the details of specific network transmission protocols. Second, we emphasize the

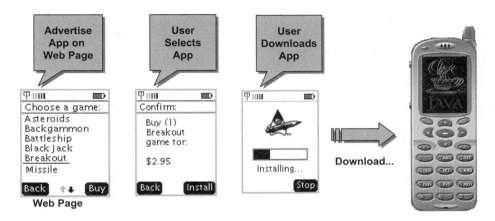

Figure 3.1   Downloading customized services

importance of generality, portability, and interoperability. The CLDC and MIDP specifications are intended to support a wide range of devices and do not focus on any specific single type or brand of devices.

3.1.3   Independence of network technology standards

The wireless communications industry has never suffered from the lack of technology standards. There is a plethora of wireless technologies in use all over the world, with varying levels of sophistication, compatibility, and interoperability. The *second generation* (2G) digital wireless network technologies include standards such as GSM, TDMA, CDMA, and PDC. *Third generation* (3G) wireless network technology standards include WCDMA, CDMA2000, and TD-SCDMA. In addition, there are several *second and a half generation* (2.5G) standards such as GPRS, CDPD, and EDGE.

One of the key goals for J2ME standardization efforts is to define solutions that can work effectively with all these network technologies and standards. Any APIs or features that would focus only on one specific type of network technology are generally avoided. An additional goal in the CLDC and MIDP standardization work was to ensure that the solutions can be used both in today's relatively low-speed wireless networks and in tomorrow's high-speed broadband wireless networks.

To reach the goals above, the CLDC standard defines a special *Generic Connection* framework for supporting networking in a coherent, extensible fashion. This is discussed in detail in Section 6.3.2, "The Generic Connection framework."

The MIDP standard utilizes the Generic Connection framework and defines one concrete network protocol, namely HTTP, that is assumed to be available in all devices supporting MIDP.

3.1.4   Compatibility with other wireless application standards

A key goal for the standards defined in this book is to provide interoperability with existing wireless application development standards and technology stacks such as *i-Mode* and *Wireless Application Protocol* (WAP). This means that the application development environments defined by CLDC and MIDP can complement existing technologies, rather than compete with them. For instance, today's wireless devices already commonly provide a simple microbrowser for finding services on the Internet. This microbrowser can be extended to locate and launch Java applications as well. A microbrowser augmented with Java application execution capabilities will provide better user interaction and graphics capabilities, support offline use of applications, and make the development of compelling applications generally much easier.

3.2   Target Devices

Potential target devices for the Mobile Information Device Profile (MIDP) include two-way communication devices such as cellular telephones, two-way pagers and wireless personal organizers. The Connected, Limited Device Configuration (CLDC) can additionally be used to support other kinds of devices such as point-of-sale terminals, barcode scanners, inventory control devices, audio/video equipment, home appliances and device controllers (for routers, sensors, vending machines, engines, and so forth). In general, CLDC is intended to be applicable to any resource-constrained device that might benefit from a portable, low-cost application development environment that supports secure, dynamic downloading of third-party applications.[1]

The characteristics of the CLDC and MIDP target devices are summarized in Figure 3.2. The technical hardware and software requirements of CLDC and MIDP target devices are defined in detail later in this chapter.

---

[1] Note that CLDC defines only general-purpose APIs, so additional APIs and/or J2ME profiles are typically necessary to address the specific needs of each device category.

Typical aspects:
- **At least 160 kB memory available to Java**
- **Processor speed starting from 8 to 32 MHz**
- **16 or 32 bit processor**
- **Limited power, usually battery operated**
- **Connectivity to network; often very limited bandwidth (9,600 bps or less)**
- **High-volume manufacturing**

Figure 3.2   CLDC and MIDP target devices

The user interaction models of CLDC and MIDP target devices vary significantly. Consider, for example, how a user interacts with today's crop of mobile information devices.

The most common example is that of "one-handed" operation. Devices of this type are typical cellular phones with small LCD displays and a standard ITU-T telephone keypad (containing at least the keys 0-9, * and #). Users interact with this type of device with one hand, usually with their thumb only. With devices of this type, smaller is better, so these devices typically have a very limited display.

Other mobile information devices are operated in "two-handed mode." These devices have a small QWERTY keyboard. Data entry for these devices is much like using a PC, although due to the small size touch typing can be problematic; consequently, many devices in this category are operated by two thumbs rather than ten fingers. Given that a QWERTY keyboard takes up more space than a telephone keypad, the display in these devices is usually larger than that found in a normal cellular phone.

As a final example of user interaction models, consider a device that depends on a touch screen. These devices primarily interact with the user by having a simple, consistent, and well-designed menu system. In addition, these devices might depend on handwriting recognition or a virtual keyboard for user-input text. Given that text input is commonly done via a stylus, these devices typically have larger LCD screens—in fact, often much larger than the other two types of devices discussed above.

Both CLDC and MIDP are designed to cater to all the different usage models presented in Figure 3.3, and consequently the CLDC and MIDP Specifications make minimal assumptions about user interaction models of the target devices.

Figure 3.3   One-handed, two-handed and stylus-operated mobile information devices

3.3   General Notes on Consumer Devices and Embedded Systems

Over the past thirty years, the performance of computer hardware has doubled approximately every 12 to 24 months. This has led to unprecedented miniaturization and widespread usage of computer technology. The price of the microprocessor in today's personal computers is only a few tens of cents per megahertz, and the price is still decreasing rapidly. Today's small wireless devices such as cell phones and two-way pagers have microprocessors that were commonly used in high-end desktop computers less than ten years ago.

Ultimately, computing power and storage capacity will become extremely cheap. Inexpensive devices, home appliances and consumer products such as microwave ovens, shopping carts, wallets and toys will include powerful processors and megabytes of storage memory.

Thanks to *Moore's Law*, software developers for desktop computers and servers haven't had to worry very much about processing power or efficiency of their software. Many performance problems have been resolved simply by waiting for a more powerful computer to become available.

However, the consumer device space and embedded software development are different. Even though the processing power of consumer devices and embedded systems is increasing, the majority of these systems are still extremely resource-constrained and limited in processing power. And unlike in the desktop and enterprise computing area, the situation is not likely to change dramatically in the next few years. There are several reasons for this:

- *Moore's Law does not apply to the battery.* Most consumer devices are battery-operated. Even though battery technology has advanced substantially in the past years, the advances in battery technology are not as dramatic and predictable as in microprocessor development. Low power consumption is very important in wireless devices, because 75 to 85 percent of the battery power typically needs to be reserved for the radio transmitter and RF signal processing. This places severe power constraints on the rest of the system.

- *High-volume production.* Typically, consumer devices such as cellular phones are manufactured in extremely large quantities (millions or even tens of millions of units). They are sold to price-conscious consumers at very low, often subsidized prices. To improve their profit margins, device manufacturers want to keep the per-unit costs of the devices as low as possible. Additional processing power or precious dynamic memory will not be added unless the consumers are willing to pay for the extra capabilities.

- *Specialized nature of devices.* Consumer devices are typically highly specialized. Each device is usually highly customized for its intended usage: cell phones for voice communication, pagers for alphanumeric message retrieval, digital cameras for photography, and so on. Again, to keep the price of the devices reasonable, device manufacturers are not willing to add general-purpose features and capabilities that would raise the cost of the device, unless the features are well-justified from the viewpoint of the target market and the consumer.

In general, a fundamental difference between desktop/enterprise computing and consumer devices is that in the consumer device space *one solution does not fit all.* Unlike personal computers, which can run tens of thousands of different kinds of applications, and are not customized particularly well for any single application, consumer devices are typically highly specialized for their intended use and are designed to do only one or a few things well. This means that unlike desktop and enterprise computers, whose performance is typically easy to measure in terms of their processing power, the performance and value of consumer devices and embedded systems is measured in terms of how well they serve their intended usage. The specialized nature of the devices has to be kept in mind when developing software for these devices.

There are further factors differentiating the consumer device space from desktop computers. These include:

- *Small screen size*. The majority of consumer devices have miniscule screens compared to desktop computers or servers. Some devices have no screens at all.

- *Different usage models*. The usage models of small devices vary considerably. Some are stylus-operated, some have tiny phone keypads that are operated by one hand only, or small QWERTY keyboards operated using two thumbs, some are voice-operated/hands-free, and so on.

- *Mobility*. Compared to personal computers, consumer devices are operated in varying and sometimes unusual circumstances, for example, while in traffic, while roller skating or skiing, at night, on a beach, in a snowstorm, and so on.

- *Limited network bandwidth with intermittent connections*. Personal computer users have become accustomed to relatively reliable, rather high-speed networks based on TCP/IP and other well-established network protocols. In contrast, many wireless devices have intermittent, low-bandwidth network connections.

In summary, the rules that apply to desktop and enterprise software development do not generally apply to consumer devices and embedded software development. Even though from the historical viewpoint it would be quite easy to predict the future of small devices to be similar to the past history of personal computers, it is by no means obvious that the history will actually repeat itself in this context. Rather, at least for the time being, a fundamentally different mindset is required to address the peculiarities of consumer devices, embedded systems, and the consumer market.

3.4   Requirements

This section introduces the technical requirements and constraints that were followed in defining the CLDC and MIDP standards. We start with the hardware and software requirements, and then discuss the specific constraints that Java 2 Micro Edition imposes on its configurations and profiles.

It should be noted that the requirements of CLDC and MIDP are different. CLDC is not targeted to any specific device category, and therefore its requirements are broader than those of MIDP. MIDP is focused specifically on two-way wireless communication devices such as cell phones, and the requirements of MIDP are specific to its target market.

3.4.1   Hardware requirements of CLDC

CLDC is intended to run on a wide variety of small devices. The underlying hardware capabilities of these devices vary considerably, and therefore the *CLDC Specification* does not impose any specific hardware requirements other than memory requirements.

The *CLDC Specification* assumes that the Java virtual machine, the configuration libraries, the profile libraries, and the applications must all fit within a *total memory budget of 160 to 512 kilobytes*. More specifically, it is assumed that:

- At least 128 kilobytes of non-volatile[2] memory is available for the virtual machine and CLDC libraries.

- At least 32 kilobytes of volatile[3] memory is available for the virtual machine runtime (for example, the object heap).

The ratio of volatile to non-volatile memory in the total memory budget can vary considerably depending on the target device and the role of the Java platform in the device. If the Java platform is used strictly for running system applications that are built in a device, then applications can be prelinked and preloaded, and a very limited amount of volatile memory is needed. If the Java platform is used for running dynamically downloaded content, then devices will need a higher ratio of volatile memory.

---

[2] The term *non-volatile* is used to indicate that the memory is expected to retain its contents between the user turning the device "on" or "off." For the purposes of the *CLDC Specification* and *MIDP Specification*, it is assumed that non-volatile memory is usually accessed in read mode, and that special setup might be required to write to it. Examples of non-volatile memory include ROM, flash, and battery-packed SDRAM. The *CLDC Specification* or *MIDP Specification* do not define which memory technology a device must have, nor do they define the behavior of such memory in a power-loss scenario.

[3] The term *volatile* is used to indicate that the memory is not expected to retain its contents between the user turning the device "on" or "off". For the purposes of the *CLDC Specification* and *MIDP Specification*, it is assumed that volatile memory can be read from and written to directly. The most common type of volatile memory is DRAM.

3.4.2   Hardware requirements of MIDP

The MIDP expert group defined a *Mobile Information Device* (MID) to be a device that should meet the following *minimum* requirements:

- Memory:
    - 128 kilobytes of non-volatile memory for the MIDP components[4]
    - 8 kilobytes of non-volatile memory for application-created persistent data
    - 32 kilobytes of volatile memory for the virtual machine runtime (for example, the object heap)
- Display:
    - Screen-size: 96x54
    - Display depth: 1-bit
    - Pixel shape (aspect ratio): approximately 1:1
- Input:
    - One or more of the following user-input mechanisms (see Figure 3.3):
        - "one-handed keypad"
        - "two-handed keyboard"
        - touch screen
- Networking:
    - Two-way, wireless, possibly intermittent, with limited bandwidth

3.4.3   Software requirements of CLDC

Like the hardware capabilities, the system software in CLDC target devices varies considerably. For instance, some of the devices might have a full-featured operating system that supports multiple, concurrent operating system processes and a hierarchical file system. Many other devices might have extremely limited system software with no notion of a file system. Faced with such variety, CLDC makes minimal assumptions about the underlying system software.

Generally, the *CLDC Specification* assumes that a minimal *host operating system* or kernel is available to manage the underlying hardware. This host operating system must provide at least one schedulable entity to run the Java virtual

---

[4.] Memory requirements cited here are for MIDP components only. MIDP runs on top of CLDC, so the static size of the CLDC implementation must be added to this figure.

machine. The host operating system does not need to support separate address spaces or processes, nor does it have to make any guarantees about the real-time scheduling or latency behavior.

3.4.4   Software requirements of MIDP

For devices meeting the MIDP hardware requirements described in previous sub-section, there is a broad range of possible system software capabilities. Unlike the consumer desktop computer model where there are large, dominant system software architectures, the Mobile Information Device (MID) space is character-ized by a wide variety of system software. For example, some MIDs might have a full-featured operating system that supports multiprocessing[5] and hierarchical file systems, while other MIDs might have small, thread-based operating systems with no notion of a file system. Faced with such variety, the *MIDP Specification*, like the *CLDC Specification*, makes minimal assumptions about system software. These requirements are as follows:

- A minimal *kernel* to manage the underlying hardware (that is, handling of in-terrupts, exceptions, and minimal scheduling). This kernel must provide at least one schedulable entity to run the Java virtual machine. The kernel does not need to support separate address spaces (or *processes*) or make any guar-antees about either real-time scheduling or latency behavior.

- A mechanism to read and write from non-volatile memory to support the MIDP persistence APIs discussed in Chapter 11.

- Read and write access to the device's wireless networking to support the MIDP networking APIs discussed in Chapter 10.

- A mechanism to provide a time base for use in time stamping the records writ-ten to persistent storage and to provide the basis of the timer APIs defined in Section 12.1, "Timer Support."

- A minimal capability to write to a bit-mapped graphics display.

- A mechanism to capture user input from one (or more) of the three input mech-anisms previously discussed.

[5.] The ability to run multiple, concurrent processes, each with a separate and distinct mem-ory map.

3.4.5   J2ME requirements

CLDC is defined as a Java 2 Micro Edition (J2ME™) *configuration*. MIDP is defined as a Java 2 Micro Edition *profile*. The rules for J2ME configurations and profiles impose certain additional constraints on the CLDC and MIDP specifications:

- A J2ME configuration shall only define a minimum complement or the "lowest common denominator" of Java technology. All the features included in a configuration must be generally *applicable to a wide variety of devices*. Features specific to a certain vertical market, device category or industry should be defined in a *profile*. This means that the scope of the Connected, Limited Device Configuration Specification is limited and must generally be complemented by profiles.

- Since the goal of the J2ME configurations and profiles is to guarantee portability and interoperability between various kinds of resource-constrained devices, the configurations and profiles do not generally define any *optional features*. This limitation has a significant impact on what can be included in the CLDC and MIDP specifications and what should not be included. More device-specific functionality should generally be avoided, but, if necessary, such functionality must be defined in manufacturer-specific *licensee open classes*, also known as *OEM-specific classes*, rather than in the J2ME configuration or profile specifications.

Note that the absence of optional features in CLDC and MIDP does not preclude the use of various *implementation-level optimizations*. For instance, at the implementation level alternative bytecode execution techniques (for example, Just-In-Time compilation) or application representation techniques can be used, as long as the observable user-level semantics of the implementation remain the same as defined by the *CLDC Specification* and *MIDP Specification*.

3.5   Scope of the CLDC and MIDP Standardization Efforts

3.5.1   Scope of CLDC

Based on the decisions of the JSR-30 expert group, the *CLDC Specification* addresses the following areas:

- Java language and virtual machine features
- core libraries (`java.lang.*`, `java.io.*`, `java.util.*`)
- input/output
- networking
- security
- internationalization

The *CLDC Specification* intentionally does *not* address the following functionality areas and features:

- application life-cycle management (application installation, launching, deletion)
- user interface functionality
- event handling
- high-level application model (interaction between the user and the application)

These features can be addressed by profiles implemented on top of the Connected, Limited Device Configuration. In general, the CLDC expert group intentionally kept small the number of areas addressed by the *CLDC Specification* in order not to exceed the strict memory limitations or to exclude any particular device category. Future versions of the Connected, Limited Device Configuration may address additional areas.

3.5.2   Scope of MIDP

Mobile Information Devices (MIDs) span a potentially wide set of capabilities. Rather than try to address all such capabilities, the MIDP expert group agreed to limit the set of APIs specified, addressing only those APIs that were considered absolute requirements to achieve broad portability. These APIs are:

- application model (that is, defining the semantics of a MIDP application and how the application is controlled)
- user interface (includes display and input)
- persistent storage
- networking
- timers

By the same reasoning, some areas of functionality were considered to be outside the scope of the MIDP. These areas include:

- *System-level APIs*: The emphasis of the Mobile Information Device Profile is on enabling *application programming*, rather than enabling *system programming*. Thus, low-level APIs that specify a system interface to, for example, power management or voice CODECs, are beyond the scope of the *MIDP Specification*.

- *Application delivery and management*: While it is assumed that a MIDP-compliant device will support dynamic application downloading, the diversity of the worldwide wireless infrastructure makes it impractical to specify how the application download occurs. For example, in a low-bandwidth wireless network, it might not be practical for applications to be delivered to the device over the wireless link. Instead, such a device might opt to enable application downloading via a serial link or other physical links. What is assumed, however, is that an application running on a mobile information device (MID) can access the network through specified network APIs. How applications are actually stored or installed on a MID is also beyond the scope of the *MIDP Specification*. For a MID that has a full-featured, hierarchical file system, storage and installation is easy to accomplish. On the other hand, for devices that do not have a file system, application storage is much more problematic.

- *Low-level security*[6]: MIDP specifies no additional low-level security features other than those provided by the CLDC.

- *Application-level security*[7]: The MIDP application model is described in Chapter 8. Other than the semantics implied by the MIDP application model and the *CLDC Specification*, the MIDP specifies no additional application-level security features.

- *End-to-end security*[8]: Given the broad diversity of wireless infrastructure in the world, the MIDP expert group found it impossible to mandate a single end-to-end security mechanism.

[6.] *Low-level security* (also known as *virtual machine* security) ensures that an ill-formed or maliciously-encoded class file does not crash the virtual machine or the device.

[7.] *Application-level security* defines which APIs and system resources the application can access.

[8.] *End-to-end security* establishes a model that guarantees that a transaction initiated on a mobile information device is protected (for instance, encrypted, and so forth) along the entire path from the device to and from the entity providing the services for that transaction.

Security issues are discussed in more detail in Section 4.2, "Security."

At first glance, the scope of the *MIDP Specification* might seem limited. However, given the broad range of devices that the *MIDP Specification* addresses, the MIDP expert group felt that it would be better to concentrate on a small set of common, required functionality, and by doing so create a "lowest common denominator" platform where none exists today. In particular, the MIDP expert group did not want to mandate features that cannot be supported easily on all the MIDP target devices and wireless networks.

CHAPTER 4

High-Level Architecture and Security

4.1 High-Level Architecture

As stated in the previous chapter, the high-level goal of the CLDC and MIDP standardization efforts is to create a highly portable, secure, small-footprint application development environment that enables third-party software development for resource-constrained, connected devices. CLDC serves as a generic, lowest common denominator platform that targets all kinds of resource-constrained devices, while MIDP builds on top of CLDC and focuses specifically on wireless two-way communication devices.

Figure 4.1 shows a high-level architectural view that illustrates the role of CLDC and MIDP in a mobile information device (MID). Not all the devices that implement the *CLDC Specification* and *MIDP Specification* will have all the elements shown in this figure, nor will every device necessarily layer its software as depicted in this figure.

In Figure 4.1, the lowest-level block represents the hardware of the mobile information device. On top of this hardware is the *native system software*. This layer includes the *host operating system* and libraries used internally by the device.

Starting at the next level, from left to right, is the next layer of software, the Connected, Limited Device Configuration (CLDC). This block represents the Java virtual machine and associated libraries defined by the *CLDC Specification*. This block provides the underlying Java execution environment upon which higher-level Java APIs may be built.

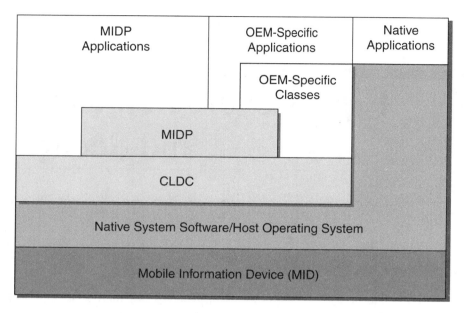

Figure 4.1   High-level architecture view

Two categories of APIs are shown on top of CLDC:

- **MIDP:** The set of APIs defined in the *MIDP Specification.*

- **OEM-specific classes:** Given the broad diversity of devices in the MIDP space, the *MIDP Specification* cannot possibly fully address all the requirements that device manufacturers and other original equipment manufacturers (OEMs) may have. These manufacturer-specific classes may be provided by an OEM to access certain functionality specific to a given device. Applications utilizing such APIs will not typically be portable to other manufacturers' devices. OEM-specific classes are sometimes also referred to as *licensee open classes.*

Note that Figure 4.1 shows CLDC as the basis for MIDP and OEM-specific classes. This does not imply that MIDP APIs or OEM-specific APIs cannot have native functionality (that is, methods declared as *native*). Rather, the intent of the figure is to show that for security reasons any native methods on a device are actually accessed through the Java virtual machine, which maps the Java-level APIs to the underlying native implementation. Also note that CLDC can be used as the basis for other J2ME profiles than just MIDP. In other words, while MIDP depends on features and APIs provided by CLDC, the reverse is not true.

The topmost blocks in Figure 4.1 represent the *application types* possible on a mobile information device. A short description of each application type is shown in Table 4.1

It is beyond the scope of this book to address OEM-specific or native applications. The MIDP application model will be discussed in more detail in Chapter 8, "MIDP Application Model."

Table 4.1   Application types

Application Type	Description
MIDP application	A MIDP application, or *MIDlet*, is one that uses only the Java libraries defined by the MIDP and CLDC specifications. This type of application is the focus of the *MIDP Specification* and is expected to be the most common type of Java application.
OEM-specific application	An OEM-specific application depends on class files that are not part of the *MIDP Specification* (that is, the OEM-specific classes). Usually, applications written using OEM-specific classes are not portable across devices from different manufacturers.
Native application	A native application is one that is not written in the Java programming language and is built on top of the existing native system software of the device.

4.2   Security

With corporations and individuals depending increasingly on critical information stored in computer systems and networks, security issues are becoming ever more important, and even more so in the context of mobile computing and wireless networks. Due to its inherent security architecture, the Java development platform is particularly well-suited to security-critical environments. The security model provided by Java 2 Standard Edition provides developers with a powerful and flexible security framework that is built into the Java platform. Developers can create fine-grained security policies and articulate independent permissions for individual applications, all while appearing transparent to the end user.

Unfortunately, the total amount of code devoted to security in Java 2 Standard Edition exceeds the memory budget available for CLDC and MIDP. Therefore, some simplifications are necessary when defining the security model for CLDC and MIDP. The security model of CLDC and MIDP is defined at three different levels:

1. *Low-level security*. Low-level security, also known as *virtual machine security*, ensures that an ill-formed or maliciously-encoded class file does not crash the mobile information device.

2. *Application-level security*. Application-level security means that a Java application running on a mobile information device can access only those libraries, system resources and other components that the device and the Java application environment allows it to access.

3. *End-to-end security*. End-to-end security refers to a model that guarantees that any transaction initiated on a mobile information device is protected along the entire path from the device to/from the entity providing the services for that transaction (*e.g*, a server located on the Internet). Encryption or other means may be necessary to achieve this.

Below we take a more detailed look at each of these levels.

4.2.1   Low-level (virtual machine) security

A key requirement for a Java virtual machine in a mobile information device is *low-level virtual machine security*. An application running in the virtual machine must not be able to harm the device in which the virtual machine is running, or crash the virtual machine itself. In a standard Java virtual machine implementation, this constraint is guaranteed by the *class file verifier*, which ensures that the bytecodes and other items stored in class files cannot contain illegal instructions, cannot be executed in an illegal order, and cannot contain references to invalid memory locations or memory areas that are outside the Java object memory (the object heap). In general, the role of the class file verifier is to ensure that class files loaded into the virtual machine do not execute in any way that is not allowed by the *Java™ Virtual Machine Specification*.

The *CLDC Specification* requires that a Java virtual machine supporting the CLDC standard must be able to reject invalid class files. This is guaranteed by the class file verification technology presented in Section 5.4.3, "Class file verification." The same technology applies also to MIDP, which typically runs on top of a virtual machine conforming to the *CLDC Specification*.

4.2.2 Application-level security

Even though class file verification plays a critical role in ensuring the security of the Java platform, the security provided by the class file verifier is insufficient by itself. The class file verifier can only guarantee that the given application is a valid Java program and nothing more. There are still several other potential security threats that will go unnoticed by the verifier. For instance, access to external resources such as the file system, printers, infrared devices, native libraries or the network is beyond the scope of the class file verifier. By *application-level security*, we mean that a Java application can access only those libraries, system resources and other components that the device and the Java application environment allows it to access.

Sandbox model

In CLDC and MIDP, application-level security is accomplished by using a metaphor of a closed "*sandbox*." An application must run in a closed environment in which the application can access only those libraries that have been defined by the configuration, profiles, and OEM-specific classes supported by the device. Java applications cannot escape from this sandbox or access any libraries or resources that are not part of the predefined functionality. The sandbox ensures that an untrusted and possibly malicious application cannot gain access to system resources.

In more technical terms, the sandbox model means that:

- Class files have been properly verified and are guaranteed to be valid Java applications. (Class file verification is discussed in more detail in Section 5.4.3, "Class file verification.")

- A closed, predefined set of Java APIs is available to the application programmer, as defined by CLDC, profiles (such as MIDP) and OEM-specific classes.

- The downloading and management of Java applications on the device takes place at the native code level inside the virtual machine and no user-definable class loaders are provided, in order to prevent the programmer from overriding the standard class loading mechanisms of the virtual machine.

- The set of native functions accessible to the virtual machine is closed, meaning that the application programmer cannot download any new libraries containing native functionality or access any native functions that are not part of the Java libraries provided by CLDC, profiles (such as MIDP) or OEM-specific classes.

Protecting system classes

A central requirement for CLDC is the ability to support dynamic downloading of Java applications to the virtual machine. A possible application-level security hole in the Java virtual machine would be exposed if the downloaded applications could override the system classes provided in packages `java.*`, `javax.microedition.*` or other profile-specific or OEM-specific packages. CLDC and MIDP implementations generally ensure that the application programmer cannot override the classes in these protected system packages. At the implementation level this can be guaranteed in different ways. One solution is to require the built-in system classes always to be searched first when performing a class file lookup. For security reasons, it is also required that the application programmer is not allowed to manipulate the class file lookup order in any way. Class file lookup order is discussed in more detail in "Class file lookup order" on page 56.

Additional restrictions on dynamic class loading

Dynamic loading of Java applications is a key feature of both CLDC and MIDP. However, both *CLDC Specification* and *MIDP Specification* define the class loading mechanism of a virtual machine conforming to CLDC to be implementation-dependent, with one important restriction: by default, a Java application can load application classes only from its own Java Archive (JAR) file. This restriction ensures that Java applications on a device cannot interfere with other or steal each others' data. Additionally, this ensures that a third-party application cannot gain access to the private or protected components of the Java classes that the device manufacturer or a service provider may have provided as part of the system applications. JAR files and applications representation formats are discussed in more detail in Section 5.4.4, "Class file format and class loading" and in the *CLDC Specification* and the *MIDP Specification*.

Together the low-level virtual machine security features and application-level security features guarantee that:

- All the classes are in the correct format.

- Application classes can only be loaded from the application's own JAR file.

- Application classes cannot override the functionality provided by system classes.

- The bytecodes of class files will not contain illegal instructions, contain instructions in an illegal order or will not refer to illegal memory addresses.

- Classes are not allowed to access protected system resources.

4.2.3   End-to-end security

A device supporting CLDC or MIDP is typically a part of an end-to-end solution such as a wireless network or a payment terminal network. These networks commonly require a number of advanced security solutions to ensure safe delivery of data and code between server machines and client devices. Given the broad diversity of wireless infrastructure in the world, the CLDC and MIDP expert groups decided not to mandate a single end-to-end security mechanism. Therefore, all the end-to-end security solutions are assumed to be implementation-dependent and outside the scope of *CLDC Specification* and *MIDP Specification*.

CHAPTER **5**

Connected Limited Device Configuration

This chapter introduces the Connected, Limited Device Configuration (CLDC), one of the core building blocks of the Java 2 Platform, Micro Edition (J2ME™). The goal of the Connected, Limited Device Configuration is to define a portable, minimum-footprint Java platform for small, resource-constrained, connected devices characterized as follows:

- 160 to 512 kilobytes of total memory budget available for the Java platform,

- a 16-bit or 32-bit processor,

- low power consumption, often operating with battery power,

- connectivity to some kind of network, often with a wireless, intermittent connection and with limited (often 9600 bps or less) bandwidth.

Cell phones, two-way pagers, personal digital assistants (PDAs), organizers, home appliances and point-of-sale terminals are some, but not all, of the devices that might be supported by the Connected, Limited Device Configuration.

The material in this chapter comes from the *CLDC Specification* document that is available from Sun's Java Community Process (JCP) web site[1]. The *CLDC Specification* defines the minimum required complement of Java technology components and libraries for small connected devices. Java language and virtual machine features, core libraries, input/output, networking and security are the primary topics addressed by the *CLDC Specification*.

---

[1] http://java.sun.com/aboutJava/communityprocess

43

5.1   CLDC Expert Group

The *CLDC Specification* is the result of the work of a Java Community Process (JCP) expert group JSR-30 consisting of a large number of industrial partners. The following 18 companies (in alphabetical order) were members of the CLDC expert group:

- America Online
- Bull
- Ericsson
- Fujitsu
- Matsushita
- Mitsubishi
- Motorola
- Nokia
- NTT DoCoMo
- Oracle
- Palm Computing
- Research In Motion (RIM)
- Samsung
- Sharp
- Siemens
- Sony
- Sun Microsystems
- Symbian

CLDC is core technology that can be used as the basis for one or more *J2ME profiles* such as MIDP.

5.2   CLDC Application Model

5.2.1   Architectural overview

The high-level architecture of a typical CLDC device is illustrated in Figure 5.1. At the heart of a CLDC implementation is the *Java virtual machine*, which, apart from specific differences defined later in this chapter, is compliant with the *Java™ Virtual Machine Specification* and *Java™ Language Specification*. The virtual machine typically runs on top of a *host operating system* that provides the necessary capabilities to manage the underlying hardware. As explained in Section 3.4.3, "Software requirements of CLDC," the *CLDC Specification* makes minimal assumptions about the capabilities of the host operating system.

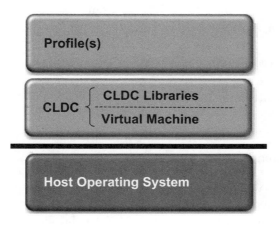

Figure 5.1   Architecture overview of a CLDC target device

On top of the virtual machine are the *Java libraries*. These libraries are divided broadly into two categories:

1. those defined by the Connected, Limited Device Configuration (CLDC Libraries),

2. those defined by profiles such as MIDP.

Libraries defined by the Connected, Limited Device Configuration are discussed in Chapter 6. Libraries defined by profiles are outside the scope of *CLDC Specification*. The libraries supported by the Mobile Information Device Profile will be discussed in Chapters 8 through 12.

5.2.2   The concept of a Java application

Connected, Limited Device Configuration is not targeted to any specific device category. Some of the target devices may have an advanced graphical user interface, some target devices may be operated from a textual, character-based user interface, while many other target devices may not have any visual user interface or display at all. To cater to such a broad variety of devices, the application model defined in the *CLDC Specification* is intentionally very simple.

In the *CLDC Specification*, the term *Java application* is used to refer to a collection of Java class files containing a single, unique method main that identifies the launch point of the application. As specified in the *Java™ Virtual Machine*

Specification (JVMS) Sections 5.2 and 2.17.1, the method `main` must be declared `public`, `static`, and `void`, as shown below:

```
public static void main(String[] args)
```

A virtual machine conforming to CLDC starts the execution of a Java application by calling the method `main`.

5.2.3   Application management

Many small, resource-constrained devices do not have a file system or any other standard mechanism for storing dynamically downloaded information on the device. Therefore, a CLDC implementation does not require that Java applications downloaded from an external source are stored persistently on the device. Rather, the implementation might just load the application and discard it immediately after execution.

However, in many potential CLDC devices, it is beneficial to be able to execute the same Java applications multiple times without having to download the applications over and over again. This is particularly important if applications are being downloaded over a wireless network, and the user could incur high downloading expenses. If a device implementing CLDC is capable of storing applications persistently, we assume that the device implementing has capabilities for managing the applications that have been stored in the device. At the high level, *application management* refers to the ability to:

- download and install Java applications,

- inspect existing Java applications stored on the device,

- select and launch Java applications,

- delete existing Java applications (if applicable).

Due to significant variations and feature differences among potential CLDC devices, the details of application management are highly device-specific and implementation-dependent. Consequently, application management capabilities are often written in the C programming language or some other low-level programming language specific to the host operating system. The actual details of application management are outside the scope of the *CLDC Specification*. Application management issues in the context of the Mobile Information Device Profile are discussed in Section 8.4, "MIDP System Software."

Also note that depending on the resources available on the device, a CLDC system may allow multiple Java applications to execute concurrently, or can restrict the system to permit the execution of only one Java application at a time. It is up to the particular implementation to decide if the execution of multiple Java applications is supported by utilizing the multiprocessing capabilities (if they exist) of the underlying host operating system, or by instantiating multiple logical virtual machines to run the concurrent Java applications.

5.3   Java Language Specification Compatibility

The general goal for a virtual machine conforming to CLDC is to be as compliant with the *Java™ Language Specification* as is feasible within the strict memory limits of CLDC target devices. This section summarizes the differences between a virtual machine conforming to CLDC and the Java virtual machine of Java 2 Standard Edition (J2SE). Except for the differences indicated herein, a virtual machine conforming to CLDC is compatible with Chapters 1 through 17 of the *The Java™ Language Specification* by James Gosling, Bill Joy and Guy L. Steele. Addison-Wesley, 1996, ISBN 0-201-63451-1.[2]

5.3.1   No floating point support

The main language-level difference between the full *Java™ Language Specification* and the *CLDC Specification* is that a virtual machine conforming to CLDC does not provide floating point support. Floating point support was removed because the majority of CLDC target devices do not have hardware floating point support, and since the cost of supporting floating point in software was considered too high by the CLDC expert group.

Note – For the remainder of this book, the *Java™ Language Specification* is referred to as JLS. Sections within the *Java™ Language Specification* are referred to using the § symbol. For example, (JLS §4.2.4).

This means that a virtual machine conforming to CLDC does not allow the use of floating point literals (JLS §3.10.2), floating point types and values (JLS

[2.] When the *CLDC Specification* was under preparation, the second edition of *Java™ Language Specification* was not yet available. For consistency with the *CLDC Specification* version 1.0, we refer to the first edition of the *Java™ Language Specification* in this book.

§4.2.3), and floating point operations (JLS §4.2.4). For further information, refer to Section 5.4.1.

5.3.2   No finalization

CLDC libraries do not include the method `java.lang.Object.finalize`. Therefore, a virtual machine conforming to CLDC does not support finalization of class instances (JLS §12.6). No application built to conform to the Connected, Limited Device Configuration can require that finalization be available.

5.3.3   Error handling limitations

A virtual machine conforming to CLDC supports *exception* handling as defined in JLS Chapter 11. However, the set of *error* classes included in CLDC libraries is limited, and consequently the error handling capabilities of CLDC are restricted. This is because:

1. In embedded systems, recovery from error conditions is usually highly device-specific. While some embedded devices may try to recover from serious error conditions, many embedded devices simply soft-reset themselves upon encountering an error. Application programmers cannot be expected to know about device-specific error handling mechanisms and conventions.

2. As specified in JLS §11.5.2, class `java.lang.Error` and its subclasses are exceptions from which programs are not ordinarily expected to recover. Implementing the error handling capabilities fully according to the *Java™ Language Specification* is rather expensive, and mandating the presence and handling of all the error classes would impose a significant overhead on the implementation given the strict memory constraints in CLDC target devices.

A virtual machine conforming to CLDC provides a limited set of error classes defined in Section 6.2.7, "Exception and error classes." When encountering any other error, the implementation will handle the error in a manner that is appropriate for the device.

5.4   Java Virtual Machine Specification Compatibility

The general goal for a virtual machine conforming to CLDC is to be as compliant with the *Java™ Virtual Machine Specification* as is possible within strict memory constraints of CLDC target devices. This section summarizes the differences between a virtual machine conforming to CLDC and the Java virtual machine of Java 2 Standard Edition (J2SE). Except for the differences indicated herein, a virtual machine conforming to CLDC is compatible with the Java virtual machine as specified in the *The Java™ Virtual Machine Specification, Second Edition* by Tim Lindholm and Frank Yellin. Addison-Wesley, 1999, ISBN 0-201-43294-3.

Note – For the remainder of this book, the *Java™ Virtual Machine Specification* is referred to as JVMS. Sections within the *Java™ Virtual Machine Specification* are referred to using the § symbol. For example, (JVMS §2.4.3).

5.4.1 No floating point support

A virtual machine conforming to CLDC does not have floating point support. Floating point support was removed because the majority of CLDC target devices do not have hardware floating point support, and since the cost of supporting floating point in software was considered too high. Consequently, a virtual machine conforming to CLDC does not support the following bytecodes:

Constants

```
fconst_0, fconst_1, fconst_2, dconst_0, dconst_1
```

Loads

```
fload, fload_1, fload_2, fload_3, dload, dload_1, dload_2, dload_3
```

Stores

```
fstore, fstore_1, fstore_2, fstore_3, dstore, dstore_1, dstore_2,
dstore_3
```

Arrays

```
faload, daload, fastore, dastore, newarray T_DOUBLE, newarray
T_FLOAT
```

Arithmetic

fadd, dadd, fsub, dsub, fmul, dmul, fdiv, ddiv, frem, drem, fneg, dneg, fcmpl, fcmpg, dcmpl, dcmpg

Conversion

i2f, f2i, i2d, d2i, l2f, l2d, f2l, d2l, f2d, d2f

Returns

freturn, dreturn

All user-supplied classes and methods running on top of a virtual machine conforming to CLDC must satisfy the following constraints:

- No method can use any of the above forbidden bytecodes.
- No field can have as its type float or double, an array of one of those types, or an array of array of one of those types.
- No method can have an argument or return type of type float or double or an array whose component type is float or double.
- No constant pool entry can be of type CONSTANT_Float or CONSTANT_Double.
- No constant pool entry can be of type CONSTANT_Class in which the class is an array of type float or double.

Due to the lack of floating point support, the following sections and subsections of the *Java™ Virtual Machine Specification* (JVMS) are not applicable to a virtual machine conforming to CLDC: §2.4.3, §2.4.4, §2.18, §3.3.2 and §3.8. In addition, all the other parts of the JVMS that refer to floating point data types (float or double) or operations are beyond the scope of the *CLDC Specification*.

5.4.2   Other differences

A number of features have been eliminated from a virtual machine conforming to CLDC because the Java libraries included in CLDC are substantially more limited than libraries in Java 2 Standard Edition, and/or the presence of the feature would have posed security problems in the absence of the full J2SE security model. The eliminated features include:

- Java Native Interface (JNI),
- user-defined class loaders,
- reflection,
- thread groups and daemon threads,
- finalization,
- weak references.

Applications written to conform to the Connected, Limited Device Configuration shall not rely on any of the features above. Each of the features in this list is discussed in more detail below.

Java Native Interface (JNI)

A virtual machine conforming to CLDC does not implement the Java Native Interface (JNI). The way in which the virtual machine invokes native functionality is implementation-dependent. Support for JNI was eliminated mainly because of two reasons:

- the limited security model provided by CLDC assumes that the set of native functions must be closed (Section 4.2.2, "Application-level security.")
- the full implementation of JNI was considered too expensive given the strict memory constraints of CLDC target devices and the additional performance overhead imposed by JNI.

User-defined class loaders

A virtual machine conforming to CLDC does not provide user-defined, Java-level class loaders (see JVMS §5.3, §2.17.2.) A virtual machine conforming to CLDC has a built-in class loader that cannot be overridden, replaced or reconfigured by the user. The actual class loading implementation as well as any error conditions occurring during class loading are implementation-dependent. The elimination of user-defined class loaders is part of the security restrictions of the *CLDC Specification*. (See Section 4.2.2, "Application-level security.")

Reflection

A virtual machine conforming to CLDC does not have reflection features, that is, features that allow a Java application to inspect the number and the contents of classes, objects, methods, fields, threads, execution stacks and other runtime structures inside the virtual machine.

An application built to conform to the Connected, Limited Device Configuration shall not rely on features that require reflection capabilities. Consequently, a virtual machine conforming to CLDC does not support remote method invocation (RMI), object serialization, JVMDI (Debugging Interface), JVMPI (Profiler Interface), or any other advanced features of Java 2 Standard Edition that depend on the presence of reflective capabilities.

Thread groups and daemon threads

A virtual machine conforming to CLDC implements multithreading, but does not have support for thread groups or daemon threads. (See JVMS §2.19, §8.12-14). Thread operations such as starting and stopping of threads can be applied only to individual thread objects. If application programmers want to perform thread operations for groups of threads, explicit collection objects must be used at the application level to store the thread objects.

Finalization

CLDC libraries do not include the method `java.lang.Object.finalize`, and therefore a virtual machine conforming to CLDC does not support finalization of class instances. (See JVMS §2.17.7). No application built to conform to the Connected, Limited Device Configuration can require that finalization be available.

Weak references

A virtual machine conforming to CLDC does not support weak references. No application built to conform to the Connected, Limited Device Configuration can require that weak references be available.

Errors

As discussed earlier in Section 5.3.3, "Error handling limitations," the error handling capabilities of a virtual machine conforming to CLDC are limited. Apart from providing the error classes defined in Section 6.2.7, "Exception and error classes," the error handling capabilities of a virtual machine conforming to CLDC are assumed to be defined in a manner that is appropriate for the target device.

5.4.3 Class file verification

Like the Java virtual machine of Java 2 Standard Edition, a virtual machine conforming to CLDC must be able to reject invalid class files. However, since the static and dynamic memory footprint of the standard class file verifier is excessive for a typical CLDC target device, an alternative solution is defined in the *CLDC Specification*. This solution is described below.

Off-device preverification and runtime verification with stack maps

The existing J2SE class file verifier defined in the *Java™ Virtual Machine Specification* JVMS §4.9 is not ideal for small, resource-constrained devices. The J2SE verifier takes a minimum of 50 kilobytes of binary code space, and typically at least 30 to 100 kilobytes of dynamic RAM at runtime. In addition, the CPU power needed to perform the complex dataflow algorithm in the conventional verifier can be substantial.

The verification approach described in this subsection is significantly smaller and more efficient in resource-constrained devices than the existing J2SE verifier. The implementation of the new verifier in Sun's KVM requires about 12 kilobytes of Intel x86 binary code, and less than 100 bytes of dynamic RAM at runtime for typical class files. The verifier performs only a linear scan of the bytecode, without the need of a costly dataflow algorithm.

The new class file verifier operates in two phases, as illustrated in Figure 5.2.

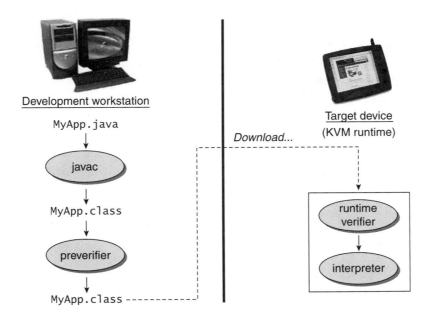

Figure 5.2   Two-phase class file verification in CLDC

- First, class files have to be run through a special *preverifier* tool in order to augment the class files with additional attributes to speed up runtime verification. The preverification phase is typically performed on the development workstation that the application developer uses for writing and compiling the applications.

- At runtime, the *runtime verifier* component of the virtual machine uses the additional attributes generated by the preverifier to perform the actual class file verification efficiently.

The interpretation of bytecodes in a class file can start only when the class file has successfully passed the runtime verifier.

Runtime class file verification guarantees type safety. Classes that pass the runtime verifier cannot, for example, violate the type system of the Java virtual machine and corrupt the memory. Unlike approaches based on code signing, such a guarantee does not rely on the verification attribute to be authentic or trusted. A missing, incorrect or corrupted verification attribute causes the class to be rejected by the runtime verifier.

The new verifier requires the methods in class files to contain a special `Stack-Map` attribute. The preverifier tool inserts this attribute into normal class files. A transformed class file is still a valid Java class file, with additional attributes (refer to the *CLDC Specification* for further details) that allow verification to be carried out efficiently at runtime. These attributes are automatically ignored by the conventional class file verifier used in Java 2 Standard Edition, so the solution is fully upward compatible with the Java virtual machine of Java 2 Standard Edition. Preprocessed class files containing the extra attributes are approximately 5 to 10 percent larger than the original, unmodified class files.

Additionally, the new verifier requires that all the *subroutines in the bytecodes of class files are inlined*. In Java class files, subroutines are special bytecode sequences that contain the bytecodes `jsr`, `jsr_w`, `ret` or `wide ret`. The inlining process removes all the `jsr`, `jsr_w`, `ret` and `wide ret` bytecodes from all the methods in class files, replacing these instructions with semantically equivalent bytecode. The inlining process makes runtime verification significantly easier and faster.

The new verification process and the format of the `StackMap` attribute have been specified in more detail in the *CLDC Specification*.

5.4.4 Class file format and class loading

An essential requirement for the Connected, Limited Device Configuration is the ability to support dynamic downloading of Java applications and third-party content. The dynamic class loading mechanism of the Java platform plays a central role in this. This section discusses the application representation formats and class loading practices required of a virtual machine conforming to CLDC.

Supported file formats

A CLDC implementation must be able to read standard class files (defined in JVMS Chapter 4) with the preverification changes discussed above. In addition, a CLDC implementation must support compressed Java Archive (JAR) files. Detailed information about the JAR format is provided at `http://java.sun.com/products/jdk/1.2/docs/guide/jar/`.

Network bandwidth conservation is very important in low bandwidth wireless networks. The compressed JAR format provides 30 to 50 percent compression over regular class files without loss of any symbolic information or compatibility problems with existing Java systems.

Public representation of Java applications and resources

A Java application is considered to be *"represented publicly"* or *"distributed publicly"* when the system it is stored on is open to the public, and the transport layers and protocols it can be accessed with are open standards. In contrast, a device can be part of a *closed network environment* where the vendor (such as the operator of a wireless network) controls all communication. In this case, the application is no longer represented publicly once it enters and is distributed via the closed network system.

Whenever Java applications intended for a CLDC device are represented publicly, the compressed JAR file representation format must be used. The JAR file must contain regular class files with the following restrictions and additional requirements:

1. `StackMap` attributes (See *CLDC Specification*, Section 4.4.3.2, "Stack map attribute definition" for details) must be included in class files.

2. The class files must not contain any of the following bytecodes: `jsr` (JVMS p. 304, `jsr_w` (JVMS p. 305), `ret` (JVMS p. 352) and `wide ret` (JVMS p. 360).

Sun's CLDC reference implementation includes a preverification tool for performing these modifications to a class file. The stack map attributes are automatically ignored by the conventional class file verifier described in JVMS §4.9. That is to say, the modified class file format is fully upward compatible with other Java environments such as J2SE or J2EE.

Additionally, the JAR file may contain *application-specific resource files* that can be loaded into the virtual machine by calling method `Class.getResourceAsStream(String name)`.

Class file lookup order

The *Java™ Language Specification* and *Java™ Virtual Machine Specification* do not specify the order in which class files are searched when new class files are loaded into the virtual machine. At the implementation level, a typical Java virtual machine implementation uses a special environment variable *CLASSPATH* to define the lookup order.

The *CLDC Specification* assumes class file lookup order to be implementation-dependent, with the restrictions described in the next paragraph. The lookup strategy is typically defined as part of the application management implementation (see Section 5.2.3, "Application management.") A virtual machine conforming to CLDC is not required to support the notion of *CLASSPATH*, but may do so at the implementation level.

Two restrictions apply to class file lookup order. First, as explained earlier in Section 4.2.2, "Application-level security," a virtual machine conforming to CLDC must guarantee that the application programmer cannot override the system classes (classes belonging to CLDC, profiles or OEM-specific libraries) in any way. Second, it is required that the application programmer must not be able to manipulate the class file lookup order in any way. Both of these restrictions are important for security reasons.

Implementation optimizations

The *CLDC Specification* mandates the use of compressed JAR files for Java applications that are represented and distributed publicly. However, in closed network environments (see the discussion above) and internally inside the virtual machine at runtime, alternative application representation formats can be used. For instance, in low bandwidth wireless networks it is often a good idea to use alternative, more compact transport formats at the network transport level in order to conserve network bandwidth. Similarly, when storing the downloaded applications in CLDC devices, more compact representations can be used, as long as the observable user-level semantics of the applications remain the same as with the public representation required by the *CLDC Specification*. The definition of more compact class file representations is assumed to be implementation-dependent and outside the scope of the *CLDC Specification*.

Preloading/prelinking ("ROMizing")

A virtual machine conforming to CLDC may choose to preload and prelink some classes to reduce class loading time at runtime. This technology is often referred to informally as *ROMizing*.[3] Typically, small virtual machine implementations choose to preload all the system classes (for instance, classes belonging to a specific configuration or profile) and perform application loading dynamically. The actual mechanisms for preloading are implementation-dependent and beyond the scope of the *CLDC Specification*. In all cases, the runtime effect and semantics of preloading/prelinking must be the same as if the actual class had been loaded in at that point. There must be no visible effects from preloading other than the possible speed-up in application launching. In particular, any class initialization that has a user-visible effect must be performed at the time the class would first have been used if it had not been preloaded into the system.

Future application representation formats

Regular Java class files are not optimized for network transport in limited bandwidth environments; each class file is an independent unit that contains its own constant pool (symbol table), method, field and exception tables, bytecodes and some other information. The self-contained nature of class files is one of the virtues of Java technology, allowing applications to be composed of multiple pieces that do not necessarily have to reside in the same location, and making it possible to extend applications dynamically at runtime. However, this flexibility has its price. If Java applications were treated as a sealed unit, a lot of space could be saved by removing the redundancies in multiple constant pools and other structures, especially if full symbolic information was left out. Also, one of the desirable features of an application transport format in a limited-power computing environment is the ability to execute applications "in-place," without any special loading or conversion process between the static representation and runtime representation. Standard class files are not designed for such execution. Future versions of the Connected, Limited Device Configuration may define a public application representation format that is more compact and better suited for in-place execution.

[3.] The term *ROMizing* is somewhat misleading, since this technology can be used independently of any specific memory technology. ROMized class files do not necessarily have to be stored in ROM.

CHAPTER 6

CLDC Libraries

J ava 2 Platform, Enterprise Edition (J2EE) and Java 2 Platform, Standard Edition (J2SE) provide a very rich set of libraries for the development of enterprise applications for desktop computers and servers. Unfortunately, these libraries require tens of megabytes of memory to run, and are therefore unsuitable for small devices with limited resources. In this chapter we introduce the Java-based libraries supported by the Connected, Limited Device Configuration.

6.1   Background and Goals

A general goal for designing the libraries for the Connected, Limited Device Configuration was to provide a minimum useful set of libraries for practical application development and profile definition for a variety of small devices. Given the strict memory constraints and differing features of today's small devices, it is virtually impossible to come up with a set of libraries that would support all devices. No matter where the bar for feature inclusion is set, the bar is inevitably going to be too low for some devices and users and too high for many others.

In defining the scope of the CLDC libraries, the original Java Specification Request JSR-30 was used as a guideline, and a lot of emphasis was placed on *connectivity*. This means that in addition to fundamental system and data type classes, the libraries included in CLDC provide an extensible set of networking features for both today's and tomorrow's small, connected devices.

To ensure upward compatibility with the larger editions of the Java 2 Platform, the majority of the libraries included in CLDC are a subset of Java 2 Standard Edition (J2SE) and Java 2 Enterprise Edition (J2EE). While upward compatibility is a very desirable goal, J2SE and J2EE libraries have strong internal dependencies that make subsetting them difficult in important areas such as security, input/output, user interface definition, networking, and storage. These dependencies are a natural consequence of design evolution and reuse that has taken place during the development of the libraries over time. Unfortunately, these dependencies make it difficult to take just one part of the libraries without including several others. For this reason, some of them have been redesigned, especially in the area of networking.

The libraries defined by the *CLDC Specification* can be divided broadly into two categories:

1. those classes that are a subset of standard J2SE libraries,

2. those classes that are specific to CLDC (but which can be mapped onto J2SE).

Classes belonging to the former category are located in packages `java.lang`, `java.util` and `java.io`. These classes have been derived from Java 2 Standard Edition version 1.3. A list of these classes is presented in Section 6.2, "Classes Derived from J2SE."

Classes belonging to the latter category are located in package `javax.micro-edition`. These classes are discussed in Section 6.3, "CLDC-Specific Classes."

6.2   Classes Derived from J2SE

CLDC provides a number of classes that have been derived from J2SE. The rules for J2ME configurations require that each class that has the same name and package name as a J2SE class must be identical to or a subset of the corresponding J2SE class. The semantics of the classes and their methods included in the subset may not be changed. The classes may not add any public or protected methods or fields that are not available in the corresponding J2SE classes.

6.2.1   System classes

J2SE class libraries include several classes that are intimately coupled with the Java virtual machine. Similarly, several commonly used Java tools assume the presence of certain classes in the system. For instance, the standard Java compiler (`javac`) generates code that requires certain methods of classes `String` and `StringBuffer` to be available. The system classes included in the *CLDC Specification* are listed below. Each of these classes is a subset of the corresponding class in J2SE.

```
java.lang.Object
java.lang.Class
java.lang.Runtime
java.lang.System
```

```
java.lang.Thread
```
java.lang.Runnable (interface)
```
java.lang.String
java.lang.StringBuffer
java.lang.Throwable
```

6.2.2   Data type classes

The following basic data type classes from package `java.lang` are supported. Each of these classes is a subset of the corresponding class in J2SE.

```
java.lang.Boolean
java.lang.Byte
java.lang.Short
java.lang.Integer
java.lang.Long
java.lang.Character
```

6.2.3   Collection classes

The following collection classes from package `java.util` are supported.

```
java.util.Vector
java.util.Stack
java.util.Hashtable
```
java.util.Enumeration (interface)

6.2.4   Input/output classes

The following classes from package `java.io` are supported. Classes `Reader`, `Writer`, `InputStreamReader` and `InputStreamWriter` are required in order to support internationalization (see Section 6.2.8, "Internationalization support").

```
java.io.InputStream
java.io.OutputStream
java.io.ByteArrayInputStream
java.io.ByteArrayOutputStream
```
java.io.DataInput (interface)
java.io.DataOutput (interface)
```
java.io.DataInputStream
java.io.DataOutputStream
java.io.Reader
```

```
java.io.Writer
java.io.InputStreamReader
java.io.OutputStreamWriter
java.io.PrintStream
```

6.2.5   Calendar and time classes

CLDC includes a small subset of the standard J2SE classes `java.util.Calendar`, `java.util.Date` and `java.util.TimeZone`. To conserve space, the *CLDC Specification* requires only one time zone to be supported. It is up to the device manufacturer to decide which time zone is supported by default. Additional time zones may be provided by manufacturer-specific implementations of CLDC.

```
java.util.Calendar
java.util.Date
java.util.TimeZone
```

6.2.6   Additional classes

Two additional utility classes are provided. Class `java.util.Random` provides a simple pseudo-random number generator that is useful for implementing applications such as games. Class `java.lang.Math` provides methods `min`, `max` and `abs` (for data types `int` and `long`) that are frequently used by other Java library classes.

```
java.util.Random
java.lang.Math
```

6.2.7   Exception and error classes

Since the libraries included in CLDC are generally intended to be compatible with J2SE libraries, the library classes included in CLDC throw precisely the same exceptions as regular J2SE classes do. Consequently, a fairly comprehensive set of exception classes has been included.

In contrast, as explained in Section 5.3.3, "Error handling limitations," the error handling capabilities of CLDC are limited. By default, a virtual machine conforming to CLDC is required to provide only the error classes listed below.

Error classes

```
java.lang.Error
java.lang.VirtualMachineError
java.lang.OutOfMemoryError
```

Exception classes

```
java.lang.Exception
java.lang.ClassNotFoundException
java.lang.IllegalAccessException
java.lang.InstantiationException
java.lang.InterruptedException
java.lang.RuntimeException
java.lang.ArithmeticException
java.lang.ArrayStoreException
java.lang.ClassCastException
java.lang.IllegalArgumentException
java.lang.IllegalThreadStateException
java.lang.NumberFormatException
java.lang.IllegalMonitorStateException
java.lang.IndexOutOfBoundsException
java.lang.ArrayIndexOutOfBoundsException
java.lang.StringIndexOutOfBoundsException
java.lang.NegativeArraySizeException
java.lang.NullPointerException
java.lang.SecurityException

java.util.EmptyStackException
java.util.NoSuchElementException

java.io.EOFException
java.io.IOException
java.io.InterruptedIOException
java.io.UnsupportedEncodingException
java.io.UTFDataFormatException
```

6.2.8   Internationalization support

A CLDC implementation is required to support Unicode characters. CLDC includes limited support for the translation of Unicode characters to and from a sequence of bytes. In J2SE this is done using objects called *Readers* and *Writers*, and this same mechanism is utilized in CLDC using the InputStreamReader and OutputStream-Writer classes with identical constructors.

```
new InputStreamReader(InputStream is);
new InputStreamReader(InputStream is, String enc)
    throws UnsupportedEncodingException;
```

```
new OutputStreamWriter(OutputStream os);
new OutputStreamWriter(OutputStream os, String enc)
    throws UnsupportedEncodingException;
```

If the enc parameter is present, it is the name of the encoding to be used. Where it is not, a default encoding (defined by the system property microedition.encoding) is used. Additional converters may be provided by manufacturer-specific implementations of CLDC. If a converter for a certain encoding is not available, an UnsupportedEncodingException is thrown. For official information on character encodings in J2SE, refer to http://java.sun.com/j2se/1.3/docs/guide/intl/ encoding.doc.html.

Note that CLDC does not provide any *localization* features. All the solutions related to the formatting of dates, times, currencies and so on are assumed to be outside the scope of CLDC.

6.2.9   Property support

CLDC libraries do not include the java.util.Properties class familiar from Java 2 Standard Edition. In J2SE, that class is used for storing system properties such as the name of the host operating system, version number of the virtual machine and so on. In CLDC, a limited set of system properties described in Table 6.1 is available. These properties can be accessed by calling the method System.getProperty(*String key*).

Table 6.1   Standard system properties

Key	Explanation	Default value
microedition.platform	Name of the host platform or device	null
microedition.encoding	Default character encoding	"ISO8859_1"
microedition.configuration	Name and version of the supported configuration	"CLDC-1.0"
microedition.profiles	Names of the supported profiles	null

Property microedition.encoding describes the default character encoding name. This information is used by the system to find the correct class for the default character encoding in supporting internationalization. Property microedition.platform characterizes the host platform or device. Property microedi-

`tion.configuration` describes the current J2ME configuration and version, and property `microedition.profiles` defines a string containing the names of the supported profiles, separated by blanks.

J2ME profiles may define additional properties not included in Table 6.1. The set of system properties defined by the Mobile Information Device Profile can be found in Section 12.2, "System Properties."

6.3   CLDC-Specific Classes

This section contains a description of the *Generic Connection framework* for supporting input/output and networking in a generalized, extensible fashion. The Generic Connection framework provides a coherent way to access and organize data in a resource-constrained environment.

6.3.1   Background and motivation

The class libraries included in Java 2 Standard Edition and Java 2 Enterprise Edition provide a rich set of functionality for handling input and output access to storage and networking systems. The package `java.io` of J2SE contains approximately 60 classes and interfaces, and more than 15 exception classes. The package `java.net` of J2SE consists of approximately 20 regular classes and 10 exception classes. The total static size of these class files is approximately 200 kilobytes. It is difficult to make all this functionality fit in a small device with only a few hundred kilobytes of total memory budget. Furthermore, a significant part of the standard I/O and networking functionality is not directly applicable to today's small devices, which often do not have TCP/IP support, or which commonly need to support specific types of connections such as IrDA (infrared) or Bluetooth.

In general, the requirements for the networking and storage libraries vary significantly from one resource-constrained device to another. Those device manufacturers who are dealing with packet-switched networks typically want datagram-based communication mechanisms, while those dealing with circuit-switched networks require stream-based connections. Due to strict memory limitations, manufacturers supporting certain kinds of networking capabilities generally do not want to support any other mechanisms. All this makes the design of the networking facilities for CLDC very challenging, especially since J2ME configurations are not allowed to define optional features. Also, the presence of multiple networking mechanisms and protocols is potentially very confusing to the application programmer, especially if the programmer has to deal with low-level protocol issues.

6.3.2   The Generic Connection framework

The requirements presented above have led to the generalization of the J2SE networking and I/O classes. The high-level goal for this generalized design is to be a precise functional subset of J2SE classes, which can easily map to common low-level hardware or to any J2SE implementation, but with better extensibility, flexibility, and coherence in supporting new devices and protocols.

The general idea is illustrated below. Instead of using a collection of different kinds of abstractions for different forms of communication, a set of related abstractions are used at the application programming level.

General form

```
Connector.open("<protocol>:<address>;<parameters>");
```

Note – These examples are provided for illustration only. CLDC itself does not define any protocol implementations (see Section 6.3.3, "No network protocol implementations defined in CLDC"). It is not expected that a particular J2ME profile would provide support for all these kinds of connections. J2ME profiles may also support protocols not shown below.

HTTP

```
Connector.open("http://www.sun.com");
```

Sockets

```
Connector.open("socket://129.144.111.222:2800");
```

Communication ports

```
Connector.open("comm:0;baudrate=9600");
```

Datagrams

```
Connector.open("datagram://129.144.111.222:2800");
```

Files

```
Connector.open("file:/foo.dat");
```

All connections are created by calling the static method open of the class javax.microedition.io.Connector. If successful, this method will return an object that implements one of the javax.microedition.io.Connection interfaces shown in Figure 6.1. The Connector.open method takes a String parameter in the general form:

```
Connector.open("<protocol>:<address>;<parameters>");
```

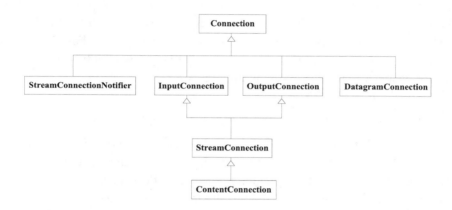

Figure 6.1   Connection interface hierarchy

The syntax of the Connector.open parameter strings should generally follow the *Uniform Resource Indicator* (URI) syntax as defined in the IETF standard RFC2396 (http://www.ietf.org/rfc/rfc2396.txt).

A central objective of this design is to isolate, as much as possible, the differences between the use of one protocol and another into a string characterizing the type of connection. This string is the parameter to the method Connector.open. A key benefit of this approach is that the bulk of the application code stays the same regardless of the kind of connection that is used. This is different from traditional implementations, in which the abstractions and data types used in applications often change dramatically when changing from one form of communication to another.

The binding of protocols to a J2ME program is done at runtime. At the implementation level, the string (up to the first occurrence of ':') that is provided as the parameter to the method Connector.open instructs the system to obtain the desired protocol implementation from a location where all the protocol implementations are stored. It is this *late binding* mechanism which permits a program to dynamically adapt to use different protocols at runtime. Conceptually this is identical to the relationship between application programs and device drivers on a personal computer or workstation.

6.3.3   No network protocol implementations defined in CLDC

The Generic Connection framework included in CLDC does not specify the actual supported network protocols or mandate implementations of any specific networking protocols. The *CLDC Specification* provides an *extensible framework* that can be customized by J2ME profiles such as MIDP to support those protocols that specific device categories might need. The actual implementations and decisions regarding supported protocols must be made at the profile level. For instance, the Mobile Information Device Profile supports the HTTP protocol only. Refer to Chapter 10 for details on MIDP networking libraries.

6.3.4   Design of the Generic Connection framework

Connections to different types of devices will need to exhibit different forms of behavior. A file, for instance, can be renamed, but no similar operation exists for a TCP/IP socket. The Generic Connection framework reflects these different capabilities, ensuring that operations that are logically the same share the same API.

The Generic Connection framework is implemented using a hierarchy of `Connection` interfaces (located in package `javax.microedition.io`) that group together classes of protocols with the same semantics. This hierarchy consists of seven interfaces. Additionally, there is the `Connector` class, one exception class, one other interface, and a number of data stream classes for reading and writing data. At the implementation level, a minimum of one class is needed for implementing each supported protocol. Often, each protocol implementation class contains simply a number of wrapper functions that call the native functions of the underlying host operating system.

There are six basic interface types that are addressed by the Generic Connection framework:

- A basic serial input device

- A basic serial output device

- A datagram oriented communications device

- A circuit oriented communications device

- A notification mechanism to inform a server of client-server connections

- A basic Web server connection

The collection of Connection interfaces forms a hierarchy that becomes progressively more capable as the hierarchy progresses from the root Connection interface. This arrangement allows J2ME profile designers or application programmers to choose the optimal level of cross-protocol portability for the libraries and applications they are designing.

The Connection interface hierarchy is illustrated in Figure 6.1. A brief summary of each interface class is provided below. For a definitive reference on the Connection interfaces, refer to the documentation that is provided as part of the CLDC reference implementation.

Interface Connection

This is the most basic connection type that can only be opened and closed. The open method is not included in the interface because connections are always opened using the static open method of the Connector class.

Methods:

```
public void close() throws IOException;
```

Interface InputConnection

This connection type represents a device from which data can be read. The openInputStream method of this interface will return an InputStream for the connection. The openDataInputStream method of this interface will return a DataInputStream for the connection.

Methods:

```
public InputStream openInputStream() throws IOException;
public DataInputStream openDataInputStream() throws IOException;
```

Interface OutputConnection

This connection type represents a device to which data can be written. The openOutputStream method of this interface will return an OutputStream for the connection. The openDataOutputStream method of this interface will return a DataOutputStream for the connection.

Methods:

```
public OutputStream openOutputStream() throws IOException;
public DataOutputStream openDataOutputStream() throws IOException;
```

Interface `StreamConnection`

This connection type combines the `InputConnection` and `OutputConnection` interfaces. It forms a logical starting point for classes that implement two-way communication interfaces.

Interface `ContentConnection`

This connection type is a sub-interface of `StreamConnection`. It provides access to some of the most basic metadata information provided by HTTP connections.

Methods:

```
public String getType();
public String getEncoding();
public long getLength();
```

Interface `StreamConnectionNotifier`

This connection type is used when waiting for a connection to be established. The `acceptAndOpen` method of this interface will block until a client program makes a connection. The method returns a `StreamConnection` on which a communications link has been established. Like all connections, the returned `StreamConnection` must be closed when it is no longer required.

Methods:

```
public StreamConnection acceptAndOpen() throws IOException;
```

Interface `DatagramConnection`

This connection type represents a datagram endpoint. In common with the J2SE datagram interface, the address used for opening the connection is the endpoint at which datagrams are received. The destination for datagrams to be sent is placed in the datagram object itself. There is no address object in this API. Instead, a string is used that allows the addressing to be abstracted in a similar way as in the `Connection` interface design.

Methods:

```
public int getMaximumLength() throws IOException;
public int getNominalLength() throws IOException;
public void send(Datagram datagram) throws IOException;
public void receive(Datagram datagram) throws IOException;
```

```
public Datagram newDatagram(int size) throws IOException;
public Datagram newDatagram(int size, String addr)
       throws IOException;
public Datagram newDatagram(byte[] buf, int size)
       throws IOException;
public Datagram newDatagram(byte[] buf, int size, String addr)
       throws IOException;
```

This `DatagramConnection` interface requires a data type called `Datagram` that is used to contain the data buffer and the address associated with it. The `Datagram` interface contains a useful set of access methods with which data can be placed into or extracted from the datagram buffer. These access methods conform to the `DataInput` and `DataOutput` interfaces, meaning that the datagram object also behaves like a stream. A current position is maintained in the datagram. This is automatically reset to the start of the datagram buffer after a read operation is performed.

6.3.5 Additional remarks

In order to read and write data to and from Generic Connections, a number of input and output stream classes are needed. The stream classes supported by CLDC are listed in Section 6.2.4, "Input/output classes." J2ME profiles may provide additional stream classes as necessary.

6.3.6 Sample code

Note – We emphasize again that the Connected, Limited Device Configuration Specification itself does *not* provide support for sockets, communication ports, HTTP, IrDA, Bluetooth, or any other networking protocols. What the *CLDC Specification* provides is an *extensible framework* that can be customized by J2ME profiles such as MIDP to support those protocols that specific device categories might need. Sun's CLDC reference implementation provides various sample implementations of such protocols. The examples below follow the parameter definition conventions supported by the reference implementation. However, the actual syntax defined by J2ME profiles can be different. Therefore, these examples are provided for illustration only.

Client-side socket connections

To open a client-side TCP/IP socket, the following kind of statement is typically executed:

```
StreamConnection sc =
  (StreamConnection)Connector.open("socket://<address>:<port>");
```

Logically this is the equivalent of the following J2SE statement:

```
Socket s = new Socket(<address>, <port>);
```

For example:

```
StreamConnection sc =
  (StreamConnection)Connector.open("socket://foo.com:2800");
```

or

```
StreamConnection sc =
  (StreamConnection)Connector.open("socket://192.168.0.1:2800");
```

A `StreamConnection` performs exactly the same kind of function that a J2SE socket does. It is also used in much the same way for deriving I/O streams:

```
InputStream  is = sc.openInputStream();
OutputStream os = sc.openOutputStream();
```

Semantically there is very little difference between the new interfaces and the J2SE APIs.

Server-side socket connections

The Generic Connection framework can also be used for supporting server-side socket connections. The following statement sets up a socket listener:

```
StreamConnectionNotifier scn =
  (StreamConnectionNotifier)Connector.open("socket://:<port>");
```

The syntax of this request is very similar to the previous example. The difference is that no host address is specified, and as a result a `StreamConnectionNotifier` object is returned rather than a `StreamConnection`. The `StreamConnectionNotifier` interface type is the equivalent of J2SE `Server-`

Socket. Only one function (other than `close`) is provided by the `StreamConnectionNotifier` type:

```
StreamConnection sc = scn.acceptAndOpen();
```

This is just like the `accept` function in the J2SE class. The *"AndOpen"* functionality has been added to preserve an invariant rule for the I/O system that a well-formed program should contain exactly the same number of *open* and *close* operations.

A more comprehensive socket example

Below is a more comprehensive program that illustrates the use of sockets. This program consists of two classes, `SocketTest` and `ServerSocketThread`, to demonstrate the use of client-side and server-side sockets communicating with each other. When the program is started, class `SocketTest` first instantiates and starts a `ServerSocketThread` object to wait for input from the main program. The main program then calls a function called `sendData` to send data to the server. The server thread stores the result in a static variable contained in the client class. Finally, the main program compares that the result string contains the same data that the client sent to the server.

```java
import java.io.*;
import javax.microedition.io.*;

public class SocketTest {

    public static String result = null;

    public static void main(String[] args) throws IOException {

        // Start the server side of the program
        ServerSocketThread sst = new ServerSocketThread();
        sst.start();

        // Wait for server to start
        sst.waitForServer();

        // Send data to server
        sendData();
```

```
        // Wait for server to complete
        sst.waitForServer();

        // Ensure that server got the correct result
        if (!result.equals("Hello World")) {
            throw new RuntimeException("Incorrect result!");
        }
    }

    static void sendData() throws IOException {

        // Open client side connection to the port 1234
        // of the local machine
        DataOutputStream os = Connector.openDataOutputStream(
                                "socket://localhost:1234");

        // Write a string out in textual form
        os.writeUTF("Hello World");

        // Close the output stream
        os.close();
    }
}


class ServerSocketThread extends Thread {

    public void run() {

        try {
            // Create the server socket for port 1234
            StreamConnectionNotifier scn =
                (StreamConnectionNotifier)Connector.open(
                                "socket://:1234");

            // Tell the client the server is ready
            signalClient();

            // Accept and open a connection
            StreamConnection sc = scn.acceptAndOpen();
```

```
                // Get the data input stream of the connection
                DataInputStream is = sc.openDataInputStream();

                // Read and save the result
                SocketTest.result = is.readUTF();

                // Close everything
                is.close();
                sc.close();
                scn.close();

                // Tell the client the server is finished
                signalClient();

            } catch (IOException x) {
                // Handle possible exceptions here...
            }
        }

        synchronized public void waitForServer() {
            try {
                wait();
            } catch(InterruptedException x) {
                throw new RuntimeException("Wait failure");
            }
        }

        synchronized void signalClient() {
            notify();
        }
    }
```

Communication ports

Communication ports are also implemented using the StreamConnection interface.

```
StreamConnection sc =
    (StreamConnection)Connector.open("comm:<unit>;<parameters>");
```

The *<unit>* part defines the number of the communication port to open. A number of other parameters such as baud rate are typically also available.

Example:

```
StreamConnection sc =
    (StreamConnection)Connector.open("comm:0;baudrate=9600");
```

A more comprehensive communication port example

Below is a more comprehensive program illustrating the use of communication ports. The program opens the serial port 0 with baud rate 38400, and reads input from that port until the character 'Z' is encountered. All the characters that have been read from the port are echoed (written back) to the communication port.

```
import java.io.*;
import javax.microedition.io.*;

public class CommTest {

    public static void main(String[] args) throws Throwable {

        StreamConnection sc =
            (StreamConnection)Connector.open(
                            "comm:0;baudrate=38400");

        InputStream is  = sc.openInputStream();
        OutputStream os = sc.openOutputStream();

        int ch = 0;
        while (ch != 'Z') {
            ch = is.read();
            os.write(ch);
        }

        is.close();
        os.close();
        sc.close();
    }
}
```

Datagrams

The Generic Connection framework includes a datagram connection type. Again, the public interface is semantically very similar to the corresponding J2SE classes, except that all the protocol-specific details have been abstracted out of the API.

Additionally, a few convenience functions have been added to simplify the management of the datagram buffer and to facilitate access to the data it contains.

Detailed information about the datagram connection type is provided in the library documentation that is available in the CLDC reference implementation. However, it is worth highlighting here how the opening of connections takes place. As with stream connection types, both client and server type datagram connections are supported. This is indicated in the `Connector.open` method calls by the presence or absence of the *<host>* parameter. If the *<host>* parameter is present, a client-side connection is opened. Otherwise, a server-side connection is opened.

A client-side datagram connection is opened as follows:

```
DatagramConnection dgc =
    (DatagramConnection) Connector.open("datagram://<host>:<port>");
```

A datagram object is used in the same way as in Java 2 Standard Edition. The target for a datagram is automatically set to the address specified in the connection. This is done by requesting a datagram object to be created by the connection object itself as follows:

```
Datagram dg = dgc.newDatagram(n);
```

In this statement, *n* is the size of the datagram buffer to be allocated.

A server-side datagram connection is opened as follows:

```
DatagramConnection dgc =
    (DatagramConnection) Connector.open("datagram://:<port>");
```

Note the absence of the *<host>* parameter above. As in J2SE, a datagram object allocated for this connection type contains the sender's address upon receipt (after a call to `receive`) and will automatically be sent back to the sender's machine and port when the `send` method is executed.

CHAPTER 7

Mobile Information Device Profile

The *Mobile Information Device Profile* (MIDP) for the Java™ 2 Platform, Micro Edition (J2ME™) is an architecture and a set of Java libraries that create an open, third-party application development environment for small, resource-constrained mobile information devices, or *MIDs*. Typical examples of MIDP target devices include cellular phones, two-way pagers and wireless personal organizers. As summarized in Chapter 3, the minimum set of hardware requirements for MIDP target devices is as follows:

- Memory:
  - 128 kilobytes of non-volatile memory for the MIDP components
  - 8 kilobytes of non-volatile memory for application-created persistent data
  - 32 kilobytes of volatile memory for the virtual machine runtime (for example, the object heap)
- Display:
  - Screen-size: 96x54
  - Display depth: 1-bit
  - Pixel shape (aspect ratio): approximately 1:1
- Input:
  - One or more of the following user-input mechanisms:
    - "one-handed keypad"
    - "two-handed keyboard"
    - touch screen

- Networking:

  - Two-way, wireless, possibly intermittent, with limited bandwidth

Any device with these capabilities can host the MIDP.

7.1   MIDP Expert Group

The *MIDP Specification* was produced by the Mobile Information Device Profile Expert Group (MIDPEG) as part of the Java Community Process (JCP) standardization effort JSR-37. The following 22 companies, listed in alphabetical order, were members of the MIDP standardization effort:

• America Online	• Nokia
• DDI	• NTT DoCoMo
• Ericsson	• Palm Computing
• Espial Group	• Research In Motion (RIM)
• Fujitsu	• Samsung
• Hitachi	• Sharp
• J-Phone	• Siemens
• Matsushita	• Sony
• Mitsubishi	• Sun Microsystems
• Motorola	• Symbian
• NEC	• Telcordia Technologies

7.2   Areas Covered by the MIDP Specification

The *Mobile Information Device Profile Specification* is designed to extend the functionality defined by the *Connected, Limited Device Configuration* (CLDC) *Specification*. The *MIDP Specification* defines a set of APIs that add a minimum set of capabilities that are common to various kinds of mobile information devices. The specific areas covered by the *MIDP Specification* include:

- user interface support (Limited Connected Device User Interface, *LCDUI*),

- networking support (based on the HTTP protocol and the Generic Connection framework introduced by CLDC),

- persistent storage support (Record Management System, *RMS*),

- miscellaneous classes such as timers and exceptions.

In addition to these areas, the *MIDP Specification* defines an extension of the CLDC application model that allows for the execution and communication of applications called *MIDlets*. In MIDP, the basic unit of execution is the *MIDlet*, which is a class that extends the class `javax.microedition.MIDlet`. The MIDlet application model and each of the areas mentioned above are discussed in detail in the subsequent chapters of this book.

CHAPTER **8**

MIDP Application Model

Due to strict memory constraints and the requirement to support application inter-action and data sharing within related applications, the Mobile Information Device Profile does not support the familiar Applet model introduced by Java™ 2 Platform, Standard Edition (J2SE™). Rather, MIDP introduces a new application model that was designed to augment the CLDC application model and to allow multiple Java applications to share data and run concurrently on the KVM.

In order to understand the MIDP application model, it is useful to first examine the limitations of the CLDC application model.

8.1   Limitations of the CLDC Application Model

The CLDC application model (see Section 5.2, "CLDC Application Model") is intentionally very simple. In the *CLDC Specification*, the term *Java application* refers to a collection of class files that contain a unique launch point identified by the method `public static void main(String[] args)`. While this model is general and is familiar to J2SE programmers, it is not suitable for environments in which a graphical user interface is needed, or in which there is a need to share data between multiple Java applications—especially in light of the security constraints defined by the CLDC security model (see Section 4.2, "Security").

The limitations of the CLDC application model arise primarily from the fact that having more than one application running in the absence of the full Java 2 Standard Edition security model could pose security risks. These security risks include the sharing of *external resources* (such as persistent storage) and *static fields of classes*. For instance, consider a situation in which a virtual machine conforming to CLDC is running two applications: `Application1` and `Application2`. Suppose that `Application1` creates a persistently stored object[1] named `Application1_data.rms`. If the application model does not prevent applications from

83

accessing data and resources created by other applications, `Application2` could now legitimately open and read `Application1_data.rms`. Similarly, if applications were allowed to share classes, then data stored in the static fields of classes of `Application1` could be accessed by `Application2`.

Several possible solutions to these issues were examined by the CLDC and MIDP expert groups. For example, one proposed solution was to make the KVM support multiple "logical virtual machines." In this solution, several logically isolated Java virtual machines would run inside the same physical virtual machine, each sharing the non-writable portion of their memory space (that is, code and read-only memory locations). Each logical virtual machine would have a separate object heap, and each virtual machine would have a separate "root" for its name space.[2]

Using the persistent storage example above, when `Application1` creates `Application1_data.rms`, the virtual machine would create it in a place that `Application2` could not access. Furthermore, since the static fields of classes would reside in separate object heaps, `Application1` and `Application2` could not interact via these shared resources.

While this idea and other proposed solutions partially or totally solved the security issues, there was still a fundamental problem: without the ability for applications to interact, designing suites of applications that work together would be impossible. Even though this restriction would not be too severe for CLDC, which does not define any APIs for accessing shared resources, it would be overly limiting for MIDP devices, in which users expect some level of data sharing and interaction. The MIDP application model was created to address this need.

Table 8.1   Classes in package `javax.microedition.midlet`

Classes in `javax.microedition.midlet`	Description
`MIDlet`	Superclass of all MIDP applications. Extended by a MIDlet to allow the system to start, stop, and destroy it.
`MIDletStateChangeException`	Thrown when the application cannot make the change requested.

---

[1] This is a hypothetical example, since CLDC does not provide any file or database APIs.

[2] For the purpose of this discussion, the term *name space* denotes a logical path by which a given object can be found in the system. For example, an RMS database might have a logical path "`/my_midlet/storage1.rms`".

8.2　MIDlets

In MIDP, the basic unit of execution is a *MIDlet*. A MIDlet is a class that extends the class javax.microedition.MIDlet (see Table 8.1).

As an example of programming with the MIDP application model, consider the following program that implements one of the simplest MIDlets possible: the canonical "Hello World" application:

```java
package examples;
import javax.microedition.midlet.*;
import javax.microedition.lcdui.*;

public class HelloWorld extends MIDlet implements CommandListener {
    private Command exitCommand;
    private TextBox tb;

    public HelloWorld() {
        exitCommand = new Command("Exit", Command.EXIT, 1);
        tb = new TextBox("Hello MIDlet", "Hello, World!", 15, 0);
        tb.addCommand(exitCommand);
        tb.setCommandListener(this);
    }

    protected void startApp() {
        Display.getDisplay(this).setCurrent(tb);
    }

    protected void pauseApp() {}
    protected void destroyApp(boolean u) {}

    public void commandAction(Command c, Displayable d) {
        if (c == exitCommand) {
            destroyApp(false);
            notifyDestroyed();
        }
    }
}
```

The output of this simple MIDlet, when run on a MIDP device emulator, is shown in the figure on the left. In this figure, the MIDlet's `startApp` method has just completed its execution. Hitting the upper-right-most button (the *Exit* command) on the phone's keypad would invoke the `commandAction` method and run the `destroyApp` and `notifyDestroyed` code.

In this example, there are a few key things that are common to all MIDlets, no matter how simple or complex the applications are. First, HelloWorld extends the class `javax.microedition.midlet.MIDlet`.[3]

Like every Java class, a MIDlet can have a constructor. In the MIDP application model, the system (see Section 8.4, "MIDP System Software") calls the public no-argument constructor of a MIDlet exactly once to instantiate the MIDlet. The functionality that needs to be defined in the constructor depends on how the MIDlet is written, but in general, any operations that must be performed only once when the application is launched should be placed in the constructor.

If no such functionality is required by the MIDlet, then there is no need to provide a constructor. Care should be taken in the constructor to catch any exceptions and handle them gracefully, since the behavior of an uncaught exception at the MIDlet level is undefined.

Class `javax.microedition.midlet.MIDlet` defines three abstract methods, `startApp`, `pauseApp`, and `destroyApp`, which must be defined by all MIDlets. The `startApp` method is generally used for starting or restarting a MIDlet. This method may be called by the system under different circumstances (see Section

---

[3.] Note that the MIDlet also implements the `CommandListener` interface. This interface, along with the `TextBox`, `Command`, and `Display` classes, is part of the `javax.microedition.lcdui` package that is discussed in Chapter 9, "MIDP User Interface Libraries."

8.2.1, "MIDlet states"), but its purpose is to acquire or re-acquire resources needed by the MIDlet and to prepare the MIDlet to handle events such as user input and timers. Note that the startApp method may be called more than once—once to start execution for the first time, and again for every time the MIDlet is "resumed"; therefore, a startApp method should be written so that it can be called under these different circumstances.

The startApp method can "fail" in two ways: transient and non-transient. A transient failure is one that might have to do with a certain point in time (such as a lack of resources, network connectivity, and so forth). Since this type of error may not be fatal, a MIDlet can tell the system that it would like to try and initialize later by throwing a javax.microedition.midlet.MidletStateChangeException. A non-transient failure is one that is caused by any other unexpected and uncaught runtime error. In this case, if the runtime error is not caught by the startApp method, it is propagated back to the system that will destroy the MIDlet immediately and call the MIDlet's destroyApp method.

A robust startApp method should distinguish between transient and non-transient exceptions and respond accordingly, as illustrated in the following code fragment:

```
void startApp() throws MIDletStateChangeException {
    HttpConnection c = null;
    int status = -1;
    try {
        c = (HttpConnection)Connector.open(...);
        status = c.getResponseCode();
        ...
    } catch (IOException ioe) {
        // Transient failure: could not connect to the network
        throw new MIDletStateChangeException(
                    "Network not available");
    } catch (Exception e) {
        // Non-transient failure: can either
        // catch this and exit here, or let the
        // exception propagate back to the system
        destroyApp(true);
        notifyDestroyed();
    }
}
```

The pauseApp method is called by the system to ask a MIDlet to "pause." The precise definition of what pause means is discussed in Section 8.2.1, "MIDlet states," but in general, the pauseApp method works in conjunction with the start-App method to release as many resources as possible so that there is more memory and/or resources available to other MIDlets or native applications. The use of the pauseApp method is illustrated in the following code fragment:

```
boolean firstTime= false;
int[] runTimeArray = null;
...
void startApp() {
    runTimeArray = new int[200];
    if (firstTime) {
        // first time, initialize array with some values, etc.
        ...
        firstTime = false;
    } else {
        // coming from a paused state, read data
        // saved from a RecordStore and put into
        // runTimeArray
        ...
    }
}

void pauseApp() {
    // open a RecordStore and save runTimeArray values;
    // set runTimeArray to null so that it is a candidate
    // for garbage collection.
    ...
    runTimeArray = null;
}
```

The last method that a MIDlet must implement is the destroyApp method. This method is called by the system when the MIDlet is about to be destroyed; it can also be called indirectly (that is, by calling notifyDestroyed) by the MIDlet itself in order to clean up before exiting. In either case, the destroyApp method should be written so that it performs all the necessary clean up operations to release all the resources (that is, close the graphical user interface components, network connections, database records) that the application had allocated during its execution. The following code fragment provides a simple example:

```
RecordStore rs = null;
...
```

```
void startApp() {
    ...
    rs = RecordStore.openRecordStore(...);
    ...
}
void destroyApp(boolean u) {
    if (rs != null) {
        // make sure all records are written to storage
        // and close the record store
        ...
    }
}
```

Taken as a whole, the aforementioned methods—startApp, pauseApp, and destroyApp—represent a state machine with each method responsible for entry or exit to a given state. The next section describes these MIDlet states and the rules that govern the transitions between the different states of a MIDlet.

8.2.1 MIDlet states

During the lifetime of a MIDlet, it may be in one of three distinct states, with well-defined rules that govern the transitions between these states (see Figure 8.1):

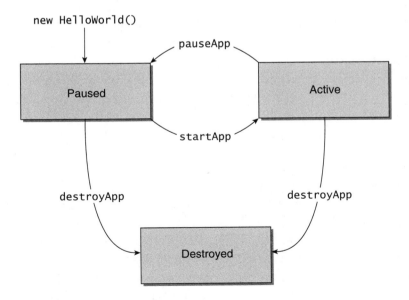

Figure 8.1   MIDlet states and state transitions

- *Paused:* A MIDlet is in the *Paused* state when it has just been started and has not yet entered its startApp method. It can also be in the *Paused* state as a result of the pauseApp or the notifyPaused methods (see below). When in the *Paused* state, a MIDlet should hold as few resources as possible. A MIDlet in the *Paused* state can receive asynchronous notifications, for example, from a timer firing (see Section 12.1, "Timer Support").

    Since CLDC does not provide guaranteed real-time behavior, the system is not required to use the *Paused* state to manage the interaction of the real-time portions of the phone and the Java environment. Consider, for example, the case where the virtual machine is running on a cellular phone, and the phone receives a call. In this scenario, the real-time operating system on the phone might suspend the virtual machine altogether rather than cycle the MIDlets to the *Paused* state.

- *Active*: A MIDlet is in the *Active* state upon entry to its startApp method. In addition, a MIDlet can transition from the *Paused* state to the *Active* state as the result of the resumeRequest method. While in the *Active* state, a MIDlet can allocate and hold all necessary resources for optimal execution.

- *Destroyed:* A MIDlet is in the *Destroyed* state when it has returned from the destroyApp or notifyDestroyed methods. Once a MIDlet enters the *Destroyed* state, it cannot reenter any other state.

The *Destroyed* state replaces the normal convention of an application calling the System.exit method to terminate. A MIDlet cannot call the System.exit method, since doing so will throw a java.lang.SecurityException (see Section 12.4, "Exiting a MIDlet.")

The MIDlet state transitions can be triggered either by the MIDP system itself or by the application programmer. Below we summarize how the MIDP system can initiate these state transitions. Note that all these method calls are synchronous in that the state changes are not complete until the method returns to the caller.

- startApp: This method is called by the system to move a MIDlet into the *Active* state for the first time, and also when a MIDlet is being resumed from the *Paused* state. When a MIDlet enters its startApp method, it is in the *Active* state. An important note: Beginning MIDlet programmers are often tempted to treat startApp as equivalent to the main method, and thus combine MIDlet initialization and main-line processing in the startApp method. In general this is not a good idea, since the startApp method may be called more than once: one time initially, and then once per each transition from *Paused* to *Active* state.

- pauseApp: During the normal operation of a mobile device, the system might run into situations where it is necessary to suspend or pause some of the MIDlets on the device. The most common example is when a device is running low on memory. In order to reclaim memory, the system may call the pauseApp method of all the *Active* MIDlets. When the pauseApp method of a MIDlet is called, the MIDlet should release as much of its resources as possible and become quiescent. Note that the system does not actually try to force any specific behavior on a MIDlet in a *Paused* state, so it is possible for an ill-behaved MIDlet to ignore this request. However, if such a situation occurs, the system may forcibly terminate the MIDlet or even the virtual machine itself, especially in a low-memory situation. In addition, note that while in the *Paused* state the MIDlet can still receive asynchronous events such as timer events.

- destroyApp: This is the normal way the system terminates a MIDlet. The destroyApp method has one boolean parameter that indicates whether or not the request is unconditional. If the request is not unconditional (that is, the boolean parameter is *false*), then the MIDlet may request a "stay of execution" by throwing a MIDletStateChangeException. In this case, if the system is able to honor the request, the MIDlet may continue in its current state (*Paused* or *Active*). If, on the other hand, the request is unconditional, then the MIDlet should give up its resource, save any persistent data it might be caching, and return. Upon return from this method, the MIDlet enters the *Destroyed* state and can be reclaimed by the system.

While the MIDP system is the primary instigator of MIDlet state changes, a MIDlet application programmer can also request state changes via the following methods:

- resumeRequest: This method can be called by a *Paused* MIDlet to indicate that it wishes to reenter the *Active* state. The primary scenario for this call is when a *Paused* MIDlet handles a timer expiration and needs to resume processing.

- notifyPaused: This method is provided to allow a MIDlet to signal to the system that it has voluntarily entered the *Paused* state (that is, it has released its resources and is now quiescent). An example use case for this call is a time-based MIDlet that sets timers and has nothing to do until those timers expire.

- notifyDestroyed: This method can be called by the MIDlet to tell the system that the MIDlet has released all its resources and has saved any cached data to persistent storage. Note that the destroyApp method of a MIDlet will *not* be called as a result of invoking this method.

8.3   MIDlet Suites

One of the central goals for the MIDP application model is to provide support for the controlled sharing of data and resources between multiple, possibly simultaneously running MIDlets. This means that the security issues discussed in the beginning of this chapter need to be addressed. To accomplish this, the *MIDP Specification* requires that in order for MIDlets to interact and share data, they must be placed into a single JAR file. This collection of MIDlets encapsulated in a JAR file is referred to as a *MIDlet suite*. MIDlets within a MIDlet suite share a common name space (for persistent storage), runtime object heap, and static fields in classes. In order to preserve the security and the original intent of the MIDlet suite provider, the MIDlets, classes, and individual files within the MIDlet suite cannot be installed, updated, or removed individually—they must be manipulated as a whole. In other words, the basic unit of application installation, updating, and removal in MIDP is a MIDlet suite.

A MIDlet suite can be characterized more precisely by its *packaging* and its *runtime environment*. These characteristics are discussed in more detail below.

8.3.1   MIDlet suite packaging

A MIDlet suite is encapsulated within a JAR file. A MIDlet suite provider is responsible for creating a JAR file that includes the appropriate components for the target user, device, network, and locale. For example, since the *CLDC Specification* does not include the full internationalization and localization support provided by Java 2 Standard Edition, a MIDlet suite provider must tailor the JAR file components to include the necessary additional resources (strings, images, and so forth) for a particular locale.

The contents of the MIDlet suite's JAR file include the following components:

- The class files implementing the MIDlet(s)

- Any resource files used by the MIDlet(s): for example, icon or image files, and so forth.

- A manifest describing the JAR contents

All the files needed by the MIDlet(s) are placed in the JAR file using the standard structure based on mapping the fully qualified class names to directory and file names within the JAR file. Each period is converted to a forward slash, '/'. For class files, the `.class` extension is appended.

The JAR manifest provides a means to encode information about the contents of the JAR file.[4] In particular, the JAR manifest specification provides for *name-value pairs* which MIDP uses to encode *MIDlet attributes*. These attributes can be retrieved by a MIDlet with the method `MIDlet.getAppProperty`. Note that MIDlet attribute names are case sensitive. Also note that all the attribute names that start with "`MIDlet-`" are reserved for use by the MIDP expert group to define MIDP-specific MIDlet attributes. MIDlet suite developers can define their own MIDlet attributes, provided that the new attributes do not start with the reserved "`MIDlet-`" prefix. The *MIDP Specification* currently defines the MIDlet attributes shown in Table 8.2.

Of the predefined attributes in Table 8.2, the following must be in the JAR manifest (the other attributes in the table may be optionally included):

- *MIDlet-Name*

- *MIDlet-Version*

- *MIDlet-Vendor*

- A `MIDlet-<n>` for each MIDlet

- *MicroEdition-Profile*

- *MicroEdition-Configuration*

As an example, the following shows a JAR manifest for a hypothetical MIDlet suite of card games provided by Motorola. The suite contains two MIDlets: `Solitaire` and `JacksWild`:

```
MIDlet-Name: CardGames
MIDlet-Version: 1.1.9
MIDlet-Vendor: Motorola
MIDlet-1: Solitaire, /Solitaire.png, com.motorola.Solitaire
MIDlet-2: JacksWild, /JacksWild.png, com.motorola.JacksWild
MicroEdition-Profile: MIDP-1.0
MicroEdition-Configuration: CLDC-1.0
```

[4.] JAR file format specifications are available at `http://java.sun.com/products/jdk/1.2/docs/guide/jar/index.html`. Refer to the JDK JAR and manifest documentation for syntax and related details.

Table 8.2   MIDlet attributes

Attribute Name	Attribute Value Description
`MIDlet-Name`	The name of the MIDlet suite that identifies the MIDlets to the user.
`MIDlet-Version`	The version number of the MIDlet suite. The format is *major.minor.micro* as described in the JDK Product Versioning Specification (see `http://java.sun.com/products/jdk/1.2/docs/guide/versioning/spec/VersioningSpecification.html`). It can be used by the system for installation and upgrade uses, as well as communication with the user. Default value is 0.0.0.
`MIDlet-Vendor`	The name of the MIDlet suite provider.
`MIDlet-Icon`	The name of a PNG file to be used as the icon to identify the MIDlet suite to the user.
`MIDlet-Description`	A short description of the MIDlet suite.
`MIDlet-Info-URL`	A URL for information further describing the MIDlet suite.
`MIDlet-<n>`	The *name*, *icon*, and *class* of the nth MIDlet in the JAR file separated by a comma. The lowest value of *<n>* must be 1 and consecutive ordinals must be used. *Name* is used to identify this MIDlet to the user. *Icon* is the name of an image (PNG) within the JAR that the system should use for the icon of the nth MIDlet. *Class* is the name of the `MIDlet` class for the nth MIDlet.
`MIDlet-Jar-URL`	The URL from which the JAR file was loaded.
`MIDlet-Jar-Size`	The size of the JAR file in bytes.
`MIDlet-Data-Size`	The minimum number of bytes of persistent data required by the MIDlet. The default is zero.
`MicroEdition-Profile`	The J2ME profile required, using the same format and value as the system property `microedition.profiles` (for example "MIDP-1.0").
`MicroEdition-Configuration`	The J2ME Configuration required using the same format and value as the system property `microedition.configuration` (for example "CLDC-1.0").

In addition to the JAR file, the MIDP provides for a separate and optional[5] file called the *application descriptor*. The application descriptor allows the system to verify that the associated MIDlet suite is suited to the device before loading the full JAR file of the MIDlet suite. It also allows MIDlet attributes to be supplied to the MIDlet suite without modifying the JAR file.

The application descriptor is a file that has a MIME type of text/ vnd.sun.j2me.app-descriptor, and file extension of .jad, and contents described by the following BNF syntax:

```
appldesc: *attrline
attrline: attrname ":" WSP attrvalue WSP newline
attrname: 1*<any Unicode char except CTLs or separators>
attrvalue: *valuechar | valuechar *(valuechar | WSP) valuechar
valuechar: <any valid Unicode character, excluding CTLs and WSP>
newline: CR LF | LF
CR = <Unicode carriage return (0x000D)>
LF = <Unicode linefeed (0x000a)>
WSP: 1*( SP | HT )
SP = <Unicode space (0x0020)>
HT = <Unicode horizontal-tab (0x0009)>
CTL = <Unicode characters 0x0000 - 0x001F and 0x007F>
separators = "(" | ")" | "<" | ">" | "@"
             | "," | ";" | ":" | "'" | <">
             | "/" | "[" | "]" | "?" | "="
```

If the application descriptor is present, then it must contain the following pre-defined attributes (again, the other attributes in Table 8.2 are optional in the application descriptor):

- *MIDlet-Name*
- *MIDlet-Version*
- *MIDlet-Vendor*
- *MIDlet-Jar-URL*
- *MIDlet-Jar-Size*

A rudimentary form of version control between the JAR file and the application descriptor is ensured by requiring that the attribute values for *MIDlet-Name*,

---

[5] Note: The application descriptor is optional for distributors of MIDlet suites (such as cellular carriers and so forth). However, all MIDP-compliant implementations must accept an application descriptor.

MIDlet-Version, and *MIDlet-Vendor* be identical in the JAR manifest and the application descriptor. If they are not, then the system will assume a version mismatch, and the MIDlet suite will not be installed. All other MIDlet attributes names may also be duplicated, but their values can differ. In this case, the value from the application descriptor will override the value from the JAR manifest.

8.3.2   MIDlet suite execution environment

The *MIDP Specification* defines the environment in which MIDlets within a suite execute. This environment is shared by all MIDlets within a MIDlet suite, and any MIDlet can interact with other MIDlets packaged in a suite. The runtime environment is logically composed of name spaces, as depicted in Figure 8.2. These name spaces determine how a MIDlet accesses an entity within that name space.

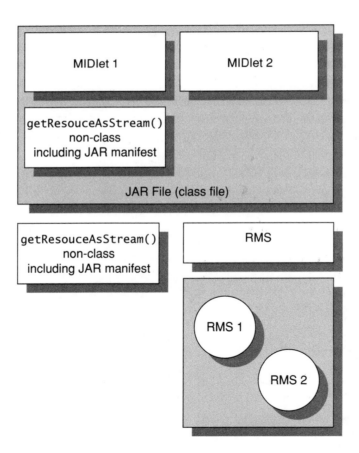

Figure 8.2   MIDlet suite name spaces

The logical name spaces in a MIDlet's runtime environment are as follows:

- Classes and native code that implement the CLDC and MIDP. This is the only name space that is shared by all MIDlet suites on the device.

- Classes within the MIDlet suite's JAR file.

- All non-class files in the MIDlet suite's JAR file, such as icon or image files, and the JAR manifest. These files are accessible via the method `java.lang.Class.getResourceAsStream`.

- The contents of the Application Descriptor File. Accessible via the method `javax.microedition.midlet.MIDlet.getAppProperty`. (Note that the JAR manifest is also accessible via this method.)

- A separate name space for RMS record stores (see Chapter 11, "MIDP Persistence Libraries").

All the classes needed by a MIDlet within a suite must be in the JAR file or in the CLDC and MIDP libraries. A MIDlet may load and invoke methods from any class in the JAR file, in the MIDP libraries, or in the CLDC libraries. All of the classes within these three scopes are shared in the execution environment, along with a single heap containing the objects created by MIDlets, MIDP libraries, and CLDC libraries. The usual locking and synchronization primitives of the Java programming language can be used where necessary to avoid concurrency problems.

The class files of the MIDlet are only available for execution and can neither be read as resources nor extracted for re-use, since the underlying CLDC implementation may store and interpret the contents of the JAR file in any manner suitable for the device.

The non-class files within the JAR file, including the JAR manifest, can be accessed using the method `java.lang.Class.getResourceAsStream`. The parameter to this method, a `String` object, represents a path that is interpreted in the following manner: If it begins with a '/', the search for the resource begins at the "root" of the JAR file; however, if it does not begin with a '/', the resource is searched for along a path relative to the class instance retrieving the resource. For example, if a JAR file has the following contents as shown in this JAR manifest:

```
META-INF/
META-INF/MANIFEST.MF
examples/
examples/HelloWorld.class
```

then, in the following code fragment, both `getResourceAsStream` calls will open an `InputStream` to the manifest file.

```
Class C = Class.forName("examples.HelloWorld");
InputStream s1 = C.getResourceAsStream("/META-INF/MANIFEST.MF");
InputStream s2 = C.getResourceAsStream("../META-INF/MANIFEST.MF");
```

8.4   MIDP System Software

In the preceding sections, frequent references were made to the piece of software called the "system," "MIDP system" or the "execution environment." For example, in Table 8.1, the description of the `MIDlet` class includes the following text: "Extended by a MIDlet to allow the *system* to start, stop, and destroy it." The *MIDP Specification* calls this software the *application management software*, or the AMS. In some documents, application management software is also referred to as the *Java Application Manager*, or the JAM. The two terms (AMS and JAM) are equivalent.

The application management software in a MIDP implementation consists of those pieces of software on the device that provide a framework in which MIDlet suites are installed, updated, removed, started, stopped, and in general, managed. Furthermore, the application management software provides MIDlets with the runtime environment discussed in Section 8.3.2, "MIDlet suite execution environment."

8.4.1   Application management functionality

In the *MIDP Specification*, the application management software is presumed to implement a minimum set of functionality listed in Table 8.3.

Before a MIDlet can be launched, the associated JAR file (MIDlet suite) must be retrieved from some source. A device may be able to retrieve MIDlet suites from multiple transport mediums. For example, a device may support retrieval via a serial cable, an IrDA (infrared) port, or a wireless network. The application management software must support a *medium-identification* step in which the retrieval medium can be selected, either automatically or by user input. After selecting the retrieval medium, the application management software can initiate the *negotiation* step, where information about the MIDlet suite

Table 8.3   Typical application management operations

Operation	Description
Retrieval	Retrieves a MIDlet suite from some source. Possible steps include *medium-identification, negotiation,* and *retrieval.*
Installation	Installs a MIDlet suite on the device. Possible steps include *verification* and *transformation.*
Launching	Invokes a MIDlet. Possible steps include *inspection* and *invocation.*
Version management	Allows installed MIDlet suites to be upgraded to newer versions. Possible steps include *inspection* and *version management.*
Removal	Removes a previously installed MIDlet suite. Possible steps include *inspection* and *deletion.*

and the device is exchanged and compared (for example, the application descriptor may be used in this step.) This information can include the device's capability (for example, available memory), the size of the MIDlet, and so forth. Upon verifying that the device can potentially[6] install the MIDlet suite, the *retrieval* step begins. In this step, the device transfers the MIDlet suite to the device.

Once the MIDlet suite has been retrieved, the installation process may begin. A MIDP implementation may need to *verify* that the retrieved MIDlet suite does not violate the device's security policies. For example, a device might enforce some sort of "code signing" mechanism to validate that the retrieved MIDlet suite is from a trusted source (the *MIDP Specification* does not require this, however.) The next step in installation is the *transformation* from the public representation of the MIDlet suite (for example, the compressed JAR file) into some device-specific, internal representation. This transformation may be as simple as storing the JAR file to persistent storage, or it may actually entail preparing the MIDlet to execute directly from non-volatile memory.

After installation, the MIDlets within the MIDlet suite can now be *launched.* Launching a MIDlet means that the user is presented with a selection of installed MIDlets that are gathered by the device performing the *inspection* step. The user may then select one of the MIDlets for the device to run (or *invoke*). Invocation is the point at which the application management software actually starts to run the

---

[6.] Potentially, because when the MIDlet suite is internalized for execution on a particular device, it may in fact be too large to fit in non-volatile memory.

MIDlet on the virtual machine. At this point, the methods discussed in Section 8.3.1, "MIDlet suite packaging" are used to control the states of MIDlet.

At some point after installation, a new version of a MIDlet suite may become available. To upgrade to this new version, the application management software must keep track of what MIDlet suites have been installed (*identification*) and their "version number" (*version management*). Using this information, the older version of a MIDlet suite can be upgraded to the newer version. Again, the *MIDP Specification* does not allow for individual MIDlets to be upgraded—rather, it specifies that the entire MIDlet suite must be upgraded as a unit. This is done to ensure that the original intent of the MIDlet suite provider is not changed, nor its security model compromised.

A related concept is MIDlet suite *removal*. This differs only slightly from the previous step in that after performing *inspection*, the application management software *deletes* the installed MIDlet suite and its related resources. This includes the removal of the records that the application has written to persistent storage via the APIs described in Chapter 11, "MIDP Persistence Libraries."

As mentioned before, the application management software is not specified by the *MIDP Specification*; therefore, all the above discussions are merely possibilities. An application programmer should not expect that every device implements all of the functionality mentioned above.

CHAPTER **9**

MIDP User Interface Libraries

In light of the wide variations in cellular phones and other MIDP target devices, the requirements for user interface support are very challenging. MIDP target devices differ from desktop systems in many ways, especially in how the user interacts with them. The following requirements must be kept in mind when designing a user interface library for mobile information devices:

- The devices and applications should be useful to users who are not necessarily experts in using computers.

- The devices and applications should be useful in situations where the user cannot pay full attention to the application. For example, many cellular phones and other wireless devices are commonly operated with one hand while the user is driving a car, cooking, fishing, skiing, and so forth.

- The form factors and user interface concepts of MIDP target devices vary considerably between devices, especially compared to desktop systems. For example, display sizes are much smaller, and input devices do not always include pointing devices.

- The Java applications for mobile information devices should have user interfaces that are compatible with the native applications so that the user finds them intuitive to use.

Given these requirements and the capabilities of devices that implement the MIDP (see Section 3.2, "Target Devices"), the MIDP expert group decided that neither the Abstract Windowing Toolkit (AWT) provided by Java™ 2 Standard Edition nor a subset would meet the requirements. Reasons for this decision include:

- AWT was designed and optimized for desktop computers. Desktop requirements and assumptions are not appropriate for smaller screens.

- When a user interacts with AWT, event objects are created dynamically. These objects are short-lived and exist only until each associated event is processed by the system. The event object then becomes garbage and must be reclaimed by the system's garbage collector. The limited CPU and memory subsystems of a mobile information device (MID) typically cannot afford the overhead of unnecessary garbage objects.

- AWT has a rich but desktop-oriented feature set. This feature set includes support for features not found on MIDs. For example, AWT has extensive support for window management (such as overlapping windows, window resize, and so forth). MIDs have small displays that are not large enough for multiple overlapping windows. Limited display size also makes window resizing impractical. As such, the windowing and layout manager support within AWT is not required for MIDs.

- AWT assumes certain desktop user interaction models. The component set of AWT was designed to work with a *pointer device* (for instance, a mouse or pen input). As mentioned earlier, this assumption is valid for a small subset of MIDs, since many of these devices have only a keypad for user input.

9.1   Structure of the MIDP User Interface API

9.1.1   Screen model

The central abstraction of the MIDP user interface is the *screen*. Simple screens help organize the user interface into manageable pieces. This results in user interfaces that are easy to use and learn. Each MIDP application has a `Display` on which a single screen is shown. The application sets and resets the current screen on the `Display` for each step of the task, based on user interactions. The application is notified of commands selected by the user and changes the screen as necessary. The device software manages the sharing of the physical display between the native applications and the MIDP applications.

The rationale behind the screen-oriented approach is based on the wide variations in display and keypad configurations found in MIDP devices. Each device provides a consistent look and feel by handling the component layout, painting, scrolling, and focus traversal. If an application needed to be aware of these details, portability would be difficult to achieve, and smooth integration with the look and feel of the device and its native applications would place a heavy burden on application developers.

Each `Screen` (technically, each `Displayable` object) is a functional user interface element that encapsulates device-specific graphics rendering and user input handling. Figure 9.1 shows the hierarchy of the classes.

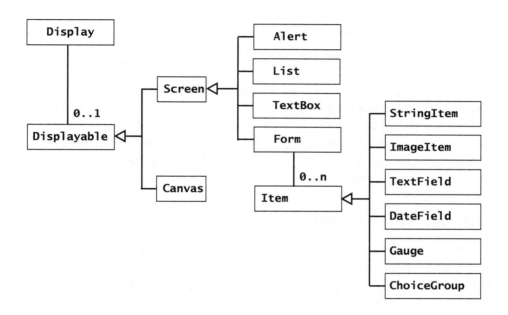

Figure 9.1   MIDP user interface class hierarchy

There are two types of `Displayable` object:

- `Canvas`: low-level objects that allow the application to provide the graphics and handle input.

- `Screen`: high-level objects that encapsulate a complete user interface component (for example, classes `Alert, List`, `TextBox`, or `Form`).

Any application may use combinations of `Screens` and `Canvases` to present an integrated user interface. For instance, in a game application, `Lists` and `Forms` can be used to select or configure the options of a game, while `Canvas` can be used for the interactive game components.

9.1.2   Low-level user interface

The *low-level* user interface API for Canvas is designed for applications that need precise placement and control of graphic elements, as well as need access to low-level input events. Typical examples are a game board, a chart object, or a graph. Using the low-level user interface API, an application can:

- Control what is drawn on the display

- Handle primitive events like key presses and releases

- Access concrete keys and other input devices

Applications that program to the low-level API can be portable if the application uses only the standard features; applications should stick to the platform-independent part of the low-level API whenever possible. This means that applications should not directly assume the presence of any keys other than those defined in class Canvas. Also, applications should inquire about the size of the display and adjust behavior accordingly.

9.1.3   High-level user interface

The *high-level* user interface API is designed for business applications whose client components run on mobile information devices. For these applications, portability across devices is important. To achieve such portability, the high-level user interface API employs a high level of abstraction and provides very little control over look and feel. In addition:

- Drawing to the display is performed by the device's system software. Applications do not define the visual appearance (such as shape, color, font, and so forth) of the components.

- Navigation, scrolling, and other primitive interactions with the user interface components are performed by the device. The application is not aware of these interactions.

- Applications cannot access concrete input mechanisms, such as individual keys.

The high-level API is provided through the Screen classes such as:

- List: select from a predefined set of choices

- TextBox: ask for textual input

- `Alert`: display temporary messages containing text and images
- `Form`: display multiple, closely-related user interface elements

The class `Form` is defined for cases where a screen with a single function is not sufficient. Class `Form` is designed to contain a small number of closely related user interface elements, or `Items`. For example, an application might have two `Text-Fields`, or a `TextField` and a simple `ChoiceGroup`. If all the `Items` of a `Form` do not fit on the screen, the implementation might either make the `Form` scrollable, expand each `Item` automatically when the user edits it, or it might use a "pop up" representation. Each `Form` can contain a combination of the following `Item` subclasses:

- `StringItem`, used for strings and text

- `ImageItem`, used for images

- `TextField`, used for textual input with constraints

- `DateField`, used to display time and dates

- `Gauge`, used to display a value graphically

- `ChoiceGroup`, used for single and multiple selections

Although the `Form` class allows creation of arbitrary combinations of components, developers should keep in mind the limited display size and make forms simple and functional.

9.2   Abstract Commands

9.2.1   Commands and command types

Since the MIDP user interface is highly abstract, it does not dictate any concrete user interaction technique such as soft buttons or menus. An abstract command mechanism is provided to adjust to the widely varying input mechanisms of MIDP target devices, and to allow the applications to be unaware of device specifics, such as number of keys, key locations, and key bindings. Low-level user interactions such as traversal or scrolling are not visible to the application. MIDP applications define `Commands`, and the implementation can provide user control over these with buttons, menus, or whatever mechanisms are appropriate for the device. Commands must be added to each screen using `Displayable.addCommand`.

Command types and priorities allow the device to place the commands to match the native style of the device, and the device might put certain types of commands in standard places. For example, the "GO BACK" operation might always be mapped to the right soft button. The Command class allows the application to communicate the semantic meaning to the implementation so that the standard mappings can be used.

The Command object has three parameters:

1. **Label**: Shown to the user as a hint.

2. **CommandType**: The meaning of the command. The most commonly used hint is *BACK*, which causes the application to go back to a previous state. Most device designs have a standard policy on which button is used for this operation.

3. **Priority**: Allows the implementation to make high priority commands more accessible.

There is one predefined command (List.SELECT_COMMAND) for selection within a list that could be, for example, implemented with *GO, SELECT* or a similar button. The physical button does not need to have a label, but the meaning of a button should always be obvious to the user. For example, if the user is presented with a set of mutually exclusive options, the *SELECT* operation should choose one of these options in an obvious manner.

9.2.2   Command listeners

The application-level handling of commands is based on a *listener* model. Each Displayable object has a single listener. When the user invokes a Command on a Screen, its listener is called. Listeners are registered using the method Displayable.setCommandListener. To define itself as a listener, an object must implement the interface CommandListener and its method, commandAction.

9.3   Interactions with MIDlet Application Lifecycle

User interface components play a key role in a MIDP application. When a MIDlet starts, the initialization of the user interface components is one of the first tasks for the application. The MIDlet application lifecycle is described in Section 8.2, "MIDlets."

The application management software of a MIDP system assumes that the application is well behaved with respect to the MIDlet events. The bullets below summarize what a well behaved MIDlet is expected to do when each of its methods is called:

- **constructor:** The constructor initializes the application state. The method can access the `Display` for the `MIDlet` by calling `MIDlet.getDisplay`. It can create screens and objects needed when the application is started. It does not have access to the user interface, so information or alerts cannot be shown. The method can set the first screen to be shown to the user. The initialization performed should be brief; lengthy delays caused by long operations such as network access should be performed in the background or delayed until the user can be informed appropriately.

- **startApp:** The application manager calls this function to notify the MIDlet that it has been started (or restarted) and makes the screen set with `Display.setCurrent` visible when `startApp` returns. Note that `startApp` can be called several times if `pauseApp` is called in between. This means that objects or resources freed by `pauseApp` might need to be recreated.

- **pauseApp:** The application should release any unneeded resources that can be reinitialized if the application is restarted. The application should pause its threads unless they are needed for background activities. Also, if the application should restart with another screen when the application is reactivated, the new screen should be set with `Display.setCurrent`.

- **destroyApp:** The application should close all active resources, stop any active threads, and unregister or free any objects that would not be freed by a normal garbage collection cycle.

9.4   Graphics and Canvas in the Low-Level API

To directly use the display and the low-level user interface API, the developer uses the `Graphics` and `Canvas` classes. The `Graphics` class provides methods to paint lines, rectangles, arcs, text, and images to a `Canvas` or an `Image`. The `Canvas` class provides the display surface, its dimensions, and callbacks used to deliver events for key and pointer events and for painting the display when requested. Applications may draw by using this graphics object only for the duration of the `paint` method. The application implements a subclass of `Canvas`. The methods of this class must be overridden by the developer to respond to events and to paint the screen when requested.

The combination of the event handling capabilities of the Canvas and the drawing capabilities of the Graphics class allows applications to have complete control over the application region of the screen.[1] These low-level classes can be used, for example, to create new screens, implement highly interactive games, and manipulate images to provide rich and compelling displays for MIDP device owners.

9.4.1   Redrawing mechanism

The application is responsible for redrawing the screen whenever repainting is requested. The application implements the paint method in its subclass of Canvas. Painting of the screen is done on demand so that the device can optimize the use of graphics and screen resources, for example by coalescing several repaint requests into a single call to the paint method of the Canvas. To request a repaint of the entire display, the application calls the repaint method of the Canvas object. If only part of the screen needs to be updated, another repaint method can be given the origin, width, and height of the region that needs to be updated. The performance of graphic-intensive applications can be enhanced greatly by requesting repaints only for the region of the Canvas that changed, and implementing the paint method to only paint the area within the clip region.

Since painting is done asynchronously, the application might need to wait for repaint requests to be completed before it can continue. The Canvas.service-Repaints method blocks until all of the repaint requests queued have resulted in a paint call.

If the device is double buffering the display, the Graphics.isDoubleBuffered method returns true. If so, the application need not separately buffer the drawing to get a clean update of the display. An Image can be used for off-screen buffering for immutable and mutable images. Use of images is described in Section 9.7, "Creating and Using Images." If double buffering is not in use, the application might be able to optimize its display updates by creating images before they are needed, and then drawing them to the display in its paint method.

9.4.2   Drawing model

The only operation on pixels is pixel replacement. The destination pixel value is replaced by the pixel value specified in the Graphics object that is used for rendering. A MIDP implementation provides no facility for combining pixel values, such as raster operations, transparency, or alpha blending.

---

[1]. MIDP target devices often reserve certain areas of the screen for system use. Therefore, a MIDP application may not be able to draw on all the parts of the screen.

Graphics may be rendered either directly to the display or to an off-screen `Image`. The destination of rendered graphics depends on the source of the `Graphics` object. A `Graphics` object for rendering to the display is passed to the `Canvas` object's `paint` method. This is the only way to obtain a `Graphics` object whose destination is the display. Only for the duration of the `paint` method may applications draw using this `Graphics` object.

A `Graphics` object for rendering to an off-screen image is obtained by calling the `Image.getGraphics` method on the desired image. The `Graphics` object may be held indefinitely by the application, and drawing methods may be invoked on these `Graphics` objects at any time.

9.4.3   Coordinate system

The origin (0,0) of the available drawing area and images is in the upper-left corner of the display (see Figure 9.2.)

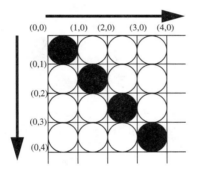

Figure 9.2   Pixel coordinate system

All coordinates are specified as integers. The numeric values of the *x*-coordinates monotonically increase from left to right, and the numeric values of the *y*-coordinates monotonically increase from top to bottom. The maximum values in *x* and *y* are available from the `getWidth` and `getHeight` methods of classes `Canvas` and `Image`. Applications may assume that horizontal and vertical distances in the coordinate system represent equal distances on the actual device display. If the shape of the pixels of the device is significantly different from square, the device does the required coordinate transformation. A MIDP implementation provides a facility for translating the origin of the coordinate system.

The coordinate system represents locations between pixels, not the pixels themselves. Therefore, the first pixel in the upper-left corner of the display lies in the square bounded by coordinates (0,0), (1,0), (0,1), (1,1).

An application can inquire about the available drawing area by calling the methods `Canvas.getWidth` and `Canvas.getHeight`. Applications should take advantage of the available screen pixels and adapt to the size as provided by the device.

9.4.4   Clipping and translation

The coordinate system described above can be translated through the use of horizontal and vertical offsets. The method `Graphics.translate` moves the location of the origin. When it is called, the offsets are added to every *x* and *y* value. The current origin can be retrieved from `Graphics.getTranslateX` and `Graphics.get-TranslateY`.

There is a single clipping rectangle. Operations are provided for intersecting the current clip rectangle with a given rectangle (`Graphics.clipRect`) and for setting the current clip rectangle outright (`Graphics.setClip`). The only pixels touched by graphics operations are those that lie entirely within the clip rectangle. Pixels outside the clip rectangle are not affected by any graphics operations. Clipping is done in the same coordinates as the drawing so the clipping is relative to the untranslated coordinates. The methods `Graphics.getClipWidth`, `Graphics.getClipHeight`, `Graphics.getClipX`, and `Graphics.getClipY` are used for obtaining the current clipping region.

Clipping can be used to copy regions of `Images` from one `Image` to another or to the `Screen`. For an example, see Section 9.7.3, "Animation using images." For another complete example, see Section 13.1, "The PhotoAlbum Application."

9.4.5   Color model

Both color and grayscale models are supported concurrently. The 24-bit color model has eight bits for each of red, green, and blue. The current color is set using the method `Graphics.setColor`. The current color is used for all lines, text, and fills for rectangles and arcs. Separate background and foreground colors are not supported.

Few devices support full 24 bits of color. The device maps the color requested by the application into a color available on the device. The details of the mapping are device specific. The `Display.isColor` method returns `true` if the display is capable of supporting multiple colors, and `false` if the display supports grayscale or black and white only. The number of distinct color or gray levels is available by calling the method `Display.numColors`. The color values are converted to grayscale values by the device. The grayscale equivalent can be retrieved with method `getGrayScale` after a color has been set.

Grayscale is supported with values within the range of 0 to 255. The current grayscale value is set with method `Graphics.setGrayScale`. The device maps the values into the number of gray levels in the display. The corresponding color is available after setting a grayscale value by calling method `Graphics.getColor`.

9.4.6 Line styles

Lines, arcs, rectangles, and rounded rectangles can be drawn with either a *SOLID* or a *DOTTED* stroke style, as set by the `Graphics.setStrokeStyle` method. The stroke style does not affect the fill, text and image operations.

For the *SOLID* stroke style, drawing operations are performed with a one pixel-wide pen that fills the pixel immediately below and to the right of the specified coordinate. Drawn lines touch pixels at both endpoints.

Drawing operations under the *DOTTED* stroke style touches a subset of pixels that would have been touched under the *SOLID* stroke style. The frequency and length of dots is device-dependent. The endpoints of lines and arcs might not be drawn. Similarly, the corner points of rectangles might not be drawn. Dots are drawn by painting with the current color. Spaces between dots are left untouched.

9.4.7 Fonts

MID devices typically have a limited number of fonts with a fixed set of styles, sizes, and faces. The `Font.getFont` method returns the `Font` associated with a given style, size, and face. It is up to the device to select a font that most closely matches the requested attributes. The following attributes can be used to request a font (from the `Font` class):

- **Size**: *SMALL, MEDIUM, LARGE.*
- **Face**: *PROPORTIONAL, MONOSPACE, SYSTEM.*
- **Style**: *PLAIN, BOLD, ITALIC, UNDERLINED.*

The `Font` class provides methods to access the font metrics, including `getHeight` and `getBaselinePosition`. For the widths of strings and sequences of chars the `Font` class methods `charWidth`, `charsWidth`, `stringWidth`, and `substringWidth` can be used. The whitespace for interline and intercharacter spacing is included in the metrics and is below and to the right of the characters, respectively. The metrics allow an application to precisely place text relative to graphics.

The methods `Graphics.setFont` and `Graphics.getFont` are used to set and get the current `Font`. Each `Graphics` object always has a font set with a default chosen by the device.

9.4.8   Canvas visibility

The display on a device is shared among native applications and MIDP applications. A particular application might or might not be displayed on the screen. When the application's choice of current screen is a `Canvas`, the canvas is notified when its visibility changes. The `Canvas.showNotify` and `Canvas.hideNotify` methods are invoked automatically on the `Canvas` when it is shown and hidden, respectively. The application should override these methods to be informed of changes in visibility. When made visible, the `paint` method of the `Canvas` is called, so the application does not need to call `repaint` explicitly. Show and hide notifications are useful if, for example, the `Canvas` is providing an animation that it could start animating when shown and stop animating when hidden.

9.5   Low-level API for Events in Canvases

9.5.1   Key events

If the application needs to handle key events in its `Canvas`, it must override the `Canvas` methods `keyPressed`, `keyReleased`, and `keyRepeated`. When a key is pressed, the `keyPressed` method is called with the key code. If the key is held down long enough to repeat, the `keyRepeated` method is called for each repeated `keyCode`. When the key is released, the `keyReleased` method is called. Some devices might not support repeating keys, and if not, the `keyRepeated` method is never called. The application can check the availability of repeat actions by calling the method `Canvas.hasRepeatEvents`.

MIDP target devices are required to support the ITU-T telephone keys. Key codes are defined in the `Canvas` class for the digits 0 through 9, *, and #. Although an implementation may provide additional keys, applications relying on these keys may not be portable. For portable applications, the action key mappings described below should be used whenever possible, since other key codes are device-specific.

9.5.2   Action keys

The `Canvas` class has methods for handling portable *action events* (also known as *game actions*) from the low-level user interface. The API defines a set of action events: *UP, DOWN, LEFT, RIGHT, FIRE, GAME_A, GAME_B, GAME_C,* and *GAME_D.* The device maps the action events to suitable key codes on the device. For example, a device with four navigation keys and a *SELECT* key in the middle could use those keys for mapping the action events, but a simpler device might use keys on the numeric keypad (such as 2, 4, 5, 6, 8) instead.

The mapping between keys and the abstract action events does not change during the execution of an application. An application can get the mapping of the key codes to action events by calling the method `Canvas.getGameAction`. If the logic of the application is based on the values returned by this method, the application is portable and runs regardless of the keypad design.

Action events are mapped to device-specific key codes that can be retrieved with method `Canvas.getKeyCode`. The application may choose to determine the key codes once during initialization for each action it uses, and later utilize those key codes in the `keyPressed` methods.

9.5.3   Pointer events

The `Canvas` class has methods that the application can override to handle pointer events. If the application needs to handle pointer events, it must override and implement the methods `pointerPressed`, `pointerReleased`, and `pointerDragged`.

Not all MIDP target devices support pointer events, and therefore the pointer methods might never be called. The application can check whether the pointer and pointer motion events are available by calling `Canvas.hasPointerEvents` and `Canvas.hasPointerMotionEvents`.

9.6   Graphics Drawing Primitives

The `Graphics` class provides various low-level drawing primitives. In general, drawing is started by calling the various methods of the `Graphics` object to set the color, translation, and clipping. Methods are available for drawing lines, filled and outlined rectangles, filled and outlined rounded rectangles, text, and images. Each of the drawing primitives is explained below, along with figures that illustrate the result of the sample drawing calls. The figure on the right shows the cumulative effect of these sample drawing calls.

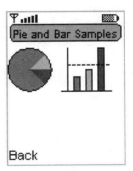

9.6.1   Scaling to the Canvas

Typically, before any low-level drawing operations can be used, the application should perform certain initialization operations and calculations based on the size of the `Canvas` or `Image` and the `Fonts` to be used. The code snippet below illustrates how to compute the relevant size and position information for the drawing examples that we provide in this section. Below, the constructor for the sample `Canvas` computes and saves the width and height of the `Canvas`, the `Font`, the height of the `Font`, a padding amount, and the height of the title bar based on the Font size. It uses the remaining screen space for the pie chart example (Section 9.6.3, "Drawing and filling arcs") by subtracting the title height from the screen height and padding. The size of the charts may be reduced so that the pie and bar charts can fit side by side with padding in between. The size of the bar chart is set to be the same as the pie chart. These layout computations are different for every use of a Canvas, and might need some adjustments to look good on various devices.

```
int w = getWidth();
int h = getHeight();
int font = Font.getFont(Font.FACE_SYSTEM,
                        Font.STYLE_PLAIN, Font.SIZE_SMALL);
int fh = font.getHeight();
int pad = 2;
int titleHeight = fd + pad * 2;
int barSize = h - (titleHeight + pad);
if (barSize > (w - pad) / 2)
    barSize = (w - pad) / 2;
int pieSize = barSize;
```

9.6.2   Drawing lines

The Graphics.drawLine method draws lines from a starting (x, y) coordinate to an ending (x, y) location, touching each pixel below and to the right of the coordinates that the line touches. The pixels are set to the value of the current color value. The lines are drawn with the current stroke style (see Section 9.4.6, "Line styles.")

For example, here is the code to draw the axes for the bar chart in the figure on the right:

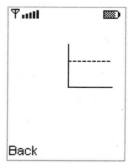

```
Graphics g = ...
int h1 = barSize / 3, h2 = barSize / 2,
    h3 = barSize; // Scaled data
int avg = (h1 + h2 + h3) / 3;
int yorig = barSize;
g.translate((w + pad) / 2, titleHeight + pad);
g.setGrayScale(0);
g.drawLine(0, 0, 0, yorig);
g.drawLine(0, yorig, barSize, yorig);
g.setStrokeStyle(Graphics.DOTTED);
g.drawLine(0, yorig-avg, barSize, yorig-avg);
```

9.6.3   Drawing and filling arcs

The `Graphics.drawArc` method draws the outline of a circular or elliptical arc covering the specified rectangle, using the current color and stroke style. The resulting arc begins at *startAngle* degrees and extends for *arcAngle* degrees. Angles are interpreted such that 0 degrees is at the 3 o'clock position. A positive value indicates a counter-clockwise rotation, while a negative value indicates a clockwise rotation.

The center of the arc is the center of the rectangle whose origin is (*x,y*) and whose size is specified by the *width* and *height* arguments. The resulting arc covers an area *width+1* pixels wide by *height+1* pixels tall. If either *width* or *height* is less than zero, nothing is drawn.

The angles are specified relative to the non-square extents of the bounding rectangle such that 45 degrees always falls on the line from the center of the ellipse to the upper-right corner of the bounding rectangle. As a result, if the bounding rectangle is noticeably longer in one axis than the other, the angles to the start and end of the arc segment are skewed farther along the longer axis of the bounds.

The `Graphics.fillArc` method draws and fills a circular or elliptical arc covering the specified rectangle. The filled region consists of the "pie wedge" region bounded by the arc segment as if drawn by `drawArc`, the radius extending from the center to this arc at *startAngle* degrees, and radius extending from the center to this arc at *startAngle + arcAngle* degrees.

For example, here is the code to fill the arcs and draw the outlines of the chart shown at right:

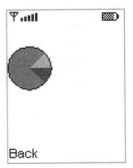

```
Graphics g = ...
g.translate(0, titleHeight + pad);
g.setColor(255, 0, 0);
g.fillArc(0, 0, pieSize, pieSize, 45, 270);
g.setColor(0, 255, 0);
g.fillArc(0, 0, pieSize, pieSize, 0, 45);
g.setColor(0, 0, 255);
g.fillArc(0, 0, pieSize, pieSize, 0, -45);
g.setColor(0);
g.drawArc(0, 0, pieSize, pieSize, 0, 360);
```

9.6.4   Drawing and filling rectangles

The `Graphics.drawRect` method draws a rectangle with the current color and stroke style. The resulting rectangle covers an area *width+1* pixels wide by *height+1* pixels tall. If either *width* or *height* is less than zero, nothing is drawn.

The `Graphics.fillRect` method fills rectangles with the current color. If either *width* or *height* is less than zero, nothing is drawn.

For example, see below for the code to draw the bar chart (shown in the figure) using filled and outlined rectangles. Note that the widths and spacing of the bars is computed from the size of the chart so they scale to the screen area available.

```
Graphics g = ...
int h1 = barSize / 3, h2 = barSize / 2,
    h3 = barSize; // Scaled data
// width of spaces and bars
int bw = barSize / 7;
// translate to right half of screen
g.translate((w + pad) / 2, titleHeight + pad);
g.setColor(255, 0, 0);
g.fillRect(bw, yorig-h1, bw+1, h1);
g.setColor(0, 255, 0);
g.fillRect(bw*3, yorig-h2, bw+1, h2);
g.setColor(0, 0, 255);
g.fillRect(25, yorig-h3, bw+1, h3);
g.setColor(0);
g.drawRect(bw, yorig-h1, bw, h1);
g.drawRect(bw*3, yorig-h2, bw, h2);
g.drawRect(bw*5, yorig-h3, bw, h3);
```

9.6.5   Drawing and filling rounded rectangles

The `Graphics.drawRoundRect` method draws a rectangle with rounded corners in the current color and stroke style. The resulting rectangle covers an area *width+1* pixels wide by *height+1* pixels tall. If either *width* or *height* is less than zero, nothing is drawn. The corners are rounded using *width* and *height* diameter measurements of the curve.

The `Graphics.fillRoundRect` method fills rectangles with rounded corners in the current color. If either *width* or *height* is less than zero, nothing is drawn.

For example, to draw the title bar shown in the figure at the top of the next page, the font metrics of the title string are used to compute the size of the filled and drawn rounded rectangles, as follows:

```
Graphics g = ...
Font font = g.getFont();
int swidth = pad * 2 +
    font.stringWidth("Pie and Bar Samples");
int title_x = (w - swidth) / 2;
g.setGrayScale(128);
g.fillRoundRect(title_x, 0, swidth, fh, 5, 5);
g.setGrayScale(0);
g.drawRoundRect(title_x, 0, swidth, fh, 5, 5);
```

9.6.6   Drawing text and images

The drawing of text is based on anchor points instead of the standard notion of baseline, as illustrated in Figure 9.3.

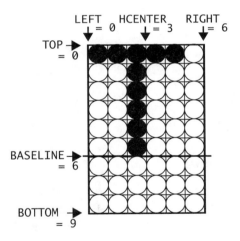

Figure 9.3   Text anchor points

Anchor points are used to minimize the amount of computation required when placing text. The Graphics.drawString method draws text in the current foreground color using the current font with its anchor point at (*x, y*). The anchor point should be one of the horizontal constants (*LEFT, HCENTER, RIGHT*), logically combined (OR-ed) with one of the vertical constants (*TOP, BASELINE, BOTTOM*). The default anchor point is 0, which signifies that the upper-left corner of the text's bounding box is used.

The position of the bounding box of the text relative to the (x, y) location is determined by the anchor point. These reference points occur at named locations along the outer edge of the bounding box.

For text drawing, character and line spacing are included in the values returned in the `Font.stringWidth` and `Font.getHeight` method calls. The interline and intercharacter space is below and to the right of the pixels belonging to the characters drawn. Reasonable vertical spacing is achieved simply by adding the font height to the y-position of subsequent lines.

The positioning of `Images` using anchors is the same as for text, but the *BASE-LINE* anchor is not used and the *VCENTER* anchor is allowed.

For example, to draw the title text shown in the figure on the right, the text is positioned with padding relative to the top and left anchor point:

```
Graphics g = ...
g.setColor(0, 0, 0);
g.drawString("Pie and Bar Samples", pad, pad,
          Graphics.TOP | Graphics.LEFT);
```

9.7   Creating and Using Images

9.7.1   Mutable and immutable images

Images in a MIDP implementation may be either *immutable* or *mutable*. Immutable images can be used in `Alert`, `List`, and `Form` screens. By allowing only immutable images in these screens, the screen update mechanism is kept simple, and the implementation is easier and smaller. Immutable images can be created directly from resource files, from binary data provided by the application, or from other images.

- The `Image.createImage(String name)` method is used to load and create an immutable image from a resource file bundled with the application in the application's JAR file. The name must begin with "/" and include the full name of the PNG image within the JAR file.

- The `Image.createImage(byte[], int offset, int length)` method is used to create an immutable image from binary PNG format data.

- The `Image.createImage(Image image)` method is used to create an immutable image from another `Image` (which could be either mutable or immutable).

In the first two cases the image data must be in Portable Network Graphics (PNG) as specified by the W3C-PNG (Portable Network Graphics) Specification, Version 1.0. W3C Recommendation, October 1, 1996. This specification is available at `http://www.w3.org/TR/REC-png.html` and as RFC 2083, available at `http://www.ietf.org/rfc/rfc2083.txt`.

9.7.2   Drawing to a mutable image

Mutable images are created with the method `Image.createImage(int width, int height)`. The `Image.getGraphics` method returns a `Graphics` object that can be used for drawing into the `Image`. All normal graphics methods operate on the `Image`. The `Image` has the same characteristics as the display of the device: for example, whether the is color or grayscale, and the number of available colors or gray levels.

For a complete example that illustrates the use of mutable and immutable images, refer to Section 13.1, "The PhotoAlbum Application." The code excerpt below demonstrates the creation of a new mutable image. An immutable image read from a resource from the JAR file is drawn on the mutable image; in addition, a rectangle is drawn for a border.

The figure shows the result when the image is drawn to the screen.

```
Image image = Image.createImage(50, 50);
Image icon = Image.createImage(
                "/icons/icon.png");
Graphics g = image.getGraphics();
g.drawImage(icon, 10, 10, TOP | LEFT);
g.setColor(128 128, 128);
g.drawRect(9, 9, icon.getWidth()+1,
                icon.getHeight())+1);
```

9.7.3   Animation using images

A very useful technique for animating graphics takes advantage of the clipping and translation capabilities of the `Graphics` object to move a region of one `Image` to another `Image`. This technique can improve the performance of graphics intensive applications considerably. In other graphics systems, this technique is known as *bitblt*.

For example, the figure to the right shows a sequence of images that, if seen in rapid succession at the same location on the screen, provide an animation of a running dog. The images and techniques are courtesy of Mark Patel at Motorola.

The series of images are stacked in a single Portable Network Graphics (PNG) image and stored in the application JAR. The general technique is to set the clipping region and translation coordinates in the destination image. Drawing the region is performed by calling the method Graphics.draw-Image by picking the region in the source image that aligns with the target. For each iteration, the next image is selected and its offset on the screen is selected. A separate thread is used to advance the *frameIndex* and to issue the repaint requests at the proper time, with the region to erase the previous image as well as to draw the new image.

```
package examples.animation;
import javax.microedition.lcdui.Graphics;
import javax.microedition.lcdui.Canvas;
import javax.microedition.lcdui.Image;


/**
 * This Canvas subclass demonstrates how to create a simple
 * animation sequence using the MIDP graphics APIs.
 *
 * @author Mark A. Patel - Motorola, Inc.
 **/
public class Doggy extends Canvas implements Runnable {

    /**
     * Number of frames in the animation
     **/
    static final int FRAME_COUNT = 17;


    /**
     * Normal frame delay (milliseconds)
     **/
    static final int FRAME_DELAY = 180;


    /**
     * Frame delay for the last frame where the dog is sleeping
     **/
    static final int LAST_FRAME_DELAY = 3000;
```

```
/**
 * Relative horizontal position where each of the frames
 * should be rendered. 0 represents the left edge of the
 * screen and 1024 represents the right edge of the run
 * distance (1024 is used so that scaling can be performed
 * using simple bit shifts instead of division operations).
 **/
static final int[] framePositions = {
    0, 50, 186, 372, 558, 744, 930, 1024, 1024,
    834, 651, 465, 279, 93, 0, 0, 0
};

/**
 * An Image containing the 17 frames of the dog running,
 * stacked vertically.
 * Using a single image is much more efficient than using
 * several images with each containing a single frame.
 * Each frame can be rendered separately by setting the clip
 * region to the size of a single frame, and then
 * rendering the image at the correct position so that the
 * desired frame is aligned with the clip region.
 **/
Image doggyImages = null;

/**
 * Width of a single animation frame
 **/
int frameWidth = 0;

/**
 * Height of a single animation frame
 **/
int frameHeight = 0;

/**
 * Index of the current frame
 **/
int frameIndex = 0;
```

```
/**
 * The distance, in pixels, that the dog can run
 * (screen width less the width of a single frame)
 **/
int runLength = 0;

/**
 * Indicates if the animation is currently running
 **/
boolean running = false;

/**
 * Called when this Canvas is shown. This method starts the
 * timer that runs the animation sequence.
 **/
protected void showNotify() {
    if (doggyImages == null) {
        try {
            doggyImages =
             Image.createImage("/examples/animation/Doggy.png");
            frameWidth = doggyImages.getWidth();
            frameHeight = doggyImages.getHeight()/FRAME_COUNT;
        } catch (Exception ioe) {
            return; // no image to animate
        }
    }
    runLength = getWidth() - frameWidth;
    running = true;
    frameIndex = 0;

    new Thread(this).start();
}


/**
 * Called when this Canvas is hidden. This method stops
 * the animation timer to free up processing
 * power while this Canvas is not showing.
 **/
protected void hideNotify() {
    running = false;
}
```

```java
public void run() {

    // Need to catch InterruptedExceptions
    // and bail if one occurs
    try {
        while (running) {
            Thread.sleep((frameIndex == FRAME_COUNT - 1) ?
                         LAST_FRAME_DELAY : FRAME_DELAY);

            // Remember the last frame index so we can
            // compute the repaint region
            int lastFrameIndex = frameIndex;

            // Update the frame index
            frameIndex = (frameIndex + 1) % FRAME_COUNT;

            // Determine the left edge of the repaint region
            int repaintLeft = framePositions[lastFrameIndex];
            int repaintRight = framePositions[frameIndex];
            if (framePositions[lastFrameIndex] >
                    framePositions[frameIndex]) {
                repaintLeft = framePositions[frameIndex];
                repaintRight = framePositions[lastFrameIndex];
            }


            // Scale repaint coordinates to width of screen
            repaintLeft = (repaintLeft * runLength) >> 10;
            repaintRight = (repaintRight * runLength) >> 10;

            // Trigger repaint of the affected portion
            // of screen. Repaint the region where the
            // last frame was rendered
            // (ensures that it is cleared)
            repaint(repaintLeft, 0,
                    frameWidth + repaintRight - repaintLeft,
                    frameHeight);
        }
    } catch (InterruptedException e) {}
}
```

```
public void paint(Graphics g) {

    // Clear the background (fill with white)
    // The clip region limits the area that actually
    // gets cleared to save time
    g.setColor(0xFFFFFF);
    g.fillRect(0, 0, getWidth(), frameHeight);

    // Translate the graphics to the appropriate position
    // for the current frame
    g.translate((framePositions[frameIndex]*runLength)
                >> 10, 0);

    // Constrain the clip region to the size
    // of a single frame
    g.clipRect(0, 0, frameWidth, frameHeight);

    // Draw the current frame by drawing the entire image
    // with the appropriate vertical offset so that the
    // desired frame lines up with the clip region.
    g.drawImage(doggyImages, 0, -(frameIndex*frameHeight),
                Graphics.LEFT + Graphics.TOP);
}
}
```

9.8   Using Screens

Each subclass of Screen is a complete functional user interface element. The software in a given MIDP device implements each kind of Screen using the look and feel of the device. The device software takes care of all events that occur as the user navigates in a Screen. When user action causes a command invocation event, the event is passed to the application, which brings about a transition to a different Screen. Each Screen can have a title, multiple commands, and a Ticker. It is up to the device software to include these elements in the visual presentation to the user. The four kinds of Screens (List, TextBox, Alert and Form) are described below.

9.8.1   List

The List class is a Screen that contains a list of choices. Each choice has an associated string and may have an icon (an Image). When a List is being displayed, the user can interact with it, for instance, by traversing and possibly scrolling from element to element. These traversing and scrolling operations are handled by the system and do not generate any events that are visible to the MIDP application. The system notifies the application only when a Command is fired. The notification to the application is carried out via the CommandListener of the Screen.

There are three types of Lists: *implicit*, *exclusive* and *multiple choice*. The type of the List is selected when the List is constructed, and cannot be changed during the lifetime of the List object. The look and feel of Lists varies from one type of List to another, as illustrated by the examples below. Also note that different MIDP implementations may render the Lists differently.

Operations on List objects include insert, append and delete, and operations to get the String or the Image from any element. Elements can be added and removed from the List at any time. The selected elements in the List can be retrieved or changed. However, changing the List while the user is viewing it or trying to select an item is not recommended since it might cause confusion.

Most of the behavior for managing a List of elements is common with class ChoiceGroup; the common API is defined in the interface class Choice. Elements in the List are manipulated with the methods append, delete, getImage, getString, insert and set. Item selection is handled with setSelectedIndex, setSelected-Flags, getSelectedFlags, getSelectedIndex, isSelected and getSelectedIndex.

An example:

```
List list = new List(null,
                     Choice.IMPLICIT);
list.append("Canvas", null);
list.append("Form", null);
list.append("Alert", null);
list.append("TextBox", null);
list.append("Exclusive List", null);
list.append("Multiple Choice", null);
list.setCommandListener(this);
list.addCommand(exitCommand);
```

Implicit List

An *Implicit* List is used for a quick selection when the only action that is needed from the user is to select an element. The List is presented like a menu from which the user can pick one of the elements. The device's default *SELECT* key is used as the trigger to deliver the predeclared Command.SELECT_COMMAND to the List's CommandListener. To be notified of the selection, the List must have a CommandListener set. The application can add other Commands to the List, and the user may choose one of them instead of selecting one of the elements in the List.

```
public void commandAction(Command cmd, Displayable d) {
    if (cmd == Command.SELECT_COMMAND) {
        int i = (List)d.getSelectedIndex();
        // Act on the item selected
    } else if (cmd == ...) {
        // Check for and handle other commands
    }
}
```

Exclusive Choice List

An *Exclusive* List allows the user to select a single element. This type of a List is commonly rendered to the screen as a group of radio buttons. When the user selects an element, any previously selected element is automatically deselected. Selecting an element does not notify the application. Notification to the List's CommandListener occurs when a Command on the List is chosen. When the listener is invoked, it can determine which element is selected with the List.getSelected method. An exclusive List *must* have Commands added to it, or the user will not be able to trigger the action and will be stuck on the screen. In the example below, the user is able to pick one choice and then can select either the *OK* or *BACK* command.

```
List list = new List("Border Style",
                     Choice.EXCLUSIVE);
list.append("None", null);
list.append("Plain", null);
list.append("Fancy", null);
list.addCommand(backCommand);
list.addCommand(okCommand);
...

public void commandAction(Command cmd,
                          Displayable d) {
    if (cmd == okCommand) {
        int i = (List)d.getSelectedIndex();
        // Use the index of selected list element...
    } else if (cmd == backCommand) {
        // handle the back command
    }
}
```

Multiple Choice `List`

A *Multiple Choice* List allows the user to select zero or more elements. Each element can be selected or deselected individually. Typically, this type of a List is presented on the screen as a set of check boxes. Each element has an indicator displaying whether the element it is currently selected or not, and the user can toggle individual elements on or off. Toggling the selection of an element does not notify the application. Notification to the List's CommandListener occurs when a Command on the List is chosen. When the listener is invoked, it can determine which element(s) are selected with the List.getSelectedFlags or List.isSelected method. A multiple choice List *must* have Commands added to it, or the user will not be able to trigger the action and will be stuck on the screen.

In this example, the user can select and deselect individually choices for "*Red*", "*Green*", and "*Blue*". When satisfied with their choices, users can select either the *OK* or *BACK* command to exit the screen.

```
List list = new List("Colors to mix",
                     Choice.MULTIPLE);
list.append("Red", null);
list.append("Green", null);
list.append("Blue", null);
text.addCommand(backCommand);
text.addCommand(okCommand);
...


public void commandAction(Command cmd,
                          Displayable d) {
    if (cmd == okCommand) {
        List list = (List)d;
        for (int i = 0; i < list.size(); i++) {
            boolean selected = list.isSelected(i);
            // If selected, take action...
        }
    }
}
```

9.8.2   TextBox

The TextBox class defines a Screen that allows the user to enter and edit text. The application sets the maximum number of characters that the text box can contain and the defines the input constraints. The characters in the TextBox can be modified and retrieved either as a String or a sequence of characters by the application.

The application can set the input constraint individually for each TextBox. The available input constraint modes are *ANY, NUMERIC, PASSWORD, PHONENUMBER, URL,* and *EMAILADDR.* Each mode defines a specific set of characters that are valid to be entered. However, the mode does not automatically validate the format or syntax of the input.

The device can use the input constraints to make it easier for the user to input allowed characters, or can use them to format the field value for display. For example, in a *PHONENUMBER* TextBox, the numeric keypad could perhaps be automatically enabled for direct input of numbers, and the output can be formatted as a phone number. The device may also enable the *"TALK"* button on the phone to dial the number. This provides applications a simple way to present a phone number to the user and to allow them to dial that number.

A TextBox *must* have Commands added to it, or the user will not be able to trigger any action and will be stuck editing text in the TextBox.

For example, the TextBox created with the code below is created to with an initial phone number that can be edited and it has two commands. (Refer to the figure at the left.)

```
TextBox text = new TextBox("Phone",
                    "18005551212", 10,
                    TextField.PHONENUMBER);
    text.addCommand(backCommand);
    text.addCommand(okCommand);
```

9.8.3   Alert

An Alert is a Screen that shows a message and an optional Image to the user for a certain period of time before proceeding to the next screen. Alerts are used to inform the user about errors and other exceptional conditions. When an Alert is displayed, the application can choose the Screen to be displayed after the Alert is complete. By default, after an Alert exits, the display reverts to the current screen.

The AlertType of an Alert can be set to indicate the nature of the information provided in the Alert. There are five AlertTypes; *ALARM, CONFIRMATION, ERROR, INFO,* and *WARNING.* AlertTypes can have sounds associated with them so that the device can audibly alert the user. The specific sound or whether a sound is used at all is device dependent. The sound associated with the `AlertType` can be played anytime by calling the method `AlertType.playSound`.

The application can set the alert time to be infinite with the method `setTimeout(Alert.`*FOREVER*`)`. In this case, the `Alert` is considered to be *modal*, and the device provides a feature that allows the user to dismiss the alert, whereupon the next screen is displayed.

Timed `Alert`s can be used when the user does not need to be aware of the information presented and can safely ignore it. `Alert`s without a time-out should be used when the user must be made aware of the information or condition. `Alert`s cannot be used if the user must be able to choose from multiple responses, because `Commands` are not allowed on `Alert`s. In that case, another type of `Screen` should be used to present the information to the user instead of an `Alert`.

An example:

```
Alert alert = new Alert("Warning");
alert.setString("This window will
                dismiss in two seconds.");
alert.setTimeout(2000);
display.setCurrent(alert);
```

9.8.4   Ticker

A `Ticker` contains a `String` that scrolls continuously across the display. The direction and the speed of scrolling are determined by the device. When the `String` finishes scrolling off the display, the message starts over at the beginning of the `String`. `Ticker`s can be set on any `Screen`. A `Ticker` object can be shared between `Screen`s, so that when switching between `Screen`s the message appears continuously.

For example, a `Ticker` can be added to a `List` and is displayed across the top.

```
Ticker ticker = new Ticker("Select an item to display");
List list = new List("", List.IMPLICIT);
... // Add choices to the List and set command listener
list.addCommand(okCommand);
list.setTicker(ticker);
display.setCurrent(list);
```

9.8.5   Form

A Form is a Screen that may contain a combination of Items including Strings, Images, editable TextFields, editable DateFields, Gauges and ChoiceGroups. Any of the subclasses of Item defined by the *MIDP Specification* may be contained within a Form. The device handles layout, traversal and possible scrolling automatically. None of the Items contained within a Form has any internal scrolling; rather, the entire contents of the Form scroll up and down together. Horizontal scrolling is not usually appropriate on small screens with consumer type users. Restricting to vertical scrolling makes the layout and traversal model easier and matches the limited set of controls available on a typical mobile information device.

The methods for modifying the sequence of Items stored in a Form include insert, append, delete, get, set and size.

An example:

```
Form form = new Form("Options");
form.addCommand(backCommand);
form.addCommand(okCommand);
form.addCommandListener(this);
... // Add Items (see below)
display.setCurrent(form);
```

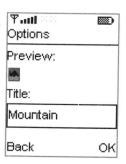

9.9   Using Items

A Form contains a sequence of Items. The different Item types are discussed below, along with a description of class ItemStateListener that can be used for listening for changes in Items.

9.9.1   Item

Class Item is a superclass for components that can be attached to a Form. All Item objects have a label field, which is a String representing the title of the Item. The label is typically displayed near the Item when the Item is visible on the screen. If the screen is scrolling, the implementation tries to keep the label visible at the same time with the Item. An Item may attached to one Form only; this simplifies the implementation since it does not have to share the internal state of Item objects.

9.9.2　String and StringItem

Read-only strings can be added to a Form either directly as Strings (Java string objects) or as StringItems. StringItem is a simple class that is used to wrap Strings so they can be treated consistently with other Items. Strings are converted to StringItems automatically when they are appended to a Form. When an Item that was appended as a String is retrieved from a Form, it is returned as a StringItem.

Continuing example:

```
form.append("The year is ");
form.append(new StringItem("2001"));
```

9.9.3　Image and ImageItem

Image objects can be added to a Form either directly as an Image or as an ImageItem. ImageItem is a simple class that wraps an Image and allows the Item to be positioned relative to the other Items of the Form. The Image can be placed *centered*, *left-justified* or *right-justified,* and with a line break either before or after the Image. Combinations of position and newline options are allowed. The ImageItem should include alternate text to be used if the Image cannot be displayed by the device.

Continuing example:

```
Image image = Image.createImage("/images/PhotoAlbum.png");
imageItem = new ImageItem("Preview:", image,
            ImageItem.LAYOUT_NEWLINE_BEFORE, "Mountain");
```

9.9.4　TextField

A TextField is an editable text component that may be placed in a Form. As with TextBox, it has a maximum size, input constraints on the valid input mode (see Section 9.8.2, "TextBox"), a label and a value. The application can set the input constraint individually for each TextField. The available input constraint modes are *ANY, NUMERIC, PASSWORD, PHONENUMBER, URL,* and *EMAILADDR.* Each mode defines a specific set of characters that are valid to be entered. The value can be retrieved and set as a sequence of characters or as a String. The number of characters displayed and their arrangement in rows and columns are determined by the device.

An example:

```
TextItem textItem =
    new TextField("Title:", "Mountain", 32, TextField.ANY);
form.append(textItem);
```

9.9.5   DateField

A `DateField` is a component that may be placed in a `Form` in order to present date and time (calendar) information. The value for a `DateField` can be initially set or left unset. If the value is not set, the `DateField.getDate` method returns `null`. The user interface must visually indicate that the date and time is unknown.

Each instance of a `DateField` can be configured to accept date or time information or both. This input mode configuration is done by choosing the `DATE`, `TIME` or `DATE_TIME` mode of this class. The `DATE` input mode configures the `DateField` to allow only date information and `TIME` only time information (hours, minutes). The `DATE_TIME` mode allows both clock time and date values to be set.

An example:

```
DateField date =
    new DateField("Date", DateField.DATE);
date.setDate(new Date());
// Set date to "now"
form.append(date);
```

9.9.6   ChoiceGroup

A `ChoiceGroup` defines a group of selectable elements that can be placed within a `Form`. A `ChoiceGroup` is similar to `List` (Section 9.8.1, "List"), but it supports only the exclusive and multiple choice modes. The device is responsible for providing the graphical representation of these modes and must provide visually different graphics for different modes. For example, it might use radio buttons for the exclusive choice mode and check boxes for the multiple choice mode.

An example:

```
ChoiceGroup choice =
    new ChoiceGroup("Size:",
                    Choice.EXCLUSIVE);
choice.append("Small", null);
choice.append("Large", null);
form.append(choice);
```

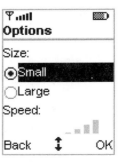

9.9.7 Gauge

The Gauge class implements a graphical value display that may be placed in a Form. A Gauge displays a visual representation of a numeric value in the range between zero and the maximum value defined by the programmer. If the Gauge is set to be interactive, the user actions can increase and decrease the value. The application can get and set the value of Gauge. Changes to the Gauge value are reported using an ItemStateListener.

An example:

```
Gauge gauge =
    new Gauge("Speed:", true, 10, 5);
form.append(gauge);
```

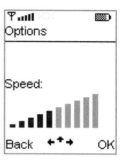

9.9.8 ItemStateListener

When the user changes an editable Item in a Form, the application can be notified of the change by implementing the ItemStateChanged interface and the itemState-Changed method. The itemStateChanged method is called automatically when the value of an interactive Gauge, ChoiceGroup, or TextField changes. The listener is set for the Form using the setItemListener method. It is not expected that the listener is called after every event that causes a change. However, if the value has changed, the listener is called sometime before it is called for another Item, or before a Command is delivered to the Form's CommandListener.

Continuing example:

```
form.setItemListener(this);
```

9.10 A Note on Concurrency

The MIDP user interface API has been designed to be thread-safe. The methods may be called from callbacks, TimerTasks, or multiple threads created by the application. The MIDP system implementation handles its own locking and synchronization to make this possible.

The application is responsible for the synchronization of its own objects and data structures. Care must be taken when calling the method `Canvas.service-Repaints` that forces the painting of the display. The `paint` method may be called by a different thread than the caller of `serviceRepaints`. If the `paint` method tries to synchronize on any object that was locked by the application when `serviceRepaints` was called, the application deadlocks. Therefore, the application should not hold any locks when it calls the method `serviceRepaints`.

The MIDP user interface API purposefully serializes callbacks to listeners and calls to the event notifications methods of class `Canvas`, so in most cases the application does not need to perform locking. The application can schedule its own activities with `Display.callSerially`. The application implements the `Runnable.run` method with the application logic and, when appropriate, the system queues this method to be called between the other events. The `run` method call requested by a call to `callSerially` is made after any pending `repaint` requests have been satisfied, so that the application can rely on the screen being up-to-date before the `run` method is invoked.

CHAPTER 10

MIDP Networking Libraries

MIDP target devices operate on a wide variety of wireless and wired networks with incompatible transport protocols. Accommodating the current and future network technologies and connected devices is an explicit goal of the *MIDP Specification*. (See Section 3.1.3, "Independence of network technology standards.") In order to reach this goal, MIDP is designed to use standard network programming mechanisms and practices, as well as to take advantage of the existing network infrastructure as much as possible.

Rather than engaging in a long discussion on the differences in wireless network technologies, we make some broad observations in terms that are applicable to the purpose of this chapter: namely, why the MIDP Expert Group chose HTTP as the protocol for wireless data, and how this protocol can be used to implement wireless data services. After that, we introduce the MIDP `HttpConnection` API and present some sample code.

10.1   Characteristics of Wireless Data Networks

Wireless data networks are different from wired data technologies. Wireless data networks have much less bandwidth, more latency, and the connections in these networks are much more likely to be disconnected or unavailable.

There are two types of wireless data networks in the market that the *MIDP Specification* addresses: *circuit-switched data*[1] (CSD) and *packet-switched data* (PSD). In a wireless circuit-switched data exchange, users are assigned a radio channel, which is dedicated to the connection until the transfer of data is completed. During the data exchange, the channel is "tied up" and cannot be used for anything else. One example of a circuit-switched data network is the GSM cellular

---

[1] Also known as *session-based* networking.

phone network. Data over a circuit-switched network is usually billed on a time basis like voice transmissions. This pricing scheme can make the use of circuit-switched wireless networks expensive for data transfer, especially since the data rates in today's wireless networks are rather low. In a GSM phone, for example, the data rate usually is only about 9.6 kilobits per second (kbps).

The other type of wireless data network is packet-switched data. In packet-switched data transmissions, the data exchange is broken up into small "packets" that usually have a fixed length. Packets from several different data exchanges, each from different users, can be sent in "time slots" of the same radio channel. These packets are intermingled during transmission, but are reassembled in the correct order at the receiving end of the data exchange. Packet-switched data provides a much more efficient use of the radio spectrum. In addition, packet-switched data is usually billed by the amount of data sent. Thus, packet-switched networks are generally much cheaper for data transfer.

The next-generation wireless network technologies promise much greater data rates than the networks that are in widespread use today. The *second and a half generation* (2.5G) wireless technologies such as the *General Purpose Radio Service* (GPRS) and *third generation* (3G) technologies such the WCDMA are generally packet-switched technologies. For example, the theoretical maximum data transfer rate of GPRS is 171.2 kilobits per second, and third generation wireless networks offer theoretical data rates up to a few megabits per second. However, it is highly unlikely that data rates this high will be available any time soon, since doing so would force a network operator to give all the possible times slots in a channel to data packets, with none left over for voice.

10.2   Network Interface Considerations

Choosing the network interface for MIDP was a study in trade-offs. For example, the MIDP Expert Group originally investigated the use of a simple datagram (UDP) interface instead of higher-level APIs. One obvious use case was the SMS (Short Message Service) capability that is in widespread usage in GSM networks. An SMS message is asynchronous—that is, a message may arrive on a phone at any time, and without the phone requesting it. Once a message arrives on the MIDP device, the native system software of the phone has to determine if this message was intended for a MIDlet, and then route it to the correct MIDlet. Furthermore, if the MIDlet (or the virtual machine) was not running, then the native system software of the device has to launch it. Complicating the adoption of a datagram interface further is the fact that not all wireless networks support an SMS interface.

Based on these kinds of considerations and challenges, the MIDP expert group decided to use *HTTP* as the network protocol for MIDP networking libraries. HTTP is a rich, widely used protocol that can be implemented relatively easily over a variety of wireless networks. HTTP makes it possible to take advantage of the extensive server side infrastructure that is already in place for wired networks. Furthermore, HTTP transmissions are synchronous in the sense that no unrequested network packets can arrive to the MIDP device. This makes the implementation of the networking interface for a MIDP device considerably easier.

Note that support for the HTTP protocol does not necessarily imply that the device must support a particular IP protocol. HTTP for a MIDP device can be implemented using either IP protocols such as TCP/IP, or non-IP protocols such as WAP or i-Mode (see Figure 10.1). In the latter case (non-IP protocol used at the implementation level), a special computer called a *gateway* is used to "bridge" the wireless protocol to and from HTTP servers on the Internet and to provide IP-based network facilities such as server name resolution (for example, DNS).

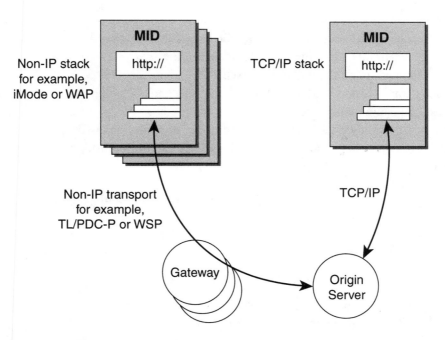

Figure 10.1   HTTP network connections

10.3   The HttpConnection Interface

The MIDP networking APIs are defined in the interface javax.micro-edition.io.HttpConnection. This interface extends the interface javax.micro-edition.io.ContentConnection and provides additional fields and methods used to parse URLs, set request headers, and parse response headers.

10.3.1   States of a network connection

HTTP is a *request-response* protocol in which the parameters of a request must be set before the actual request is sent. A connection exists in one of three states: *setup*, *connected*, or *closed*.

When first opened, but before a connection has been made to the server, a connection is in the *setup* state. In this state, information needed to connect to the server, such as the request parameters and headers, is set with one of the following methods: setRequestMethod or setRequestProperty. Similarly, this information can be retrieved with the getRequestMethod and the getRequestProperty methods.

The *connected* state is entered whenever a connection to the server has been established. In this state, the information set in the *setup* state may be sent to the server, depending on the method invoked.

The final state is the *closed* state, which is entered when the connection is closed and can no longer be used. None of the methods of HttpConnection can be used; however, any InputStream or OutputStream associated with the connection may still contain data and may be used, as illustrated in the following code fragment:

```
HttpConnection c = (HttpConnection)Connector.open(...);
InputStream is = c.openInputStream();

// Can use methods such as c.getType() or c.getLength() here.
c.close();

// Can no longer use the HttpConnection methods, but
// InputStream methods are still available.
while ((int ch = is.read()) != -1) {
        ...
}
```

10.3.2 Parsing URLs

An HttpConnection is opened with a full URL including the protocol, host, and other parameters. The various components of the URL can be parsed while the connection is open using the methods:

- getProtocol: returns the protocol component of the URL.

- getHost: returns the host component of the URL.

- getPort: returns the port number component of the URL.

- getFile: returns the file component of the URL.

- getQuery: returns the query component of the URL, that is, the text after the first question mark (?) character in the URL.

- getRef: returns the reference component of the URL, that is, the text after the crosshatch (#) character in the URL.

As an example, consider the following code fragment:

```
String HTTP_URL =
    "http://localhost:8080/myApp?first=joe?last=cool";
HttpConnection c = (HttpConnection)Connector.open(HTTP_URL);

System.out.println("Protocol: " + c.getProtocol());
System.out.println("Host: " + c.getHost());
System.out.println("Port: " + c.getPort());
System.out.println("File: " +  c.getFile());
System.out.println("Query: " + c.getQuery());
System.out.println("Reference: " + c.getRef());
```

When executed, the code above prints:

```
Protocol: http
Host: localhost
Port: 8080
File: /myApp
Query: first=joe?last=cool
Reference: null
```

10.3.3   Establishing a connection

HTTP connections are opened using the method `javax.microedition.io.Connec-`
`tor.open` inherited from CLDC. This method takes a single `String` URL parameter
in the URI (Uniform Resource Identifier) form as defined by the IETF standard
RFC2396 *Uniform Resource Identifiers.*[2] For example, the following code fragment
would open a connection to Sun's Java home page:

```
HttpConnection c =
    (HttpConnection)Connector.open("http://java.sun.com/");
```

The resulting connection supports the HTTP 1.1 protocol as defined by
RFC2616.[3]

An HTTP connection is closed using the method `javax.micro-`
`edition.io.Connector.close`. For instance, to close the connection opened above,
the following code fragment could be used:

```
try {
    c.close();
} catch (IOException e) {
    ...
}
```

10.3.4   HTTP request headers

The HTTP protocol provides a rich set of request headers that allow a MIDlet to
negotiate the form, format, language, session, and other attributes of the content
posted or retrieved. A MIDlet is responsible for the choice and processing of request
and response headers. Usually, since a MIDlet is communicating with a particular
service that is known in advance, it only needs to handle a subset of headers, and all
other headers can be omitted and ignored. The methods that are used in the *setup*
state to set the request method and headers are as follows:

- `setRequestMethod`: sets the request method to one of the following POST, GET,
  or HEAD; if not set, then the default is GET.

- `setRequestProperty`: sets the name and value of a request header.

- `getRequestMethod`: returns the current request method.

- `getRequestProperty`: returns a previously set request property.

---

[2] `http://www.ietf.org/rfc/rfc2396.txt`
[3] RFC2616 *Hypertext Transfer Protocol — HTTP/1.1*

Of the request properties that can be set, the following merit special discussion.

The User-Agent header

In the HTTP specification, a request header called *User-Agent* is used to identify the current client to the server. As specified by RFC2616, the field contains *features* separated by blanks, where each feature consists of a name and optional version number.

The *MIDP Specification* does not require that a MIDlet set the *User-Agent* field; however, this standard field can be used to identify a MIDP device to a server as in the following code fragment, which sets the *User-Agent* field to include the version number of the CLDC and MIDP running on the device:

```
String ua =
    "Profile/" +
    System.getProperty("microedition.profiles") +
    " Configuration/" +
    System.getProperty("microedition.configuration");
c.setRequestProperty("User-Agent", ua);
```

The Accept-Language header

Another important request header for MIDP devices is the Accept-Language header. For HTTP requests, this field can be set to request a document in a particular language. The *MIDP Specification* defines a system property called microedition.locale. This system property identifies the current locale of a the device (see Section 12.2, "System Properties"). This system property, then, can be used to set the Accept-Language header as in the following example:

```
String locale = System.getProperty("microedition.locale");
if (locale != null) {
    c.setRequestProperty("Accept-Language", locale);
}
```

10.3.5 Using an HTTP connection

After a MIDlet sets up the appropriate headers, it can begin to use the connection. How it uses the connection depends on what request-method was set via the setRequestMethod method: GET, POST, or HEAD.

Using the GET request method

The code fragment below illustrates the common situation in which an application opens an HttpConnection, checks the status, and then reads data from the connection using an InputStream:

```
HttpConnection c;
InputStream is;
try {
    c = (HttpConnection)Connector.open("http://java.sun.com/");

    // Get the HTTP response code, opening the connection
    // Only HTTP_OK (200) means that the content is returned
    int status = c.getResponseCode();
    if (status != HttpConnection.HTTP_OK) {
        throw new IOException("Response code not OK");
    } else {
        // Handle other recoverable responses like redirects
    }

    // Open the InputStream and read until end of file
    // (-1) is returned
    is = c.openInputStream();

    int ch;
    while ((ch = is.read()) != -1) {
        // Process the byte from the stream;
    }
} finally {
    if (is != null) {
        is.close();
    }
    if (c != null) {
        c.close();
    }
}
```

Using the POST request method

While many web-based applications use HTTP GET requests to retrieve information from a web server, these requests are limited in the amount of data they can send in the URL. For situations in which the application server expects more data or parameters, the HTTP POST request method can be used. When using HTTP POST, a MIDlet can provide parameters as part of the URL (as with HTTP GET); furthermore, a MIDlet can write a stream of bytes over the network that do a service.

The example below demonstrates an application that sets the request method to HttpConnection.POST, sets the request headers, and then opens an Output-Stream for writing additional data or commands.

```
HttpConnection c;
InputStream is;
OutputStream os;
try {
    c = (HttpConnection)Connector.open(url);

    // Set the request method
    c.setRequestMethod(HttpConnection.POST);

    // Get the output stream and write a command
    os = c.openOutputStream();
    os.write("LIST games\n".getBytes());
    os.flush();

    // Get the status code, causing the connection to be made
    // Only HTTP_OK (200) means the request was accepted
    status = c.getResponseCode();
    if (status != HttpConnection.HTTP_OK) {
        throw new IOException("Response status not OK");
}
```

Using the HEAD request method

The HEAD request method is identical to the GET request method with the exception that the server does not return a message body in the response. All information in the HTTP headers in the response to a HEAD request is identical to the information sent in response to a GET request. This method is usually used for testing purposes to see if a URL is valid or modified.

10.3.6 HTTP response headers

An HTTP server responds to any of the aforementioned requests by sending one or more headers that describe the content—the type, the encoding, the length, and so forth. The headers are sent followed by the requested content. HttpConnection parses and stores the response headers until it is closed. It is up to a MIDlet to get the headers from the open and connected HttpConnection and use them to interpret the returned content appropriately. For simplicity, the header-related methods catch exceptions that occur in making the connection and return default values. To avoid missing a network error or incorrectly acting upon it, a MIDlet should explicitly call getResponseCode, check the return value, and be prepared to handle any exceptions before getting the response headers.

For the commonly used fields, the methods that fetch and convert the field to the appropriate primitive type are:

- getResponseCode: returns the value of the response code.

- getResponseMessage: returns the value of the response message.

- getEncoding: returns the value of the content-encoding as a string.

- getType: returns the content-type header field as a string.

- getLength: returns the content-length header field as a size in bytes.

- getDate: returns the value of the date header in milliseconds.

- getExpiration: returns the value of the expires header in milliseconds.

- getLastModified: returns the value of the last-modified header in milliseconds.

Additional response headers sent by the server are available from the Http-Connection after it has been opened and is connected. These methods provide access to the fields by index or name as a String, an integer, or a time in milliseconds.

If a header may appear more than once, such as "Set-Cookie," a MIDlet must iterate through them using getHeaderFieldKey to identify which headers have multiples. The available methods are:

- getHeaderField: returns the value of the named header field as a String.

- getHeaderField: returns the value of the nth header (starting from zero).

- getHeaderFieldKey: returns the name of the nth header (starting from zero).

- getHeaderFieldInt: returns the value of the named field converted to an integer.

- getHeaderFieldDate: returns the value of the named field in milliseconds.

10.4 Sample Code (NetClientMIDlet.java)

The following application, NetClientMIDlet, demonstrates how HTTP can be used to "login" to a server, send it data, and read data back.

The HTTP protocol provides several mechanisms that can be used by a server/client pair to implement a challenge-response authentication scheme.[4] One of these mechanisms is called the *basic authentication scheme*. In this scheme, the client must authenticate itself to the server by supplying a user-ID and a password in order to access a protected resource, or *realm*. The server only services a request to access a realm if it can validate the supplied user-ID and password. A client sends these credentials to the server via the HTTP *Authorization* header. This header must contain the string "Basic", followed by a space, and then the base64[5] encoding of a string composed of the user-ID, a colon, and password. In this example, NetClientMIDlet needs to access a protected resource that requires a user-ID of "book" and a password of "bkpasswd". Thus, the MIDlet needs to send the following header field:

```
Authorization: Basic Ym9vazpia3Bhc3N3ZA==
```

where the Ym9vazpia3Bhc3N3ZA== is the base64 encoding of "book:bkpasswd".

The transformation from "book:bkpasswd" to the base64 encoded string is performed by the class BasicAuth. This class supplies a method called encode[6] that takes a user-ID and password and returns the base64 encoding.

The ConnectionManager class opens the HTTP connection to a server. The URL of the server is hard-coded in this example in the variable baseurl. For the purposes of this example, baseurl refers to a simple Java servlet that accepts HTTP POST connections. The servlet reads the POST message body and returns a string identifying itself (such as "NetServer Servlet" in the figure), followed by a date string, the original POST message body, the message body reversed, and a complete list of headers read from the POST request.

[4.] These mechanisms are defined in RFC2617, *HTTP Authentication: Basic and Digest Access Authentication.*

[5.] See RFC2045, *Multipurpose Internet Mail Extensions (MIME) Part One: Format of Internet Message Bodies.*

[6.] Note: this method defines only a subset of the functionality required by RFC2045. In particular, it does not handle strings longer than 76 characters, line breaks, and so forth.

After the connection is opened, the HTTP request type is set to `HttpConnection.POST` to allow the MIDlet to write data to the server. Before opening an output stream on the connection, the HTTP header fields are set to the values shown in Table 10.1.

The actual network connection is created when the `openOutputStream` method is invoked. At this point, the stored headers are flushed, the network connection is made, and the `msg` field is written to the server. To see if the connection was successful, the MIDlet calls the `getResponseCode` method and switches on the `status` code. There are three cases to handle:

1. The connection was opened and the data was written: `status` is `HttpConnection.HTTP_OK`.

2. The server tries to redirect the request. The `location` header is read and used a the new URL: `status` is `HttpConnection.HTTP_MOVED_TMP`, `HttpConnection.HTTP_MOVED_PERM`, or `HttpConnection.HTTP_TEMP_REDIRECT`.

3. The connection was not opened for an unexpected reason. Throw an `IOException`.

If the connection was opened successfully, an `InputStream` is opened to allow the client to read data from the server.

The main application code for the MIDlet is the class `NetClientMIDlet`. This class starts the execution by displaying an instructional screen (shown in the figure) to the user.

If the user selects OK, then the method `genDataScr` is called. In this method, a `ConnectionManager` instance is created, and its fields are set to the following values:

- `msg`: *"Esse quam videri"*[7]
- `user`: "book"
- `password`: "bkpasswd"

[7.] "To be rather than to seem"

Table 10.1 HTTP header values

Header	Value
User-Agent	The string "`Profile/MIDP-1.0 Configuration/CLDC-1.0`"
Accept-Language	The value of the system property "`microedition.locale`" or the string "`en-US`" if this property is not set
Content-Length	The length of the field `msg`
Content-Type	The string "`text/plain`"
Authorization	The string "`Basic`" + the base64 encoding of "`user:password`"

If the connection is not successful, the MIDlet displays the string "No Data Returned!," otherwise, the MIDlet displays the output from the server. As an example, the complete data displayed from the request shown in the figure is:

```
NetServer Servlet
Sun Mar 18 15:27:21 CST 2001
Esse quam videri
irediv mauq essE
User-Agent: Profile/MIDP-1.0 Configuration/CLDC-1.0
Accept: text/plain
Host: 127.0.0.1:8080
Accept-Language: en-US
Content-Type: text/plain
Authorization: Basic Ym9vazpia3Bhc3N3ZA==
Content-Length: 16
```

BasicAuth.java

```java
package examples.netclient;

/**
 * This class encodes a user name and password
 * in the format (base 64) that HTTP Basic
 * Authorization requires.
 */
```

```
class BasicAuth {
    // make sure no one can instantiate this class
    private BasicAuth() {}

    // conversion table
    private static byte[] cvtTable = {
        (byte)'A', (byte)'B', (byte)'C', (byte)'D', (byte)'E',
        (byte)'F', (byte)'G', (byte)'H', (byte)'I', (byte)'J',
        (byte)'K', (byte)'L', (byte)'M', (byte)'N', (byte)'O',
        (byte)'P', (byte)'Q', (byte)'R', (byte)'S', (byte)'T',
        (byte)'U', (byte)'V', (byte)'W', (byte)'X', (byte)'Y',
        (byte)'Z',
        (byte)'a', (byte)'b', (byte)'c', (byte)'d', (byte)'e',
        (byte)'f', (byte)'g', (byte)'h', (byte)'i', (byte)'j',
        (byte)'k', (byte)'l', (byte)'m', (byte)'n', (byte)'o',
        (byte)'p', (byte)'q', (byte)'r', (byte)'s', (byte)'t',
        (byte)'u', (byte)'v', (byte)'w', (byte)'x', (byte)'y',
        (byte)'z',
        (byte)'0', (byte)'1', (byte)'2', (byte)'3', (byte)'4',
        (byte)'5', (byte)'6', (byte)'7', (byte)'8', (byte)'9',
        (byte)'+', (byte)'/'
    };

    /**
     * Encode a name/password pair appropriate to
     * use in an HTTP header for Basic Authentication.
     *    name      the user's name
     *    passwd    the user's password
     *    returns   String   the base64 encoded name:password
     */
    static String encode(String name,
                         String passwd) {
        byte input[] = (name + ":" + passwd).getBytes();
        byte[] output = new byte[((input.length / 3) + 1) * 4];
        int ridx = 0;
        int chunk = 0;

        /**
         * Loop through input with 3-byte stride. For
         * each 'chunk' of 3-bytes, create a 24-bit
         * value, then extract four 6-bit indices.
```

```
         * Use these indices to extract the base-64
         * encoding for this 6-bit 'character'
         */
        for (int i = 0; i < input.length; i += 3) {
            int left = input.length - i;

            // have at least three bytes of data left
            if (left > 2) {
                chunk = (input[i] << 16)|
                        (input[i + 1] << 8) |
                         input[i + 2];
                output[ridx++] = cvtTable[(chunk&0xFC0000)>>18];
                output[ridx++] = cvtTable[(chunk&0x3F000) >>12];
                output[ridx++] = cvtTable[(chunk&0xFC0)    >> 6];
                output[ridx++] = cvtTable[(chunk&0x3F)];
            } else if (left == 2) {
                // down to 2 bytes. pad with 1 '='
                chunk = (input[i] << 16) |
                        (input[i + 1] << 8);
                output[ridx++] = cvtTable[(chunk&0xFC0000)>>18];
                output[ridx++] = cvtTable[(chunk&0x3F000) >>12];
                output[ridx++] = cvtTable[(chunk&0xFC0)    >> 6];
                output[ridx++] = '=';
            } else {
                // down to 1 byte. pad with 2 '='
                chunk = input[i] << 16;
                output[ridx++] = cvtTable[(chunk&0xFC0000)>>18];
                output[ridx++] = cvtTable[(chunk&0x3F000) >>12];
                output[ridx++] = '=';
                output[ridx++] = '=';
            }
        }
        return new String(output);
    }
}
```

ConnectionManager.java

```
package examples.netclient;
import java.lang.*;
import java.util.*;
```

```java
import java.io.*;
import javax.microedition.io.*;

/**
 * Manages network connection.
 *
 * This class established an HTTP POST connection
 * to a server defined by baseurl.
 * It sets the following HTTP headers:
 * User-Agent: to CLDC and MIDP version strings
 * Accept-Language: to microedition.locale or
 *                  to "en-US" if that is null
 * Content-Length:  to the length of msg
 * Content-Type:    to text/plain
 * Authorization:   to "Basic" + the base 64 encoding of
 *                  user:password
 */
class ConnectionManager {
    private HttpConnection con;
    private InputStream is;
    private OutputStream os;
    private String ua;
    private final String baseurl =
        "http://127.0.0.1:8080/Book/netserver";
    private String msg;
    private String user;
    private String password;

    /**
     * Set the message to send to the server
     */
    void setMsg(String s) {
        msg = s;
    }

    /**
     * Set the user name to use to authenticate to server
     */
    void setUser(String s) {
        user = s;
    }
```

```java
/**
 * Set the password to use to authenticate to server
 */
void setPassword(String s) {
    password = s;
}

/**
 * Open a connection to the server
 */
private void open() throws IOException {
    int status = -1;
    String url = baseurl;
    String auth = null;
    is = null;
    os = null;
    con = null;

    // Loop until we get a connection (in case of redirects)
    while (con == null) {
        con = (HttpConnection)Connector.open(url);
        con.setRequestMethod(HttpConnection.POST);
        con.setRequestProperty("User-Agent", ua);
        String locale =
            System.getProperty("microedition.locale");
        if (locale == null) {
            locale = "en-US";
        }
        con.setRequestProperty("Accept-Language", locale);
        con.setRequestProperty("Content-Length",
                        "" + msg.length());
        con.setRequestProperty("Content-Type", "text/plain");
        con.setRequestProperty("Accept", "text/plain");
        if (user != null && password != null) {
            con.setRequestProperty("Authorization",
                            "Basic " +
                            BasicAuth.encode(user,
                                    password));

        }

        // may flush headers on open connection
        os = con.openOutputStream();
```

```java
            os.write(msg.getBytes());
            os.flush();

            // check status code
            status = con.getResponseCode();
            switch (status) {
            case HttpConnection.HTTP_OK:
                // Success!
                break;
            case HttpConnection.HTTP_TEMP_REDIRECT:
            case HttpConnection.HTTP_MOVED_TEMP:
            case HttpConnection.HTTP_MOVED_PERM:
                // Redirect: get the new location
                url = con.getHeaderField("location");
                os.close();
                con.close();
                con = null;
                break;
            default:
                // Error: throw exception
                os.close();
                con.close();
                throw new IOException("Response status not OK:"+
                                        status);
            }
        }
        is = con.openInputStream();
    }


    /**
     * Constructor
     * Set up HTTP User-Agent header string to be the
     * CLDC and MIDP version.
     */
    ConnectionManager() {
        ua = "Profile/" +
            System.getProperty("microedition.profiles") +
            " Configuration/" +
            System.getProperty("microedition.configuration");
    }
```

```java
/**
 * Process an HTTP connection request
 */
byte[] Process() {
    byte[] data = null;

    try {
        open();
        int n = (int)con.getLength();
        if (n != 0) {
            data = new byte[n];
            int actual = is.read(data);
        }
    } catch (IOException ioe) {
    } finally {
        try {
            if (con != null) {
                con.close();
            }
            if (os != null) {
                os.close();
            }
            if (is != null) {
                is.close();
            }
        } catch (IOException ioe) {}
        return data;
    }
}
```

NetClientMIDlet.java

```java
package examples.netclient;

import java.lang.*;
import java.io.*;
import java.util.*;
import javax.microedition.lcdui.*;
import javax.microedition.midlet.*;
```

```java
/**
 * A simple network client.
 *
 * This MIDlet shows a simple use of the HTTP
 * networking interface. It opens a HTTP POST
 * connection to a server, authenticates using
 * HTTP Basic Authentication and writes a string
 * to the connection. It then reads the
 * connection and displays the results.
 */
public class NetClientMIDlet extends MIDlet
    implements CommandListener {

    private Display display;   // handle to the display
    private Form mainScr;      // main screen
    private Command cmdOK;     // OK command
    private Command cmdExit;   // EXIT command
    private Form dataScr;      // for display of results

    /**
     * Constructor.
     *
     * Create main screen and commands. Main
     * screen shows simple instructions.
     */
    public NetClientMIDlet() {
        display = Display.getDisplay(this);
        mainScr = new Form("NetClient");
        mainScr.append("Hit OK to make network connection");
        mainScr.append(" ");
        mainScr.append("Hit EXIT to quit");
        cmdOK = new Command("OK", Command.OK, 1);
        cmdExit = new Command("Exit", Command.EXIT, 1);
        mainScr.addCommand(cmdOK);
        mainScr.addCommand(cmdExit);
        mainScr.setCommandListener(this);
    }

    /**
     * Called by the system to start our MIDlet.
     * Set main screen to be displayed.
     */
```

```java
protected void startApp() {
    display.setCurrent(mainScr);
}

/**
 * Called by the system to pause our MIDlet.
 * No actions required by our MIDLet.
 */
protected void pauseApp() {}

/**
 * Called by the system to end our MIDlet.
 * No actions required by our MIDLet.
 */
protected void destroyApp(boolean unconditional) {}

/**
 * Gets data from server.
 *
 * Open a connection to the server, set a
 * user and password to use, send data, then
 * read the data from the server.
 */
private void genDataScr() {
    ConnectionManager h = new ConnectionManager();

    // Set message to send, user, password
    h.setMsg("Esse quam videri");
    h.setUser("book");
    h.setPassword("bkpasswd");
    byte[] data = h.Process();

    // create data screen
    dataScr = new Form("Data Screen");
    dataScr.addCommand(cmdOK);
    dataScr.addCommand(cmdExit);
    dataScr.setCommandListener(this);
    if (data == null || data.length == 0) {
        // tell user no data was returned
        dataScr.append("No Data Returned!");
    } else {
```

```java
            // loop trough data and extract strings
            // (delimited by '\n' characters
            StringBuffer sb = new StringBuffer();
            for (int i = 0; i < data.length; i++) {
                if (data[i] == (byte)'\n') {
                    dataScr.append(sb.toString());
                    sb.setLength(0);
                } else {
                    sb.append((char)data[i]);
                }
            }
        }
        display.setCurrent(dataScr);
    }


    /**
     * This method implements a state machine that drives
     * the MIDlet from one state (screen) to the next.
     */
    public void commandAction(Command c,
                                Displayable d) {
        if (c == cmdOK) {
            if (d == mainScr) {
                genDataScr();
            } else {
                display.setCurrent(mainScr);
            }
        } else if (c == cmdExit) {
            destroyApp(false);
            notifyDestroyed();
        }
    }
}
```

CHAPTER 11

MIDP Persistence Libraries

The *MIDP Specification* provides a mechanism for MIDlets to persistently store data and retrieve it later. This persistent storage mechanism, called the *Record Management System* (RMS), is modeled after a simple, record-oriented database. This chapter introduces the key features and characteristics of the Record Management System.

11.1 The Record Management System

Conceptually, RMS provides *records* and *record stores*, as shown in Figure 11.1. A record store is a collection of records that is persistent across multiple invocations of a MIDlet. Each record is an array of bytes. Each record in a record store can be of different length, and can each store data differently. For example, in Figure 11.1, the topmost record, *Record ID 1*, may contain a `String` followed by an `int`, while the second record, *Record ID 5*, may contain an array of `short` numbers.

Associated with each record in a record store is a unique identifier called the `recordId`. This identifier can be used to retrieve a record from the record store (see `getRecord` in Section 11.2.2, "Manipulating records in a record store"). In Figure 11.1, "adjacent" records in the record store do not necessarily have consecutive `recordIds`. The underlying implementation may in fact reorganize records within the store or place two consecutively placed records in "far" apart locations. All that is guaranteed is that if a record is added to the record store, it will retain its `recordId` until deleted. A `recordId` is assigned via a monotonically, increasing-by-one algorithm. There is no provision for "wrap around" of `recordIds`. However, since the data type for `recordIds` is an integer that is capable of storing a number as large as 2,147,483,647, it is highly unlikely that a given `recordId` will ever be reused within a record store, especially since mobile information devices usually have limited persistent storage.

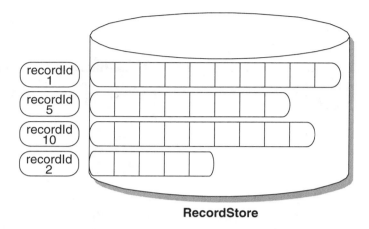

RecordStore

Figure 11.1 Structure of a record store

MIDlets within a MIDlet suite can access one another's record stores directly; however, no locking operations are provided by the RMS. Therefore, if a MIDlet suite uses multiple MIDlets or threads to access a record store, it is the developer's responsibility to coordinate these access operations with the synchronization primitives provided by the Java programming language. Note that the system software of the mobile information device is responsible for maintaining the integrity of RMS record stores throughout the normal use of the platform, including reboots, battery changes, and so forth. Therefore, the programmer does not have to worry about these issues.

The sharing of RMS record stores is controlled by the MIDP application model (See Section 8.3.2, "MIDlet suite execution environment"). Under this model, record stores are shared by all MIDlets within a MIDlet suite, but are not shared with other MIDlet suites. For example, in Figure 11.2, the record store called *Alpha* of *MIDlet_Suite_1* is separate and distinct from the record store *Alpha* of *MIDlet_Suite_2*. Therefore, *MIDlet_Suite_1* cannot access the record stores of *MIDlet_Suite_2*, and vice versa.

11.2 Manipulating Record Stores and Records

Record stores have two basic types of operations: those that deal with manipulating the record store as a whole, and those that deal with manipulating the records within the record store. A summary of different record store and record manipulation operations is provided in the following sections.

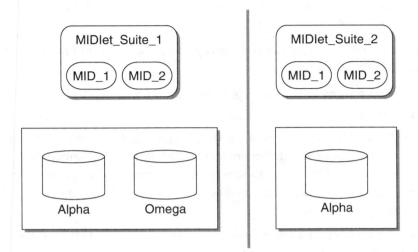

Figure 11.2 Separation of RMS name spaces

11.2.1 Manipulating a record store

The programmer accesses record stores by name. These names are case-sensitive and may be up to 32 Unicode characters in length. The name space for record stores is a flat, non-hierarchical space.[1]

Within a MIDlet suite, record store names are unique. In other words, MIDlets within a MIDlet suite are not allowed to create more than one record store with the same name. On the other hand, no such restriction applies to different MIDlet suites: a MIDlet within one MIDlet suite is allowed to have a record store with the same name as a MIDlet in another MIDlet suite. In that case, the record stores are distinct and separate. A MIDlet can obtain a list of all the record stores owned by the containing MIDlet suite by calling the class static method `listRecordStores` of class `RecordStore`.

In order to access a record store, the record store must be opened first. A record store is opened with the method `openRecordStore` that takes two parameters: a `String` containing the name of the record store, and a `boolean` indicating whether the records store should be created if it does not exist yet. The method `openRecordStore` returns an object of type `RecordStore`, which provides access to the following methods that return information about the associated record store:

---

[1] Note: The name space of record stores is separate from that of resources (resources are accessed by calling the method `java.lang.Class.getResourceAsStream`). Thus, the name of a record store can be lexically equivalent to that of a resource, but the two are separate entities.

- `getName`: returns a `String` that represents the name that this record was opened or created with.

- `getNumRecords`: returns an `int` that represents the number of records currently in the record store.

- `getSize`: returns an `int` that represents the current number of bytes contained in the record store.

- `getSizeAvailable`: returns an `int` that represents the number of remaining bytes in the device that the record store could potentially occupy. Note that the number returned by this method is not a guarantee that the record store can actually grow to this size, since another MIDlet may allocate bytes for another record store.

- `getNextRecordID`: returns an `int` that represents the `recordId` for the next record added to the record store.

- `getVersion`: returns an `int` that represents the version of the record store. Each time a record is added, deleted, or modified in the record store, the version number of the record store is incremented by 1.

- `getLastModified`: returns a `long` that represents the last modification time of the record store. The time returned is in the same format as used by method `System.currentTimeMillis`. The modification time of a record store is changed each time its version changes (see the description above.)

The two final operations on a record store are closing and deleting it. A record store is closed by invoking the method `closeRecordStore`. Note that a record store is not closed until all outstanding opens have been matched with a corresponding close operation. In other words, as long as there are open references to a record store, it will not be closed. When a record store is finally closed, all record listeners are removed (see Section 11.2.4, "Filtering, comparing, listening and enumerating records"), and any attempts to perform any operations on the record store object cause a `RecordStoreNotOpenException` to be thrown.

A record store is deleted by passing its name as a `String` to the static method `deleteRecordStore` of class `RecordStore`. A record store must be closed before it can be deleted.

11.2.2 Manipulating records in a record store

Within a record store, individual records can be added, retrieved, modified, and deleted. The most common methods for manipulating records are summarized below:

- addRecord: takes a byte array, an offset, and a length as parameters. A recordId is returned for a record created from the byte array subset starting at the given offset through the given length. Note that this is a blocking operation and the method will *not* return until the record is written to the underlying persistent storage.

- deleteRecord: takes a recordId as a parameter and removes the record represented by that recordId from the record store.

- getRecordSize: takes a recordId as a parameter and returns the size of the associated record in bytes.

- getRecord: there are two forms of this call. The first form takes a recordId as a parameter and returns a copy of the record. The second form takes a recordId, and a user-supplied byte array and offset. The method returns a copy of the record into the byte array starting at the given offset.

- setRecord: takes a recordId, a byte array, an offset, and a length as parameters. The record identified by the recordId is overwritten from the beginning with data from a subset of the byte array subset identified by the offset and length.

11.2.3 Converting record data to and from byte arrays

Before data can be saved into a record store, it must be converted into an array of bytes first. By using CLDC classes such as DataInputStream, DataOutputStream, ByteArrayInputStream or ByteArrayOutputStream, developers can pack and unpack different data types into and out of byte arrays. As an example, consider a game MIDlet that needs to record scores and names of players. The code fragment below illustrates how such a record (byte array) might be created:

```
ByteArrayOutputStream baos = new ByteArrayOutputStream();
DataOutputStream outputStream = new DataOutputStream(baos);
// Add the score (an int) then the name of the player (a UTF)
// to the DataOutputStream.
outputStream.writeInt(score);
outputStream.writeUTF(name);
```

```
// Now, extract the byte array (record)
byte[] theRecord = baos.toByteArray();
```

Once the record has been created, it can be inserted into a record store using the addRecord operation introduced in Section 11.2.2, "Manipulating records in a record store."

11.2.4   Filtering, comparing, listening and enumerating records

The records of a record store may be processed in various ways. To provide programmer-defined ways to filter, search, and sort a record store, RMS provides the four Java interfaces discussed below.

The RecordFilter interface

The RecordFilter interface allows the programmer to define filters for searching records. This interface requires the programmer to supply a method called matches that accepts one record as a parameter. This method returns a boolean indicating whether or not the given record matches the user-defined search criteria. For instance, consider the following example in which a record store contains different types of records, with the type being indicated by the first byte. In this example, Integer records are indicated by the first byte being 'I'. The following filter returns true if the candidate record is an Integer record:

```
public class IntegerFilter implements RecordFilter {
    public boolean matches(byte[] candidate)
                    throws IllegalArgumentException {
        return candidate[0] == 'I';
    }
}
```

The RecordComparator interface

The RecordComparator interface allows the programmer to define comparison operations for records. This interface defines the method compare that takes two records as parameters. This method returns one of the following class-static values from the RecordComparator class:

- EQUIVALENT: returned if the two records are considered equivalent for this sort order.

- FOLLOWS: returned if the first record follows the second for this sort order.

- PRECEDES: returned if the first record precedes the second for this sort order.

To carry forth the previous example, let's assume that the Integer records discussed above have the format of a record type indicator (in this case: 'I') followed by a four-byte Integer. Furthermore, let's assume that we want to sort the records in ascending order according to value of the four-byte Integer field. A record comparator to accomplish this could be written as follows (with error checking omitted):

```
class IntegerCompare implements RecordComparator {
    public int compare(byte[] b1, byte[] b2) {
        DataInputStream is1 = new DataInputStream(
                                new ByteArrayInputStream(b1));
        DataInputStream is2 = new DataInputStream(
                                new ByteArrayInputStream(b2));
        /**
         * Skip record type (1 byte), then read ints
         */
        is1.skip(1);
        is2.skip(1);
        int i1 = is1.readInt();
        int i2 = is2.readInt();
        if (i1 > i2) return RecordComparator.FOLLOWS;
        if (i1 < i2) return RecordComparator.PRECEDES;
        return RecordComparator.EQUIVALENT;
    }
}
```

The RecordListener interface

In order to monitor the addition and modifications of records to a record store, RMS provides the RecordListener interface. This interface defines three methods that a class must implement. Each method takes two parameters: a RecordStore, and a recordID:

- recordAdded: called when a record is added to the record store.

- recordChanged: called when a record is modified in the record store.

- recordDeleted: called when a record is deleted in the record store.

The following code fragment shows a simple record listener that prints out a line indicating what type of operation is being done to a record store:

```
/**
 * Add the listener to the record store
 */
recordStore.addRecordListener((RecordListener) new myListener());
...
public class myListener implements RecordListener {
    final private static int ADDED = 1;
    final private static int CHANGED = 2;
    final private static int DELETED = 3;

    private void handleCall(int type, RecordStore rs, int rid) {
        System.out.print("Record store " + rs.getName() +
                        " and record id " + rid +
                        " was ");
        switch (type) {
        case myListener.ADDED:
            System.out.println("added");
            break;
        case myListener.CHANGED:
            System.out.println("changed");
            break;
        case myListener.DELETED:
            System.out.println("deleted");
            break;
        }
    }

    public void recordAdded(RecordStore rs, int rid) {
        handleCall(myListener.ADDED, rs, rid);
    }
    public void recordChanged(RecordStore rs, int rid) {
        handleCall(myListener.CHANGED, rs, rid);
    }
    public void recordDeleted(RecordStore rs, int rid) {
        handleCall(myListener.DELETED, rs, rid);
    }
}
```

The RecordEnumerator interface

The final interface provided by RMS is the `RecordEnumeration` interface. A class implementing this interface provides a mechanism to enumerate over all the records in the record store. While a developer can implement this interface, the most common usage of record enumeration is simply using the `enumerateRecords` provided by the `RecordStore` class.

The `enumerateRecords` method returns an instance of a class that implements the `RecordEnumeration` interface. It takes three parameters: a `RecordComparator`, a `RecordFilter`, and a `boolean` that indicates that the returned enumerator should register itself as a listener in order to keep it updated with ongoing activity on the record store. The most efficient way to get each record in a record store is to supply neither a `RecordComparator` nor a `RecordFilter`:

```
simpleRE = recordStore.enumerateRecords(null, null, false);
while (re.hasNextElement()) {
    byte b[] = re.nextRecord();
    ...
}
```

This example would return, in an undefined order, every record in the record store while ignoring changes made to the record store by other MIDlets or threads.

A more complex example is enumerating through a subset of records in the record store and sorting them in a user-defined manner. Using our previous examples of the `RecordComparator` and the `RecordFilter`, we can construct a record enumerator that only returns the records containing `Integer` numbers in numerically ascending order with the following code fragment:

```
IntegerFilter iFilt = new IntegerFilter();
IntCompare iCompare = new IntegerCompare();
intRE = recordStore.enumerateRecords((RecordFilter)iFilt,
                                      (RecordComparator)iCompare,
                                      false);
while (IntRE.hasNextElement()) {
    byte b[] = re.nextRecord();
    ...
}
```

Suppose that our record store had two types of records: `Integer` and `String`, with the `String` records starting with an 'S', and the `Integer` records beginning with an 'I'. If our record store contained the following records:

```
Record 1: 'I', 100
Record 2: 'S', "Joy"
Record 3: 'I', 50
Record 4: 'S', "Zachary"
Record 5: 'S', "Abby"
Record 6: 'I', 25
```

then the enumeration returned by intRE would be Record 6, Record 3, then Record 1.

11.3 Sample Code (RMSMIDlet.java)

The following small sample application, RMS-MIDlet.java, demonstrates some of the capabilities of RMS. Only the main class and one non-public implementation class of this application are shown—the source code of classes SimpleRecord, SimpleFilter, and SimpleComparator is shown later in Section 13.2, "The AddressBook Application."

The RMSMIDlet example creates two record stores called Personal and Business and allows the user to view the contents of the record store and the details of the individual records, using the operations discussed in Section 11.2.1, "Manipulating a record store").

When the MIDlet begins, the application opens the screen that is depicted in the figure above.

If the user selects the OK command, then the contents of the selected database (in this case, Personal) is shown, as depicted in the figure to the right.

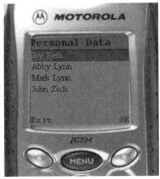

If the user navigates through the MENU command and selects the DETAIL command, then the detail screen is shown. (See the figure on the next page.)

Class RMSMIDlet is implemented as a MIDlet, so its structure and functionality follows the general guidelines defined for MIDlet classes.

This means that the class must implement the methods `startApp`, `pauseApp` and `destroyApp` to define the behavior upon application startup, pausing and exit, respectively.

The class also implements the `Command-Listener` interface in order to listen to command input from the user. The implementation of class `RMSMIDlet` utilizes a package private (non-public) class `CreateAddressBook` in order to create and populate the application's database with sample address book entries.

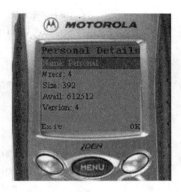

CreateAddressBook.java

```
package examples.addressbook;
import java.lang.*;
import java.io.*;
import java.util.*;
import javax.microedition.rms.*;


/**
 * Static helper class that creates a record
 * store from data in an array.
 */
class CreateAddressBook {

    // Don't allow this class to be instantiated
    private CreateAddressBook() {}
    /**
     * Helper method that creates a record
     * store from data in an array.
     * Returns:
     * true      if RMS store was created
     * false     otherwise
     * name      the name of the record store to create
     * seedData  an array w/ data to seed record store
     */
    static boolean createRecordStore(String name,
                                     String[] seedData) {
        RecordStore recordStore;
        boolean ret = false;
```

```java
        // Delete any previous record store with same name.
        // Silently ignore failure.
        try {
            RecordStore.deleteRecordStore(name);
        } catch (Exception rse) {}

        // Create new RMS store. If we fail, return false.
        try {
            recordStore = RecordStore.openRecordStore(name, true);
        } catch (RecordStoreException rse) {
            return ret;
        }

        ret = true; // assume success

        // Now, populate the record store with the seed data
        for (int i = 0; i < seedData.length; i += 3) {
            byte[] record = SimpleRecord.createRecord(seedData[i],
                                                      seedData[i+1],
                                                      seedData[i+2]);

            try {
                recordStore.addRecord(record, 0, record.length);
            } catch (RecordStoreException rse) {
                ret = false;
                break;
            }
        }

        // Get here when adds are complete, or an error occured.
        // In any case, close the record store. We shouldn't
        // have a failure, so silently ignore any exceptions.
        try {
            recordStore.closeRecordStore();
        } catch (RecordStoreException rsne) {}

        return ret;
    }
}
```

RMSMIDlet.java

```java
package examples.addressbook;
import java.lang.*;
import java.io.*;
import java.util.*;
import javax.microedition.lcdui.*;
import javax.microedition.rms.*;
import javax.microedition.midlet.*;


/**
 * A simple class that shows various functionality of RMS.
 * The general flow of this MIDlet is:
 *
 *      In the constructor (See RMSMIDlet),
 *      create and populate two record stores, one of personal
 *      contacts, the other with business contacts.
 *      Display the first screen. This screen shows a list
 *      of all RMS stores found in the MIDlet suite's name
 *      space. This screen allows the user to select a
 *      record store and either display pertinent information
 *      about the record store such as size, etc., or to view
 *      the contents of the selected store. When the contents
 *      of a record store are viewed, they are sorted by last
 *      name, though this can be changed by instantiate a
 *      SimpleComparator object with the appropriate
 *      sort order parameter.
 *
 *      Traversal from screen to screen is handled
 *      by RMSMIDlet, commandAction.
 *
 */
public class RMSMIDlet extends MIDlet implements CommandListener {
    private Display myDisplay;  // handle to the display
    private Alert alert;        // used to display errors

    // Our commands to display on every screen.
    private Command CMD_EXIT;
    private Command CMD_DETAILS;
    private Command CMD_OK;
```

```java
        // Our screens
        private List mainScr;
        private List detailScr;
        private List dataScr;

        // An array of all RMS stores found in this
        // MIDlets name space.
        private String[] recordStoreNames;

        /**
         * Seed data for creating personal contacts RMS store
         */
        private final String personalContacts[] = {
            "John", "Zach", "2225556669",
            "Mark", "Lynn", "5125551212",
            "Joy", "Beth", "2705551234",
            "Abby", "Lynn", "4085558566",
        };

        /**
         * Seed data for creating business contacts RMS store
         */
        private final String businessContacts[] = {
            "Ted", "Alan", "4125552235",
            "Sterling", "Wincle", "9995559111",
            "Deborah", "Elaine", "4445552323",
            "Suzanne", "Melissa"," 5125556064",
            "Frank", "Kenneth", "7775551212",
            "Dwight", "Poe", "1115557234",
            "Laura", "Beth", "2055558888",
            "Lisa", "Dawn", "2705551267",
            "Betty", "June", "5555551556",
            "Yvonne", "Poe", "6665558888",
            "Lizzy", "Loo", "5025557971",
            "John", "Gerald", "3335551256",
        };

        /**
         * Display a warning on the screen and revert
         * to the main screen.
         *
```

```
 * s   A warning string to display
 */
private void doAlert(String s) {
    alert.setString(s);
    myDisplay.setCurrent(alert, mainScr);
}


/**
 * Notify the system we are exiting.
 */
private void doExit() {
    destroyApp(false);
    notifyDestroyed();
}


/**
 * In our simple MIDlet, all screens have the same commands,
 * with the possible exception of the detailScr.
 *
 * Also set up the command listener to call commandAction.
 * See RMSMIDlet#commandAction
 */
private void addCommonCommands(Screen s,
                                    boolean doDetails) {
    s.addCommand(CMD_OK);
    s.addCommand(CMD_EXIT);
    if (doDetails) {
        s.addCommand(CMD_DETAILS);
    }
    s.setCommandListener(this);
}


/**
 * The public constructor. In our constructor, we get
 * a handle to our display and create two record stores.
 * In the event of an error, we display an alert.
 */
public RMSMIDlet() {
    CMD_EXIT = new Command("Exit", Command.EXIT, 3);
    CMD_DETAILS = new Command("Details", Command.SCREEN, 2);
    CMD_OK = new Command("OK", Command.OK, 1);
```

```java
        myDisplay = Display.getDisplay(this);
        alert = new Alert("Warning");
        alert.setTimeout(2000);

        CreateAddressBook.createRecordStore("Personal",
                                            personalContacts);
        CreateAddressBook.createRecordStore("Business",
                                            businessContacts);

        // Now, get a list of RMS stores and add their
        // names to the mainScr.
        recordStoreNames = RecordStore.listRecordStores();
        mainScr = new List("Select RMS Store", List.IMPLICIT,
                        recordStoreNames, null);
        addCommonCommands(mainScr, true);
    }

/**
 * Called by the system to start our MIDlet.
 */
protected void startApp() {
    myDisplay.setCurrent(mainScr);
}

/**
 * Called by the system to pause our MIDlet.
 * No actions required by our MIDLet.
 */
protected void pauseApp() {}

/**
 * Called by the system to end our MIDlet.
 * No actions required by our MIDLet.
 */
protected void destroyApp(boolean unconditional) {}

/**
 * Generate a screen with a sorted list of the contents
 * of the selected RMS store identified by index
 * If any errors encountered, display an alert and
 * redisplay the mainScr.
```

```
 *
 * index   an index into recordStoreNames
 */
public void genDataScr(int index) {
    SimpleComparator rc;
    RecordEnumeration re;
    RecordStore rs;
    dataScr;
    byte record[];

    try {
        rs = RecordStore.openRecordStore(
                            recordStoreNames[index], false);
    } catch (RecordStoreException e) {
        doAlert("Could not open " + recordStoreNames[index]);
        return;
    }

    // Create an enumeration that sorts by last name
    rc = new SimpleComparator(
                SimpleComparator.SORT_BY_LAST_NAME);
    try {
        re = rs.enumerateRecords(null, rc, false);
    } catch (RecordStoreNotOpenException e) {
        doAlert("Could not create enumeration: " + e);
        return;
    }

    // Create a screen and append the contents of the
    // selected RMS store.
    dataScr = new List(recordStoreNames[index] + " Data",
                    List.IMPLICIT);
    addCommonCommands(dataScr, false);

    try {
        while (re.hasNextElement()) {
            byte[] b = re.nextRecord();
            dataScr.append(SimpleRecord.getFirstName(b) +
                        " " + SimpleRecord.getLastName(b),
                        null);
        }
```

```
        } catch (Exception e) {
            doAlert("Could not build list: " + e);
            dataScr = null;
        } finally {
            try {
                rs.closeRecordStore();
            } catch (RecordStoreException e) {}
        }
    }


    /**
     * Generate a screen that shows some of the details
     * of the selected RMS store.
     *
     * RMS store information displayed:
     * - name
     * - number of records
     * - size, in bytes
     * - available size, in bytes
     * - version number
     *
     * index  an index into recordStoreNames
     */
    public void genDetailScr(int index) {
        RecordStore rs;
        detailScr = null;

        try {
            rs = RecordStore.openRecordStore(
                                recordStoreNames[index],
                                false);
        } catch (Exception e) {
            doAlert("Could not open " + recordStoreNames[index]);
            return;
        }

        detailScr = new List(recordStoreNames[index] + " Details",
                        List.IMPLICIT);
        addCommonCommands(detailScr, false);
```

```java
        try {
            detailScr.append("Name: " + rs.getName(), null);
            detailScr.append("# recs: " +
                            rs.getNumRecords(), null);
            detailScr.append("Size: " + rs.getSize(), null);
            detailScr.append("Avail: " +
                            rs.getSizeAvailable(),null);
            detailScr.append("Version: " +
                            rs.getVersion(), null);
        } catch (Exception e) {
            detailScr = null;
            doAlert("Failed to retrieve data");
            return;
        } finally {
            try {
                rs.closeRecordStore();
            } catch (RecordStoreException e) {}
        }
    }


/***
 * Respond to command selections.
 * Commands are:
 * EXIT: if selected, then exit
 *       (see RMSMIDlet, doExit)
 * OK:   if selected, interpreted in the context of
 *       the current screen.
 *
 * This method implements a state machine that drives
 * the MIDlet from one state (screen) to the next.
 */
public void commandAction(Command c,
                          Displayable d) {

    // Every screen has an EXIT command.
    // Handle this consistently for all screens.
    if (c == CMD_EXIT) {
        doExit();
        return;
    }
```

```
            // switch based on screen.
            if (d == mainScr) {

                // main screen: two commands to handle. If
                // OK was selected, then generate the dataScr
                // and make it active. If DETAILS was selected,
                // generate the detailScr and make it active.
                if ((c == List.SELECT_COMMAND) || (c == CMD_OK)) {
                    genDataScr(mainScr.getSelectedIndex());
                    myDisplay.setCurrent(dataScr);
                } else if (c == CMD_DETAILS) {
                    genDetailScr(mainScr.getSelectedIndex());
                    myDisplay.setCurrent(detailScr);
                }

            } else if (d == detailScr) {

                // If OK selected, go back to mainScr
                if (c == CMD_OK) {
                    myDisplay.setCurrent(mainScr);
                }

            } else if (d == dataScr) {

                // If OK selected, go back to mainScr
                if (c == CMD_OK) {
                    myDisplay.setCurrent(mainScr);
                }

            }
        }
    }
```

CHAPTER 12

Additional MIDP APIs

In addition to the application model, user interface, networking, and persistence libraries discussed earlier in this book, the *MIDP Specification* defines some additional APIs that do not belong to any of the categories discussed earlier. Also, the *MIDP Specification* intentionally modifies, refines or augments the behavior of certain functions that it inherits from CLDC.

This chapter introduces the MIDP Timer APIs. Furthermore, this chapter discusses the system properties and resource access mechanisms defined by the *MIDP Specification*, as well as explains how the *MIDP Specification* overrides the behavior of the System.exit method inherited from CLDC.

12.1 Timer Support

MIDlets may need to delay or schedule activities to be performed at a later time. To accomplish this, the *MIDP Specification* provides classes Timer and TimerTask that include functions for several types of timers. The general setup of a timer is illustrated below. In order to define a task to run, the programmer first defines a new timer task class by inheriting class TimerTask. The code to be executed by the timer is defined in the run method of the TimerTask subclass (see class MyTask below). In order to set up the actual timer, instances of class Timer and the new timer task class are created (objects myTimer and myTask in this example), and the schedule method of the timer object is then called with the task object and the appropriate time values as parameters. In this example, the timer will start executing in 10 milliseconds and will then repeat every 500 milliseconds.

```
class MyTask extends TimerTask {
    public void run() {

        . . .
```

```
        }
    }
    ...
    myTimer = new Timer();
    myTask = new MyTask();
    myTimer.schedule(myTask, 10, 500);
```

There are two basic types of timers in MIDP: *one-shot* timers and *repeating* timers. The key difference between these two types of timers is the scheduling approach. A one-shot timer executes the specified task only once. A repeating timer continues executing the specified task repeatedly at a specific interval.

12.1.1   Using one-shot timers

A one-shot timer can be set up to execute a task in two different ways. In the first approach, a `java.util.Date` object is passed into the `schedule` method of the `Timer` object. When the time specified by the `Date` object occurs, the timer task is run. If the `Date` passed in to the `Timer` object has already passed, then the timer task is run immediately. The following code fragment illustrates a timer whose task will be executed after 1000 milliseconds have passed after the current time (that is, after the time when the timer scheduling took place):[1]

```
    myTimer.schedule(myTask,
                    new Date(System.currentTimeMillis() + 1000);
```

The second way to schedule a one-shot timer is by passing it a `long` value that contains the number of milliseconds to wait before executing the timer task. For instance, the following piece of code defines another timer whose task will be executed after 1000 milliseconds have passed:

```
    myTimer.schedule(myTask, 1000);
```

12.1.2   Using repeating timers

The second type of timer supported by MIDP is a repeating timer. In this type of timer, the timer task is run repeatedly with a fixed period until the timer is canceled. Like one-shot timers, repeating timers can be set up to start executing the given task

---

[1]   Keep in mind that *MIDP Specification* does not provide any real-time guarantees. There is no guarantee that the scheduled task would start *exactly* at the specified time. Usually, the scheduled tasks will start executing *as soon as possible after* the specified time.

at a fixed time in the future (using a Date object as a parameter) or after a delay of a given number of milliseconds (using a long value as a parameter). In either case, the timer scheduling methods take an additional long parameter that indicates the repeat period of the timer. This period is interpreted either as a *fixed-delay* or a *fixed-rate* period, depending on whether the scheduling of the task is done using method schedule or scheduleAtFixedRate, respectively.

```
myTimer.schedule(myTask, 10, 500); // Fixed-delay repeating timer
myTimer.scheduleAtFixedRate(myTask, 10, 500); // Fixed-rate timer
```

In the fixed-delay case, each execution of the timer task is scheduled relative to the actual execution time of the previous timer task. If an execution is delayed for any reason, such as garbage collection or other background activity, subsequent executions will be delayed as well. This means that the execution of a fixed-delay timer may drift if, for example, the system is under a heavy execution load.

The fixed-rate case is different in that the execution of each timer task is scheduled relative to the *scheduled* execution time of the initial timer task. Thus, if an execution of a timer task is delayed for any reason, two or more executions will occur in rapid succession to "catch up" with the timer.

12.1.3 Sample code (TimerMIDlet.java)

The following example illustrates the use of timers and timer tasks in more detail. In this example, two graphical gauges are created using the javax.micro-edition.lcdui APIs, and these gauges are incremented or decremented by timer tasks. (See the figure.) The MIDlet has two abstract commands attached: OK and EXIT. If the OK command is selected, then the state of the timers is changed from nonactive to active, or from active to nonactive, depending on the current state of the timers. The MIDlet will exit if the EXIT command is selected.

TimerMIDlet.java

```
package examples.timermidlet;

import java.lang.*;
import java.io.*;
```

```java
import java.util.*;
import javax.microedition.lcdui.*;
import javax.microedition.midlet.*;

/**
 * A simple class that shows an example of using a Timer and
 * a TimerTask.
 *
 * This MIDlet creates two gauges. One gauge gaugeOne,
 * sets elements from low to high. The other, gaugeTwo,
 * set elements from high to low. In effect, this has
 * gaugeOne "going up", and gaugeTwo "going down."
 *
 * The two timers fire at different intervals.
 *
 * There are two commands on our form:
 *
 * OK: toggles whether the times are active or not.
 * EXIT: exits the MIDlet.
 */

public class TimerMIDlet extends MIDlet implements CommandListener {
    // number of elements in gauge
    final private static int GAUGE_MAX = 10;

    private boolean timersRunning; // tracks state of timers
    private Display myDisplay;     // handle to the display

    private Gauge gaugeOne;         // "going up" gauge
    private Gauge gaugeTwo;         // "going down" gauge

    private Form myScreen;          // form on which to
                                    // place gauges
    private Command cmdOK;          // OK command
    private Command cmdExit;        // EXIT command

    private Timer timer;
    private MyTimerTask timerTaskOne;
    private MyTimerTask timerTaskTwo;

    /**
     * Internal class that provides a TimerTask.
     */
```

```
private class MyTimerTask extends TimerTask {
    private Gauge myGauge; // reference to gauge
    private boolean goUp;  // if true, go up
    private int num;       // number of times called

    /**
     * Public constructor: stores "direction" and a reference to
     * a gauge.
     */
    public MyTimerTask(Gauge g, boolean up) {
        myGauge = g;
        goUp = up;
    }

    /**
     * As the timer fires, this method is invoked. Set gauge
     * based on goUp
     */
    public void run() {
        num++;
        myGauge.setValue(goUp ?
                        GAUGE_MAX -(num % GAUGE_MAX) :
                        num % GAUGE_MAX);
    }
}

/**
 * Public constructor: gets handle to display,
 * creates form, gauges, and commands.
 */
public TimerMIDlet() {
    myDisplay = Display.getDisplay(this);
    myScreen = new Form("TimerMIDlet");
    gaugeOne = new Gauge("Up Gauge",
                        false,
                        GAUGE_MAX,
                        0);
    myScreen.append(gaugeOne);

    gaugeTwo = new Gauge("Down Gauge",
                        false,
```

```
                            GAUGE_MAX,
                            GAUGE_MAX);
    myScreen.append(gaugeTwo);

    cmdOK = new Command("OK", Command.OK, 1);
    cmdExit = new Command("Exit", Command.EXIT, 1);
    myScreen.addCommand(cmdOK);
    myScreen.addCommand(cmdExit);
    myScreen.setCommandListener(this);
}


/**
 * Changes the state of timers to/from active to/from
 * not-active.
 */
private void flipFlop() {
    if (timersRunning) {
        timerTaskOne.cancel();
        timerTaskTwo.cancel();
        timer.cancel();
        timersRunning = false;
    } else {
        timer = new Timer();
        timerTaskOne = new MyTimerTask(gaugeOne, false);
        timerTaskTwo = new MyTimerTask(gaugeTwo, true);
        timer.schedule(timerTaskOne, 0, 1000);
        timer.schedule(timerTaskTwo, 0, 1500);
        timersRunning = true;
    }
}


/**
 * Called by the system to start our MIDlet.
 * @exception MIDletStateChangeException
 */
protected void startApp() throws MIDletStateChangeException {
    myDisplay.setCurrent(myScreen);
    flipFlop();
}
```

```
/**
 * Called by the system to pause our MIDlet.
 * No actions required by our MIDLet.
 */
protected void pauseApp() {}

/**
 * Called by the system to end our MIDlet.
 * No actions required by our MIDLet.
 */
protected void destroyApp(boolean unconditional) {}

/***
 * Respond to command selections. Process two commands:
 *
 * OK: flip flop the timers to/from active
 * EXIT: exit this MIDlet
 *
 */
public void commandAction(Command c, Displayable d) {
    if (c == cmdOK) {
        flipFlop();
    } else if (c == cmdExit) {
        destroyApp(false);
        notifyDestroyed();
    }
  }
}
```

12.2 System Properties

MIDP inherits the system property mechanism from CLDC (see Section 6.2.9, "Property support"). In addition to the properties provided by the CLDC, the *MIDP Specification* defines the following additional properties that can be retrieved by calling the method java.lang.System.getProperty (see Table 12.1).

The microedition.locale property is a String that consists of the language, country code and variant separated by "-" (for example, "fr-FR" or "en-US").

Table 12.1 System properties defined by MIDP

System Property	Description
microedition.locale	The current locale of the device (returns `null` by default)
microedition.profiles	Must contain at least "MIDP-1.0"

This locale string can be used by a MIDlet to determine which locale the underlying device is configured for.

The `microedition.profiles` property can be used by a MIDlet to ensure that the underlying platform supports the necessary profile and profile version that the application requires.

12.3   Application Resource Files

MIDP provides the capability of storing *resources* in the application's JAR file that can be accessed by a MIDlet at runtime. An example of such a resource might be a locale bundle, an icon or a graphical image; however, any *thing* that can be accessed as an `InputStream` can also be stored. These resources are accessed using the method `getResourceAsStream(String name)` of class `java.lang.Class`.

The rules and the parameter string format for accessing resources inside a JAR file have been discussed in Section 8.3.2, "MIDlet suite execution environment." As a general rule, if the parameter string to the `getResourceAsStream` method begins with a '/', the search for the resource begins at the "root" of the JAR file; however, if it does not begin with a '/', the resource is searched for along a path relative to the class instance retrieving the resource.

12.4   Exiting a MIDlet

The *CLDC Specification* states that a call to the method `java.lang.System.exit` is effectively equivalent to calling the method `Runtime.getRuntime().exit`. This means that in a CLDC program, calling the `System.exit` method will exit the virtual machine. However, since MIDP defines its own application model, this behavior is not desirable. For instance, it is not desirable that a single MIDlet in a MIDlet suite, upon exiting, would shut down the entire virtual machine (and therefore shut down the other MIDlets as well.) Rather, a well-behaved MIDlet should exit by calling the `destroyApp` and `notifyDestroyed` methods.

In order to prevent MIDP applications from accidentally shutting down the entire virtual machine, the *MIDP Specification* redefines the behavior of the `System.exit` method. In MIDP, calling this method will always throw a `java.lang.SecurityException`.

CHAPTER 13

Sample Applications

The CLDC and MIDP standards provide a compact but rich set of Java class libraries for application development. Together these standards enable the development of highly interactive, graphical, network-enabled applications for resource-constrained, wireless devices. The types of applications that we are likely to see in the near future include games and entertainment, information service applications (such as weather forecasts, stock quotes and graphs, street maps, travel and traffic information, news headlines), e-mail and instant messaging applications, transactions and mobile commerce applications (banking, stock trading, shopping, auctions, ticket reservations), enterprise applications (corporate database access, corporate address book and calendar access, corporate intranet/extranet applications) and advertising.

In this chapter we present three sample applications that illustrate the use of CLDC and MIDP. We start with a simple *PhotoAlbum* application that demonstrates the use of the `javax.microedition.midlet` application model and the `javax.microedition.lcdui` graphics classes. The next sample (see Section 13.2, "The AddressBook Application") illustrates the use of the networking capabilities and the MIDP record management system (RMS). The final sample (Section 13.3, "The Sokoban Game Application") illustrates the use of the MIDP graphics classes, and also demonstrates the RMS in implementing a game application.

This chapter concludes with an overview of the application development tools and environments that are emerging for J2ME.

13.1   The PhotoAlbum Application

The *PhotoAlbum* application presented in this section allows a collection of photographs or other graphical images to be displayed on a small device. Simple, optional animation and timing capabilities are included so that the application can automatically switch from one image to the next after a certain time period has passed.

When the application is started, a list of available images is first shown to the user, as seen in Figure 13.1. In this case, three images, "Flashing Light House," "Java Fly Through," and "Test Pattern," are available. When the user chooses one of these images from the list, the application loads the corresponding image resource (a PNG file) from the application's JAR file, and displays it on the screen.

Figure 13.1   The image list screen of the PhotoAlbum application

In Figure 13.2, the user has chosen the image called "Flashing Light House," and the corresponding image is now visible on the screen. Two command buttons, *Back* and *Options* are also available. Pressing the *Back* button takes the user back to the image list screen. Pressing the *Options* button allows the user to control the animation and frame display options.

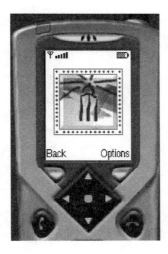

Figure 13.2   The image display screen of the PhotoAlbum application

The animation options of the *PhotoAlbum* application are illustrated in Figure 13.3. Four animation options are available: *Stop* (no animation), *Slow, Medium* and *Fast*. These options have been implemented as a ChoiceGroup, which, when used in the Choice.EXCLUSIVE mode, is typically rendered to the screen as a set of radio buttons. In addition, the options screen contains a set of frame style options that are not visible in Figure 13.3. In order to access those options, the user can scroll the options screen down.

The *PhotoAlbum* application consists of three classes: PhotoAlbum, PhotoFrame and Animation. The main class PhotoAlbum (a MIDlet class) defines the commands and screens that are used for driving the application. Class PhotoFrame provides the picture frame for the image view, and defines a thread for driving the animation of the images. Class Animation contains the set of images to display. It reads the images from resource files that are supplied in the application's JAR file, and stores them in memory for display.

A more detailed description of each class is provided below, along with the source code of each class.

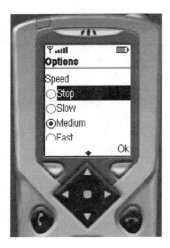

Figure 13.3   The animation options screen of the PhotoAlbum application

13.1.1   Class PhotoAlbum

Class PhotoAlbum is the main class of the *PhotoAlbum* application. The class defines all the commands and screens that are used for driving the *PhotoAlbum* application.

The PhotoAlbum class is implemented as a MIDlet. The class must define the startApp, pauseApp and destroyApp methods for starting, pausing and destroying the application, respectively. These methods are discussed in more detail below.

Let us take a look at the constructor of class PhotoAlbum first. The constructor method PhotoAlbum creates all the necessary command button objects that are needed by the application. It then creates and initializes a PhotoFrame object for displaying the images, and overrides some of the default values defined by the constructor of class PhotoFrame. It also activates a command listener that allows the *PhotoAlbum* application to respond to the commands from the user. Additionally, the constructor defines an alert object for later use, and then initializes the list of image names to be shown by calling method setupImages.

When the PhotoAlbum MIDlet is launched, its startApp method gets called automatically. In this implementation, the startApp method simply sets the display to show the earlier initialized image list by calling method display.set-Current with the object imageList as a parameter. In this implementation, methods pauseApp and destroyApp are defined simply to discard the images that have been cached by the PhotoFrame object. These methods get called automatically by the system when the MIDlet is paused or destroyed, respectively.

In order to understand the behavior of class `PhotoAlbum` in detail, it is important to take a look at the implementation of two additional methods: `commandAction` and `itemStateChanged`. Method `CommandListener.commandAction` defines the behavior of the *PhotoAlbum* application instance when it receives a command (such as a key press) from the system. In this case, the method is implemented so that the application reacts to three user-defined commands `exitCommand`, `optionsCommand` and `backCommand`, and one system-defined command `List.SELECT_COMMAND`.

The first three commands are mapped onto specific hard keys or soft keys by the underlying MIDP system implementation; the actual location of these buttons might vary on different devices. Command `List.SELECT_COMMAND` is provided as part of the implementation of the `javax.microedition.lcdui.List` user interface class. This command gets invoked automatically whenever the user chooses an item from the image list.

Method `ItemStateListener.itemStateChanged` is called automatically by the system when the state of any of the user interface components on display changes. In this case, the *PhotoAlbum* application is defined to respond to the changes in border choice and speed choice options.

```
package examples.photoalbum;
import javax.microedition.midlet.*;
import javax.microedition.lcdui.*;
import java.util.Vector;


/**
 * The PhotoAlbum MIDlet class provides the commands and screens
 * that implement a simple Photo and Animation Album.
 * The images and animations to be displayed are configured
 * in the descriptor file with attributes.
 *
 * It provides simple options to vary the speed of display
 * and the picture frames used.
 *
 */
public class PhotoAlbum extends MIDlet implements CommandListener,
ItemStateListener {

    private Display display;  // The display for this MIDlet
    private PhotoFrame frame; // The Frame and Canvas for images

    private ChoiceGroup borderChoice; // List of border choices
    private ChoiceGroup speedChoice;  // List of speed choices
```

```
    private Form optionsForm;    // The form holding the options
    private Alert alert;         // The Alert used for errors

    private Vector imageNames;   // Strings with the image names
    private List imageList;      // List of Image titles

    private Command exitCommand;    // The exit command
    private Command okCommand;      // The ok command
    private Command optionsCommand; // The command to edit options
    private Command backCommand;    // The command to go back

 /**
  * Construct a new PhotoAlbum MIDlet and initialize the base
  * options and main PhotoFrame to be used when the MIDlet is
  * started.
  */
 public PhotoAlbum() {
     display = Display.getDisplay(this);
     exitCommand = new Command("Exit", Command.EXIT, 1);
     optionsCommand = new Command("Options",Command.SCREEN,1);
     okCommand = new Command("Ok", Command.OK, 3);
     backCommand = new Command("Back", Command.SCREEN, 3);

     frame = new PhotoFrame();
     frame.setStyle(2);
     frame.setSpeed(2);
     frame.addCommand(optionsCommand);
     frame.addCommand(backCommand);
     frame.setCommandListener(this);
     alert = new Alert("Warning");
     setupImages();
 }


 /**
  * Start up the MIDlet by setting the display
  * to show the image name list.
  */
 protected void startApp() {
     display.setCurrent(imageList);
 }
```

```
/**
 * Pausing is easy since there are no background activities
 * or record stores that need to be closed.
 */
protected void pauseApp() {
    frame.reset(); // Discard images cached in the frame
}


/**
 * Destroy must clean up everything not handled by the
 * garbage collector.
 */
protected void destroyApp(boolean unconditional) {
    frame.reset(); // Discard images cached in the frame
}


/**
 * Respond to commands, including exit.
 * On the exit command, clean up and notify that
 * the MIDlet has been destroyed.
 */
public void commandAction(Command c, Displayable s) {
    if (c == exitCommand) {
        destroyApp(false);
        notifyDestroyed();
    } else if (c == optionsCommand) {
        display.setCurrent(genOptions());
    } else if (c == okCommand && s == optionsForm) {
        display.setCurrent(frame);
    } else if (c == List.SELECT_COMMAND) {
        int i = imageList.getSelectedIndex();
        String image = (String)imageNames.elementAt(i);

        try {
            frame.setImage(image);
            display.setCurrent(frame);
        } catch (java.io.IOException e) {
            alert.setString("Unable to locate " + image);
            display.setCurrent(alert, imageList);
        }
```

```
        } else if (c == backCommand) {
            display.setCurrent(imageList);
        }
    }


    /**
     * Listener for changes to options.
     */
    public void itemStateChanged(Item item) {
        if (item == borderChoice) {
            frame.setStyle(borderChoice.getSelectedIndex());
        } else if (item == speedChoice) {
            frame.setSpeed(speedChoice.getSelectedIndex());
        }
    }


    /**
     * Generate the options form with speed and style choices.
     * Speed choices are stop, slow, medium, and fast.
     * Style choices for borders are none, plain, fancy.
     */
    private Screen genOptions() {
        if (optionsForm == null) {
            optionsForm = new Form("Options");
            optionsForm.addCommand(okCommand);
            optionsForm.setCommandListener(this);
            optionsForm.setItemStateListener(this);

            speedChoice = new ChoiceGroup("Speed",
                                          Choice.EXCLUSIVE);
            speedChoice.append("Stop", null);
            speedChoice.append("Slow", null);
            speedChoice.append("Medium", null);
            speedChoice.append("Fast", null);
            speedChoice.setSelectedIndex(2, true);
            optionsForm.append(speedChoice);

            borderChoice = new ChoiceGroup("Borders",
                                           Choice.EXCLUSIVE);
            borderChoice.append("None", null);
            borderChoice.append("Plain", null);
```

```
            borderChoice.append("Fancy", null);
            borderChoice.setSelectedIndex(2, true);
            optionsForm.append(borderChoice);
        }

        return optionsForm;
    }


    /**
     * Check the attributes in the Descriptor that identify
     * images and titles and initialize the lists imageNames
     * and imageList.
     */
    private void setupImages() {
        imageNames = new Vector();
        imageList = new List("Images", List.IMPLICIT);
        imageList.addCommand(exitCommand);
        imageList.setCommandListener(this);

        for (int n = 1; n < 100; n++) {
            String nthImage = "PhotoImage-"+ n;
            String image = getAppProperty(nthImage);
            if (image == null || image.length() == 0)
                break;

            String nthTitle = "PhotoTitle-" + n;
            String title = getAppProperty(nthTitle);
            if (title == null || title.length() == 0)
                title = image;

            imageNames.addElement(image);
            imageList.append(title, null);
        }
    }
}
```

13.1.2 Class PhotoFrame

Class PhotoFrame defines the picture frame and drives the animation of the images
on the display. It handles the starting and stopping of the animation, and contains the
Java thread that is used for handling the timing and the periodical repainting of the

screen. Class `PhotoFrame` is implemented as an extension of class `Canvas`, that is, it inherits all the methods that class `Canvas` has.

When a new `PhotoFrame` object is created, the constructor of class `PhotoFrame` first creates a new `Animation` instance for future use. It also creates a new `Image` object and defines some values that `PhotoFrame` instances have by default.

The drawing functionality of class `PhotoFrame` is defined in methods `setImage`, `paint`, `paintFrame` and `paintBorder`. These functions call various lower-level graphics functions to draw the image and the surrounding border. The `paint` method takes care to use the clipping information in the `Graphics` object to optimize the painting of the border and current image. If the clipping region only includes the image displayed in the center of the frame then it does not redraw the border. It checks that the clipping region includes the `Image` to avoid drawing the image unless it is necessary. When the current image to be displayed in the frame changes, the repaint only includes the region that contains the `Image`. See the code in the `run` method. Repainting only the necessary part of the screen can improve performance.

The animation capabilities of class `PhotoFrame` are defined in methods `keyPress`, `setSpeed`, `showNotify`, `hideNotify`, and `run`. As defined in method `keyPress`, when the user presses the *FIRE* key, the application creates a new Java thread for timing the animation. This new thread executes code defined in method `run`. The code in that method compares the current time to the time when an image was last drawn, and draws the next image when sufficient time has elapsed. Methods `setSpeed` makes it possible to control the speed of animation. Methods `hideNotify` and `showNotify` are used for stopping and restarting the animation thread in case the animation display becomes inactive (for example, the user presses a button to go to the options display) or is reactivated again, respectively. Class `Animation` contains the code to paint the next image in sequence.

```
package examples.photoalbum;
import javax.microedition.lcdui.*;
import java.io.IOException;

/**
 * This class provides the picture frame and drives the
 * animation of the frames and the picture. It handles the
 * starting and stopping of the Animation and contains the
 * Thread used to do the timing and requests that the Canvas
 * is repainted periodically. Additionally, it has controls for
 * border style and animation speed.
 */
```

```
class PhotoFrame extends Canvas implements Runnable {

    private Animation animation; // The Animation sequencer
    private int speed;           // Animation speed set

    private Thread thread;  // Thread for triggering repaints
    private long paintTime; // Time of most recent paint

    private Image image;    // Buffer image of screen
    private Image bimage;   // Pattern used for border
    private int style;      // Border style

    /*
     * Mapping of speed values to delays in milliseconds.
     * Indices map to those in the ChoiceGroup.
     */
    private final static int speeds[] =
        {999999999, 500, 250, 100};

    /**
     * Create a new PhotoFrame. Creates an offscreen mutable
     * image into which the border is drawn.
     * Border style is none (0).
     * Speed is stopped (0) until set.
     */
    PhotoFrame() {
        animation = new Animation();
        image = Image.createImage(getWidth(), getHeight());
        setStyle(0);
        setSpeed(0);
    }

    /**
     * Load a new photo into the frame.
     * Load the images into the Animation and pick
     * where the image should be placed on the canvas.
     * Also draw the frame into the buffered image based
     * on the animation size.
     * If the images can't be loaded, just reset the origin
     * and throw an IOException.
     * name the prefix of the resource to load.
```

```
 * throws IOException when no images can be loaded.
 */
void setImage(String prefix) throws IOException {
    try {
        animation.loadImage(prefix);
        animation.x = (getWidth() - animation.width) / 2;
        animation.y = (getHeight() - animation.height) / 2;
        paintFrame(style, animation.x, animation.y,
                   animation.width, animation.height);
    } catch (java.io.IOException ex) {
        // No image to display. Just show an empty frame.
        animation.x = 0;
        animation.y = 0;
       paintFrame(style, 10, 10, getWidth()-20, getHeight()-20);
        throw ex;
    }
}


/**
 * Reset the PhotoFrame so it holds minimal resources
 * by resetting the animation.
 * The animation thread is stopped.
 */
void reset() {
    animation.reset();
    image = null;
    thread = null;
}


/**
 * Handle key events. FIRE events toggle between
 * running and stopped.  LEFT and RIGHT key events
 * when stopped show the previous or next image.
 */
protected void keyPressed(int keyCode) {
    int action = getGameAction(keyCode);

    switch (action) {
    case RIGHT:
        if (thread == null) {
            animation.next();
```

```
                    repaint();
                }
            break;
        case LEFT:
            if (thread == null) {
                animation.previous();
                repaint();
            }
            break;
        case FIRE:
            // Use FIRE to toggle the activity of the thread
            if (thread == null) {
                thread = new Thread(this);
                thread.start();
            } else {
                synchronized (this) {
                    // Wake up the thread to change the timing
                    this.notify();
                    thread = null;
                }
            }
            break;
    }
}

/**
 * Handle key repeat events as regular key events.
 */
protected void keyRepeated(int keyCode) {
    keyPressed(keyCode);
}

/**
 * Set the animation speed.
 * speed speedo of animation 0-3;
 * 0 == stop; 1 = slow, 2 = medium, 3 = fast.
 */
void setSpeed(int speed) {
    this.speed = speed;
}
```

```
/**
 * Set the frame style.
 * Recreate the photo frame image from the current animation
 * and the new style.
 */
void setStyle(int style) {
    this.style = style;
    paintFrame(style, animation.x, animation.y,
            animation.width, animation.height);
}


/**
 * Notified when Canvas is made visible.
 * Create the thread to run the animation timing.
 */
protected void showNotify() {
    thread = new Thread(this);
    thread.start();
}


/**
 * Notified when the Canvas is no longer visible.
 * Signal the running Thread that it should stop.
 */
protected void hideNotify() {
    thread = null;
}


/**
 * Paint is called whenever the canvas should be redrawn.
 * It clears the canvas and draws the frame and
 * the current frame from the animation.
 * g the Graphics context to which to draw
 */
protected void paint(Graphics g) {
    paintTime = System.currentTimeMillis();
    if (image != null) {
        // Draw the frame unless only the picture is
        // being redrawn
        // This is the inverse of the usual clip check.
        int cx = 0, cy = 0, cw = 0, ch = 0;
```

```
        if ((cx = g.getClipX()) < animation.x ||
            (cy = g.getClipY()) < animation.y ||
            ((cx + (cw = g.getClipWidth())) >
             (animation.x + animation.width)) ||
            ((cy + (ch = g.getClipHeight())) >
             (animation.y + animation.height))) {

            g.drawImage(image, 0, 0,
                        Graphics.LEFT | Graphics.TOP);
        }


        // Draw the image if it intersects
        // the clipping region
        if (intersectsClip(g,
                 animation.x, animation.y,
                 animation.width, animation.height)) {
            animation.paint(g);
        }
    }
}

/**
 * Return true if the specified rectangle does intersect the
 * clipping rectangle of the graphics object. If it returns
 * true then the object must be drawn. Otherwise it would
 * be clipped completely.
 * The checks are done in a order with early exits to make
 * this as inexpensive as possible.
 * g the Graphics context to check
 * x the upper left corner of the rectangle
 * y the upper left corner of the rectangle
 * w the width of the rectangle
 * h the height of the rectangle
 * return true if the rectangle intersects the clipping region
 */
boolean intersectsClip(Graphics g, int x, int y, int w, int h) {

    int cx = g.getClipX();
    if (x + w <= cx)
        return false;
```

```
        int cw = g.getClipWidth();
        if (x > cx + cw)
            return false;

        int cy = g.getClipY();
        if (y + h <= cy)
            return false;

        int ch = g.getClipHeight();
        if (y > cy + ch)
            return false;
        return true;
    }


    /**
     * Paint the photo frame into the buffered screen image.
     * This avoids drawing each of its parts on each repaint.
     * Paint only needs to put the image into the frame.
     * style of the style of frame to draw.
     * Parameters:
     *    x       the x offset of the image.
     *    y       the y offset of the image
     *    width  the width of the animation image
     *    height the height of the animation image
     */
    private void paintFrame(int style, int x, int y,
                            int width, int height) {

        Graphics g = image.getGraphics();

        // Clear the entire canvas to white
        g.setColor(0xffffff);
        g.fillRect(0, 0, getWidth()+1, getHeight()+1);

        // Set the origin of the image and
        // paint the border and image.
        g.translate(x, y);
        paintBorder(g, style, width, height);
    }
```

```
/**
 * Runs the animation and makes the repaint requests.
 * The thread exits when it is no longer the current
 * Animation thread.
 */
public void run() {
    Thread me = Thread.currentThread();
    long scheduled = System.currentTimeMillis();
    paintTime = scheduled;

    while (me == thread) {
        synchronized (this) {
            try {
                // Update when the next frame should be drawn
                // and compute the delta till then
                scheduled += speeds[speed];
                long delta = scheduled - paintTime;
                if (delta > 0)  {
                    this.wait(delta);
                }
                animation.next();
                // Request a repaint only of the image,
                // not the frame
                repaint(animation.x, animation.y,
                        animation.width, animation.height);
            } catch (InterruptedException e) {
            }
        }
    }
}

/**
 * Draw a border of the selected style.
 * Style:
 * - Style 0: No border is drawn.
 * - Style 1: A simple border is drawn
 * - Style 2: The border is outlined and an image
 *            is created to tile within the border.
 * Parameters:
 *   g  graphics context to which to draw.
 *   x  the horizontal offset in the frame of the image.
```

```
 *    y   the vertical offset in the frame
 *    w   the width reserved for the image
 *    h   the height reserved of the image
 */
private void paintBorder(Graphics g, int style, int w, int h) {
    if (style == 1) {
        g.setColor(0x808080);
        g.drawRect(-1, -1, w + 1, h + 1);
        g.drawRect(-2, -2, w + 3, h + 3);
    }


    if (style == 2) {
        // Draw fancy border with image between outer
        // and inner rectangles
        if (bimage == null)
            bimage = genBorder();
        int bw = bimage.getWidth();
        int bh = bimage.getHeight();
        int i;

        // Draw the inner and outer solid border
        g.setColor(0x808080);
        g.drawRect(-1, -1, w + 1, h + 1);
        g.drawRect(-bw - 2, -bh - 2,
                   w + bw * 2 + 3, h + bh * 2 + 3);

        // Draw it in each corner
        g.drawImage(bimage, -1, -1,
                    Graphics.BOTTOM|Graphics.RIGHT);
        g.drawImage(bimage, -1, h + 1,
                    Graphics.TOP|Graphics.RIGHT);
        g.drawImage(bimage, w + 1, -1,
                    Graphics.BOTTOM|Graphics.LEFT);
        g.drawImage(bimage, w + 1, h + 1,
                    Graphics.TOP|Graphics.LEFT);

        // Draw the embedded image down left and right sides
        for (i = ((h % bh ) / 2); i < h - bh; i += bh) {
            g.drawImage(bimage, -1, i,
                        Graphics.RIGHT|Graphics.TOP);
```

```
            g.drawImage(bimage, w + 1, i,
                    Graphics.LEFT|Graphics.TOP);
        }

        // Draw the embedded image across the top and bottom
        for (i = ((w % bw) / 2); i < w - bw; i += bw) {
            g.drawImage(bimage, i, -1,
                    Graphics.LEFT|Graphics.BOTTOM);
            g.drawImage(bimage, i, h + 1,
                    Graphics.LEFT|Graphics.TOP);
        }
    }
}


/**
 * Create an image for the border.
 * The border consists of a simple "+" drawn in a 5x5 image.
 * Fill the image with white and draw the "+" as magenta.
 */
private Image genBorder() {
    Image image = Image.createImage(5, 5);
    Graphics g = image.getGraphics();
    g.setColor(255,255,255);
    g.fillRect(0, 0, 5, 5);
    g.setColor(128, 0, 255);
    g.drawLine(2, 1, 2, 3);    // vertical
    g.drawLine(1, 2, 3, 2);    // horizontal
    return image;
}
}
```

13.1.3 Class Animation

Class `Animation` implements support for displaying a set of images sequentially (one after another). Also, this class implements the low-level code for reading the images from the resource files that are supplied in the JAR file of the *PhotoAlbum* application. The sample implementation provided below is not particularly memory-efficient because it keeps the loaded images in memory (stored in a `java.util.Vector` object) while the *PhotoAlbum* application is running.

The methods `next` and `loadImage` in the implementation below perform certain name manipulation operations that map the images used by the application to resource files that are provided in the application's JAR file. In this case, it is assumed that each resource file is of type .png (a PNG graphics image). Loading of the images is accomplished by calling image.createImage.

```
package examples.photoalbum;
import java.io.IOException;
import java.util.Vector;
import javax.microedition.lcdui.Image;
import javax.microedition.lcdui.Graphics;


/**
 * An Animation contains the set of images to display.
 * Images are read from resource files supplied in the
 * JAR file.
 * This implementation keeps the Images in the heap.
 * If memory is short, a more deliberate management
 * of Image may be required.
 */
class Animation {
    /**
     * Location to draw the animation, set these fields to
     * change the location where the image is drawn.
     */
    int x, y;

    /**
     * The width and the height of the images (max of all
     * if they are different). They are set when images
     * are loaded and should not be changed.
     */
    int width, height;

    /**
     * Vector of images in the sequence.
     */
    private Vector images;

    /**
     * Current index into the sequence of images.
     */
    private int index;
```

```
/**
 * Size of sequence of images. Set to a large number until
 * the last image of the sequence has been read.
 */
private int size;

/**
 * Prefix or name of the image.
 */
private String prefix;

/**
 * Create a new Animation.
 */
Animation() {
    images = new Vector(30);
}


/**
 * Advance to the next image.
 * If the number of images is known, just advance
 * and wrap around if necessary.
 * If the number of images is not known, when
 * advancing off the end of the known images try to
 * create a new image using the pattern.
 * When an attempt fails, this sets the number of images.
 */
void next() {
    int nextindex = index + 1;
    if (nextindex >= size) {
        index = 0;
    } else if (nextindex >= images.size()) {
        // Try to read the next image
        // If that works, put it into the images vector
        try {
            String name = prefix + nextindex + ".png";
            Image image = Image.createImage(name);
            images.setSize(nextindex+1);
            images.setElementAt(image, nextindex);
            index = nextindex;
```

```
        } catch (IOException ex) {
            // No more images, set the size of the sequence.
            size = nextindex;
            index = 0;
        } catch (Exception e) {
            size = nextindex;
            index = 0;
        }
    } else {
        // Index is within range of Images already read
        index = nextindex;
    }
}


/**
 * Back up to the previous image.
 * If at the beginning, wrap around to the end.
 */
void previous() {
    index--;
    if (index < 0) {
        index = images.size()-1;
    }
}


/**
 * Paint the current image in the sequence.
 * The image is drawn to the target graphics context
 * at the x, and y of the Animation.
 * g graphics context to which the next image is drawn.
 */
public void paint(Graphics g) {
    if (images.size() > 0) {
        g.drawImage((Image)images.elementAt(index), x, y, 0);
    }
}


/**
 * Load Images from resource files using
 * Image.createImage.
 * The first image is loaded to determine whether it is a
 * single image or a sequence of images, and to make sure
```

```
 * it exists.
 * Subsequent images are loaded on demand when they are
 * needed. If the name given is the complete name of the
 * image then it is a singleton.
 * Otherwise it is assumed to be a sequence of images
 * with the name as a prefix. Sequence numbers (n) are
 * 0, 1, 2, 3, .... The full resource name is the
 * concatenation of name + n + ".png".
 *
 * Subsequent images are loaded when they are needed.
 * See next and previous for details.
 * name the name or prefix of the resource image names
 * @exception IOException is thrown if the image or the first
 * of the sequence cannot be found.
 * @exception OutOfMemoryError if no memory can be allocated
 * for the image.
 */
void loadImage(String prefix) throws IOException {
    this.prefix = prefix;
    Image image;
    images.setSize(0);
    index = 0;

    try {
        // Try the name supplied for the single image case.
        // If it is found, then do the set up and return
        image = Image.createImage(prefix);
        size = 1;
    } catch (IOException ex) {
        // Use the prefix + "0.png" to locate the first of
        // a series of images.
        String name = prefix + "0.png";
        image = Image.createImage(name);
        size = 999999999;
    }

    width = image.getWidth();
    height = image.getHeight();
    images.addElement(image);
}
```

```
/**
 * Reset the Animation to reduce memory usage.
 * Discard all but the first image.
 */
void reset() {
    if (images.size() > 0) {
        for (int i = 0; i < images.size(); i++)
            images.setElementAt(null, i);
    }
}
}
```

13.1.4 Descriptor file PhotoAlbum.jad

The *MIDP Specification* requires each MIDlet suite to have a descriptor file. The descriptor file is commonly generated automatically by the application development environment that is used for developing and compiling the application. Here is a sample descriptor file, PhotoAlbum.jad:

```
MIDlet-Name: PhotoAlbum
MIDlet-Vendor: Riggs
MIDlet-Version: 1.0
MIDlet-1: PhotoAlbum, /PhotoAlbum.png,
         examples.photoalbum.PhotoAlbum
MIDlet-Description: Displays images in an album.
MIDlet-Jar-Size: 408206
MIDlet-Jar-URL: PhotoAlbum.jar
MIDlet-Data-Size: 0
MicroEdition-Configuration: CLDC-1.0
MicroEdition-Profile: MIDP-1.0
PhotoImage-1: /j2mebook/images/LightHouse-
PhotoTitle-1: Flashing Light House
```

The descriptor file provides information about various aspects of the application, including the name, address, and icon of the MIDlet suite, its author, version number, JAR file size, supported J2ME configuration and profile, and so on. This information is used for determining whether the MIDlet suite can be downloaded and executed in the target device.

13.2 The AddressBook Application

This example, `AddressBookMIDLet`, implements a simple address book application similar to address book applications found in most cellular phones. It has the ability to search both the local address book and a remote one located on the network. It also supports the addition of new address book entries and the browsing of the local address book. The application is composed of five classes: `AddressBookMIDlet`, `SimpleRecord` (see 13.2.2), `SimpleFilter` (13.2.3), `SimpleComparator` (13.2.4), and `NetworkQuery` (13.2.5).

13.2.1 Class AddressBookMIDlet

Class `AddressBookMIDlet` is the main class of the *AddressBook* application. This class defines how the application interacts with the user. When this class is invoked, it opens the local address book, and displays the screen shown in Figure 13.4.

Figure 13.4   AddressBookMIDlet main screen

The user can select one of five actions:

1. Search the local or network address book.

2. Add a new entry to the local address book.

3. Browse the local address book.

4. Set the sort options for browses and searches.

5. Exit.

If the user selects the *Search* option, the screen depicted in Figure 13.5 is presented.

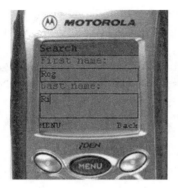

Figure 13.5   AddressBookMIDlet search entry screen

The user can then enter a partial or complete first and/or last name, then select the *Menu* command. This brings up the screen shown in Figure 13.6, where the user can choose whether to search the local address book or the one on the network.

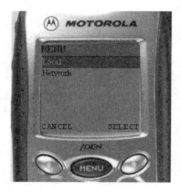

Figure 13.6   AddressBookMIDlet search options screen

In either case, a screen with matches from the desired address book is displayed, as shown in Figure 13.7.

Figure 13.7   AddressBookMIDlet search results screen

Any screen that displays the results of a browse or a search has a *Dial* command attached to it. If this command is selected, then the MIDlet creates a TextBox screen with the input constraint of TextField.PHONENUMBER. Depending on the implementation, such a TextBox might display a confirmation dialog to the user asking for confirmation before dialing the phone number. Not all MIDP devices implement this feature, since this feature is not required by the specification.

On the main screen, if the *Add New* command is selected, the user is presented a screen much like the search entry screen, with the exception that an additional TextField is also displayed to allow entry of a phone number. After entering the first name, last name and phone number, the user selects the *Add* command to create a new record in the address book.

The *Browse* option simply displays a list of entries, in the selected order, from the local address book. The results are sorted either by last name or first name. This choice of sort order is made by selecting the Option entry on the main screen, which brings up a ChoiceGroup, as shown in Figure 13.8.

Figure 13.8   AddressBookMIDlet sort order options screen

```java
package examples.addressbook;

import java.lang.*;
import java.io.*;
import java.util.*;
import javax.microedition.lcdui.*;
import javax.microedition.midlet.*;
import javax.microedition.rms.*;

/**
 * This MIDlet implements a simple address book with
 * the following functionality: browsing, entry,
 * deletion, and searching (both on device and over
 * the network).
 */
public class AddressBookMIDlet extends MIDlet
    implements CommandListener, ItemStateListener {

    private RecordStore addrBook;

    private static final int FN_LEN = 10;
    private static final int LN_LEN = 20;
    private static final int PN_LEN = 15;
    final private static int ERROR = 0;
    final private static int INFO = 1;

    private Display display;
    private Alert alert;
    private Command cmdAdd;
    private Command cmdBack;
    private Command cmdCancel;
    private Command cmdDial;
    private Command cmdExit;
    private Command cmdSelect;
    private Command cmdSearchNetwork;
    private Command cmdSearchLocal;
    private List mainScr;
    private String[] mainScrChoices = {"Search",
                                       "Add New",
                                       "Browse",
                                       "Options" };
```

```
private Form searchScr;
private TextField s_lastName;
private TextField s_firstName;

private Form entryScr;
private TextField e_lastName;
private TextField e_firstName;
private TextField e_phoneNum;

private List nameScr;
private Vector phoneNums;

private Form optionScr;
private ChoiceGroup sortChoice;
private TextBox dialScr;

private int sortOrder = 1;

/**
 * Public no-argument constructor. Called by the system to
 * instantiate our class. Caches reference to
 * the display, allocate commands, and tries to open
 * the address book.
 */
public AddressBookMIDlet() {
    display = Display.getDisplay(this);

    cmdAdd = new Command("Add", Command.OK, 1);
    cmdBack = new Command("Back", Command.BACK, 2);
    cmdCancel = new Command("Cancel", Command.BACK, 2);
    cmdDial = new Command("Dial", Command.OK, 1);
    cmdExit = new Command("Exit", Command.EXIT, 2);
    cmdSelect = new Command("Select", Command.OK, 1);
    cmdSearchNetwork = new Command("Network",
                                    Command.SCREEN, 4);
    cmdSearchLocal = new Command("Local", Command.SCREEN, 3);

    alert = new Alert("", "", null, AlertType.INFO);
    alert.setTimeout(2000);
```

```java
        try {
            addrBook = RecordStore.openRecordStore("TheAddressBook",
                                                    true);
        } catch (RecordStoreException e) {
            addrBook = null;
        }
    }


    /**
     * Called by the system to start our MIDlet.
     * If the open of the address book fails, display
     * an alert and continue.
     *
     * @exception MIDletStateChangeException
     */
    protected void startApp() throws MIDletStateChangeException {
        if (addrBook == null) {
            displayAlert(ERROR,
                            "Could not open address book", null);
        } else {
            genMainScr();
        }
    }


    /**
     * Called by the system to pause our MIDlet.
     * No actions required by our MIDlet.
     */
    protected void pauseApp() {}

    /**
     * Called by the system to end our MIDlet.
     * No actions required by our MIDlet.
     */
    protected void destroyApp(boolean unconditional) {
        if (addrBook != null) {
            try {
                addrBook.closeRecordStore();
            } catch (Exception e) { }
        }
    }
```

```java
/**
 * Display an Alert on the screen
 *
 *   type     One of the following: ERROR, INFO
 *   msg      Message to display
 *   s        screen to change to after displaying alert.
 *            if null, revert to main screen
 */
private void displayAlert(int type, String msg, Screen s) {
    alert.setString(msg);

    switch (type) {
    case ERROR:
        alert.setTitle("Error!");
        alert.setType(AlertType.ERROR);
        break;
    case INFO:
        alert.setTitle("Info");
        alert.setType(AlertType.INFO);
        break;
    }
    display.setCurrent(alert,
                        s == null ? display.getCurrent() : s);
}


/**
 * Notify the system that we are exiting.
 */
private void midletExit() {
    destroyApp(false);
    notifyDestroyed();
}


/**
 * Create the first screen of our MIDlet.
 * This screen is a list.
 */
private Screen genMainScr() {
    if (mainScr == null) {
        mainScr = new List("Menu",
```

```
                              List.IMPLICIT,
                              mainScrChoices,
                              null);
        mainScr.addCommand(cmdSelect);
        mainScr.addCommand(cmdExit);
        mainScr.setCommandListener(this);
    }
    display.setCurrent(mainScr);
    return mainScr;
}


/**
 * Sort order option screen.
 * Allows us to set sort order to either sorting by
 * last name (default), or first name.
 */
private Screen genOptionScr() {
    if (optionScr == null) {
        optionScr = new Form("Options");
        optionScr.addCommand(cmdBack);
        optionScr.setCommandListener(this);

        sortChoice = new ChoiceGroup("Sort by",
                                    Choice.EXCLUSIVE);
        sortChoice.append("First name", null);
        sortChoice.append("Last name", null);
        sortChoice.setSelectedIndex(sortOrder, true);
        optionScr.append(sortChoice);
        optionScr.setItemStateListener(this);
    }
    display.setCurrent(optionScr);
    return optionScr;
}


/**
 * Search screen.
 *
 * Displays two TextFields: one for
 * first name, and one for last name.
 * These are used for searching the address book.
 *
```

```
 * @see AddressBookMIDlet#genNameScr
 */
private Screen genSearchScr() {
    if (searchScr == null) {
        searchScr = new Form("Search");
        searchScr.addCommand(cmdBack);
        searchScr.addCommand(cmdSearchNetwork);
        searchScr.addCommand(cmdSearchLocal);
        searchScr.setCommandListener(this);
        s_firstName = new TextField("First name:", "",
                                    FN_LEN, TextField.ANY);
        s_lastName = new TextField("Last name:", "",
                                    LN_LEN, TextField.ANY);
        searchScr.append(s_firstName);
        searchScr.append(s_lastName);
    }

    s_firstName.delete(0, s_firstName.size());
    s_lastName.delete(0, s_lastName.size());
    display.setCurrent(searchScr);
    return searchScr;
}


/**
 * Name/Phone number entry screen
 *
 * Displays three TextFields: one for
 * first name, one for last name, and one for phone number.
 * These are used to capture data to add to the address book.
 *
 * @see AddressBookMIDlet#addEntry
 */
private Screen genEntryScr() {
    if (entryScr == null) {
        entryScr = new Form("Add new");
        entryScr.addCommand(cmdCancel);
        entryScr.addCommand(cmdAdd);
        entryScr.setCommandListener(this);

        e_firstName = new TextField("First name:", "",
                                    FN_LEN, TextField.ANY);
```

```
                    e_lastName = new TextField("Last name:", "",
                                        LN_LEN, TextField.ANY);
                    e_phoneNum = new TextField("Phone Number", "",
                                        PN_LEN, TextField.PHONENUMBER);
                    entryScr.append(e_firstName);
                    entryScr.append(e_lastName);
                    entryScr.append(e_phoneNum);
                }

                e_firstName.delete(0, e_firstName.size());
                e_lastName.delete(0, e_lastName.size());
                e_phoneNum.delete(0, e_phoneNum.size());

                display.setCurrent(entryScr);
                return entryScr;
            }


    /**
     * Generates a list of first/last/phone numbers.
     * Can be called as a result of a browse command
     * (genBrowseScr) or a search command
     * (genSearchScr).
     *
     *   title   title of this screen (since it can be called
     *           from a browse or a search command.
     *   f       if not null, first name to search on
     *   l       if not null, last name to search on
     */
    private Screen genNameScr(String title,
                              String f,
                              String l,
                              boolean local) {
        SimpleComparator sc;
        SimpleFilter sf;
        RecordEnumeration re;
        phoneNums = null;

        if (local) {
            sc = new SimpleComparator(sortOrder == 0 ?
                    SimpleComparator.SORT_BY_FIRST_NAME :
                    SimpleComparator.SORT_BY_LAST_NAME);
```

```java
        if (f != null || l != null) {
            sf = new SimpleFilter(f, l);
        }

        try {
            re = addrBook.enumerateRecords(sf, sc, false);
        } catch (Exception e) {
            displayAlert(ERROR,
                "Could not create enumeration: " + e, null);
            return null;
        }
    } else {
        re = new NetworkQuery(f,l, sortOrder);
    }

    nameScr = null;
    if (re.hasNextElement()) {
        nameScr = new List(title, List.IMPLICIT);
        nameScr.addCommand(cmdBack);
        nameScr.addCommand(cmdDial);
        nameScr.setCommandListener(this);
        phoneNums = new Vector(6);

        try {
            while (re.hasNextElement()) {
                byte[] b = re.nextRecord();
                String pn = SimpleRecord.getPhoneNum(b);
                nameScr.append(SimpleRecord.getFirstName(b) +
                    " " + SimpleRecord.getLastName(b) +
                    " " + SimpleRecord.getPhoneNum(b), null);
                phoneNums.addElement(pn);
            }
        } catch (Exception e) {
            displayAlert(ERROR,
                "Error while building name list: " + e, null);
            return null;
        }
        display.setCurrent(nameScr);

    } else {
```

```
                displayAlert(INFO, "No names found", null);
        }

        return nameScr;
    }

    /**
     * Generate a screen with which to dial the phone.
     * Note: this may or may not be implemented
     * on a given implementation.
     */
    private void genDialScr() {
        dialScr =  new TextBox("Dialing",
                               (String)phoneNums.elementAt(
                                   nameScr.getSelectedIndex()),
                               PN_LEN,
                               TextField.PHONENUMBER);
        dialScr.addCommand(cmdCancel);
        dialScr.setCommandListener(this);
        display.setCurrent(dialScr);
    }

    /**
     * Add an entry to the address book.
     * Called after the user selects the addCmd
     * while in the genEntryScr screen.
     */
    private void addEntry() {
        String f = e_firstName.getString();
        String l = e_lastName.getString();
        String p = e_phoneNum.getString();

        byte[] b = SimpleRecord.createRecord(f,l,p);
        try {
            addrBook.addRecord(b, 0, b.length);
            displayAlert(INFO, "Record added", mainScr);
        } catch (RecordStoreException rse) {
            displayAlert(ERROR, "Could not add record" + rse,
                        mainScr);
        }
    }
```

```
/***
 * This method implements a state machine that drives the
 * MIDlet from one state (screen) to the next.
 */
public void commandAction(Command c,
                          Displayable d) {
    if (d == mainScr) {
        // Handle main sceen
        if (c == cmdExit) {
            midletExit(); // exit
        } else if ((c == List.SELECT_COMMAND)
                     || (c == cmdSelect)) {
            switch (mainScr.getSelectedIndex()) {
            case 0:
                // display search screen
                genSearchScr();
                break;
            case 1:
                // display name entry screen
                genEntryScr();
                break;
            case 2:
                // display all names
                genNameScr("Browse", null, null, true);
                break;
            case 3:
                // display option screen
                genOptionScr();
                break;
            default:
                displayAlert(ERROR, "Unexpected index!",
                             mainScr);
            }
        }
    } else if (d == nameScr) {
        // Handle a screen with names displayed, either
        // from a browse or a search
        if (c == cmdBack) {
            // display main screen
            genMainScr();
```

```
            } else if (c == cmdDial) {
                // dial the phone screen
                genDialScr();
            }
        } else if (d == entryScr) {
            // Handle the name entry screen
            if (c == cmdCancel) {
                // display main screen
                genMainScr();
            } else if (c == cmdAdd) {
                // display name entry screen
                addEntry();
            }
        } else if (d == optionScr) {
            // Handle the option screen
            if (c == cmdBack) {
                // display main screen
                genMainScr();
            }
        } else if (d == searchScr) {
            // Handle the search screen
            if (c == cmdBack) {
                // display main screen
                genMainScr();
            } else if (c == cmdSearchNetwork ||
                       c == cmdSearchLocal) {

                // display search of local addr book
                genNameScr("Search Result",
                        s_firstName.getString(),
                        s_lastName.getString(),
                        c == cmdSearchLocal);
            }
        } else if (d == dialScr) {
            if (c == cmdCancel) {
                // display main screen
                genMainScr();
            }
        }
    }
}
```

```
/**
 * Gets called when the user is viewing the sort options
 * in the optionScr. Takes the new selected index and
 * changes the sort order (how names are displayed
 * from a search or a browse).
 *
 *   item    An item list
 */
public void itemStateChanged(Item item) {
    if (item == sortChoice) {
        sortOrder = sortChoice.getSelectedIndex();
    }
}
}
```

13.2.2   Class SimpleRecord

The class SimpleRecord provides static methods that allow records for the address book to be created and parsed.

A record in the address book has three fields: *first name*, *last name* and *phone number*. This format is shown in Figure 13.9. Each field within the record is at a fixed offset to allow for easy sorting and filtering.

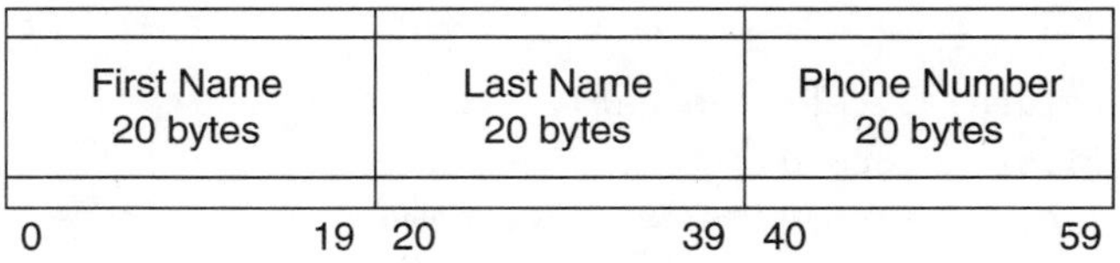

First Name 20 bytes	Last Name 20 bytes	Phone Number 20 bytes

```
0              19 20             39 40             59
```

Figure 13.9   AddressBook record format

```
package examples.addressbook;
import java.lang.*;
import java.io.*;
import java.util.*;
import javax.microedition.rms.*;

/**
 * This class provides static methods that allow us
 * to hide the format of a record.
 * N.B. no synchronized access is provided
 */
```

```java
public final class SimpleRecord {

    private final static int FIRST_NAME_INDEX = 0;
    private final static int LAST_NAME_INDEX = 20;
    private final static int PHONE_INDEX = 40;
    private final static int MAX_REC_LEN = 60;

    private static StringBuffer recBuf =
        new StringBuffer(MAX_REC_LEN);

    // Don't let anyone instantiate this class
    private SimpleRecord() {}

    // Clear internal buffer
    private static void clearBuf() {
        for (int i = 0; i < MAX_REC_LEN; i++) {
            recBuf.insert(i, ' ');
        }
        recBuf.setLength(MAX_REC_LEN);
    }

    /**
     * Takes component parts and return a record suitable
     * for our address book.
     *
     * return   byte[] the newly created record
     * first    record field: first name
     * last     record field: last name
     * num      record field: phone number
     */
    public static byte[] createRecord(String first,
                                      String last,
                                      String num) {
        clearBuf();
        recBuf.insert(FIRST_NAME_INDEX, first);
        recBuf.insert(LAST_NAME_INDEX, last);
        recBuf.insert(PHONE_INDEX, num);
        recBuf.setLength(MAX_REC_LEN);
        return recBuf.toString().getBytes();
    }
```

```
/**
 * Extracts the first name field from a record.
 *   return  String contains the first name field
 *   b       the record to parse
 */
public static String getFirstName(byte[] b) {
    return new String(b, FIRST_NAME_INDEX, FIELD_LEN).trim();
}


/**
 * Extracts the last name field from a record.
 *   return  String contains the last name field
 *   b       the record to parse
 */
public static String getLastName(byte[] b) {
    return new String(b, LAST_NAME_INDEX, FIELD_LEN).trim();
}


/**
 * Extracts the phone number field from a record.
 *   return  String contains the phone number field
 *   b       the record to parse
 */
public static String getPhoneNum(byte[] b) {
    return new String(b, PHONE_INDEX, FIELD_LEN).trim();
}
```

13.2.3 Class SimpleFilter

Class `SimpleFilter` is used to return a subset of the local address book during a search
(network searches are handled separately in Section 13.2.5, "Class NetworkQuery").
The `SimpleFilter` class implements the `javax.microedition.rms.RecordFilter`
interface. A MIDlet that wants to use this class would first instantiate it, then pass a reference to that `SimpleFilter` object to the `javax.microedition.rms.Record-
Store.enumerateRecords` method as the first parameter.

When the constructor of the `SimpleFilter` class is called, the filter parameters, `first` and `last`, are saved as lowercase strings to allow case-insensitive filtering. Later, when a `javax.microedition.rms.RecordEnumeration` is performed,
these fields are used to compare against the first name and last name in the record.

```
package examples.addressbook;

import java.lang.*;
import java.io.*;
import java.util.*;
import javax.microedition.rms.*;

/**
 * This class implements the RecordFilter interface.
 * It works on the records created by SimpleRecord.
 * It filters on first name and/or last name.
 */
public class SimpleFilter implements RecordFilter {

    // first and last names on which to filter
    private String first;
    private String last;

    /**
     * Public constructor: stores the first and last
     * names on which to filter. Stores first/last
     * names as lower case so that filters are
     * are case-insensitive.
     */
    public SimpleFilter(String f, String l) {
        first = f.toLowerCase();
        last = l.toLowerCase();
    }

    /**
     * Takes a record, (r), and checks to see if it matches
     * the first and last name set in our constructor.
     *
     * Extracts the first and last names from the record,
     * converts them to lower case, then compares them
     * with the values extracted from the record.
     *
     * return true if record matches, false otherwise
     */
    public boolean matches(byte[] r) {
```

```
        String f = SimpleRecord.getFirstName(r).toLowerCase();
        String l = SimpleRecord.getLastName(r).toLowerCase();

        return f.startsWith(first) && l.startsWith(last);
    }
}
```

13.2.4   Class SimpleComparator.

Class SimpleComparator is used for comparing records. This class implements the
javax.microedition.rms.RecordComparator interface. Like the SimpleFilter
class, the constructor of class SimpleComparator stores a parameter (sortOrder),
which is used during a record enumeration. The compare method extracts the appropriate fields (as indicated by sortOrder) from the two records it receives, compares
them, and returns the results of that comparison encoded as defined by the
javax.microedition.rms.RecordComparator interface.

```
package examples.addressbook;
import java.lang.*;
import java.io.*;
import java.util.*;
import javax.microedition.rms.*;


/**
 * This class implements the RecordComparator interface.
 * It works on the records created by SimpleRecord.
 * It sorts on either first name or last name.
 */
class SimpleComparator implements RecordComparator {

    /**
     * Sorting values (sort by first or last name)
     */
    public final static int SORT_BY_FIRST_NAME = 1;
    public final static int SORT_BY_LAST_NAME = 2;

    /**
     * Sort order.  Set by constructor.
     */
    private int sortOrder = -1;
```

```
/**
 * Public constructor: sets the sort order to be
 * used for this instantiation.
 *
 * Sanitize s: if it is not one of the
 * valid sort codes, set it to SORT_BY_LAST_NAME
 * silently.
 *   s   the desired sort order
 */
SimpleComparator(int s) {
    switch (s) {
    case SORT_BY_FIRST_NAME:
    case SORT_BY_LAST_NAME:
        this.sortOrder = s;
        break;
    default:
        this.sortOrder = SORT_BY_LAST_NAME;
        break;
    }
}


/**
 * This is the compare method. It takes two
 * records, and depending on the sort order
 * extracts and lexicographically compares the
 * subfields as two Strings.
 *
 *   r1   First record to compare
 *   r2   Second record to compare
 * return one of the following:
 *
 * RecordComparator.PRECEDES
 *     if r1 is lexicographically less than r2
 * RecordComparator.FOLLOWS
 *     if r1 is lexicographically greater than r2
 * RecordComparator.EQUIVALENT
 *     if r1 and r2 are lexicographically equivalent
 */
public int compare(byte[] r1,
                   byte[] r2) {
```

```
        String n1 = null;
        String n2 = null;

        // Based on sortOrder, extract the correct fields
        // from the record and convert them to lower case
        // so that we can perform a case-insensitive compare.
        if (sortOrder == SORT_BY_FIRST_NAME) {
            n1 = SimpleRecord.getFirstName(r1).toLowerCase();
            n2 = SimpleRecord.getFirstName(r2).toLowerCase();
        } else if (sortOrder == SORT_BY_LAST_NAME) {
            n1 = SimpleRecord.getLastName(r1).toLowerCase();
            n2 = SimpleRecord.getLastName(r2).toLowerCase();
        }

        int n = n1.compareTo(n2);
        if (n < 0) {
            return RecordComparator.PRECEDES;
        }
        if (n > 0) {
            return RecordComparator.FOLLOWS;
        }

        return RecordComparator.EQUIVALENT;
    }
}
```

13.2.5 Class NetworkQuery

In addition to searching a local address book, the AddressBookMIDlet application also supports searching a network URL for contacts. After entering information on the search screen, the user may select one of two locations: *Local* or *Network*. If the user selects *Network*, a new instance of the NetworkQuery is created.

When instantiated, this class constructs a String that is used as a URL. This URL encodes the last name, first name, and which field to sort upon. For example, if the connection is made to a service called AddrBookServer on the local machine's port 8080, and the search is to return all entries, sorted by last name, where the first name starts with "Joh" and the last name with "Do", then the URL would be:

```
http://127.0.0.1:8080/AddrBookServer?last=Do&first=Joh=&sort=1
```

The AddrBookServer service on the local machine would then be expected to construct an enumeration of all records that matched this criterion.

Class NetworkQuery implements the javax.microedition.rms.Record-Enumeration interface, but only the methods pertinent to this example—namely the hasNextElement and nextRecord methods—are included in the implementation shown here. Other methods in this interface are simple stubs in this example.

```java
package examples.addressbook;
import java.io.*;
import java.util.*;
import javax.microedition.rms.*;


/*
 * Class to query a network service for address book entries
 * and parse the result. Uses HttpConnection to fetch
 * the entries from a server.
 *
 * The http request is made using a base url provided by the caller
 * with the query arguments for last name and first name
 * encoded in the query parameters of the URL.
 */
public class NetworkQuery implements RecordEnumeration {
    private StringBuffer buffer = new StringBuffer(60);
    private String[] fields = new String[3];
    private String empty = new String();
    private Vector results = new Vector(20);
    private Enumeration resultsEnumeration;

    final static String baseurl =
        "http://127.0.0.1:8080/Book/netaddr";

    /**
     * Create a RecordEnumeration from the network.
     *
     * Query a network service for addresses matching the
     * specified criteria. The base URL of the service
     * has the query parameters appended. The request is
     * made and the contents parsed into a Vector which
     * is used as the basis of the RecordEnumeration.
     * lastname  the last name to search for
     * firstname the first name to search for
```

```
 * sortorder the order in which to sort
 *         1 is by last name, 0 is by first name
 */
NetworkQuery(String firstname,
             String lastname,
             int sortorder) {
    HttpConnection c;
    int ch;
    InputStream is;
    InputStreamReader reader;
    String url;

    // Format the complete URL to request
    buffer.setLength(0);
    buffer.append(baseurl);
    buffer.append("?last=");
    buffer.append((lastname != null) ? lastname : empty);
    buffer.append("&first=");
    buffer.append((firstname != null) ? firstname : empty);
    buffer.append("&sort=" + sortorder);

    url = buffer.toString();

    // Open the connection to the service
    try {
        c = open(url);
        results.removeAllElements();

        /*
         * Open the InputStream and construct a reader to
         * convert from bytes to chars.
         */
        is = c.openInputStream();
        reader = new InputStreamReader(is);
        while (true) {
            int i = 0;
            fields[0] = empty;
            fields[1] = empty;
            fields[2] = empty;
            do {
                buffer.setLength(0);
```

```
                    while ((ch = reader.read()) != -1 &&
                        (ch != ',') && (ch != '\n')) {
                        if (ch == '\r') {
                            continue;
                        }
                        buffer.append((char)ch);
                    }

                    if (ch == -1) {
                        throw new EOFException();
                    }

                    if (buffer.length() > 0) {
                        if (i < fields.length) {
                            fields[i++] = buffer.toString();
                        }
                    }
                } while (ch != '\n');

                if (fields[0].length() > 0) {
                    results.addElement(
                        SimpleRecord.createRecord(
                            fields[0], fields[1], fields[2]));
                }
            }
        } catch (Exception e) {

        } finally {
            try {
                if (is != null) {
                    is.close();
                }
                if (c != null) {
                    c.close();
                }
            } catch (Exception e) {
            }
        }
        resultsEnumeration = results.elements();
    }
```

```
/**
 * Read the HTTP headers and the data using HttpConnection.
 * Check the response code to ensure successful open.
 *
 * Connector.open is used to open url and a HttpConnection
 * is returned.
 * The HTTP headers are read and processed.
 *  url the URL to open
 * throws IOException for any network related exception
 */
private HttpConnection open(String url) throws IOException {
    HttpConnection c;
    int status = -1;

    // Open the connection and check for redirects
    while (true) {
        c = (HttpConnection)Connector.open(url);

        // Get the status code,
        // causing the connection to be made
        status = c.getResponseCode();

        if ((status == HttpConnection.HTTP_TEMP_REDIRECT) ||
            (status == HttpConnection.HTTP_MOVED_TEMP) ||
            (status == HttpConnection.HTTP_MOVED_PERM)) {

            // Get the new location and close the connection
            url = c.getHeaderField("location");
            c.close();
        } else {
            break;
        }
    }

    // Only HTTP_OK (200) means the content is returned.
    if (status != HttpConnection.HTTP_OK) {
        c.close();
        throw new IOException("Response status not OK");
    }
    return c;
}
```

```java
/**
 * Returns true if more elements exist in enumeration.
 */
public boolean hasNextElement() {
    return resultsEnumeration.hasMoreElements();
}

/**
 * Returns a copy of the next record in this enumeration,
 */
public byte[] nextRecord() {
    return (byte[])resultsEnumeration.nextElement();
}

/**
 * The following are simply stubs that we don't
 * implement...
 */
public boolean hasPreviousElement() {return false;}
public void destroy() {}
public boolean isKeptUpdated() {return false;}
public void keepUpdated(boolean b) {return;}
public int nextRecordId() {return 0;}
public int numRecords() {return 0;}
public byte[] previousRecord() {return null;}
public int previousRecordId() {return 0;}
public void rebuild() {return;}
public void reset() {return;}
}
```

13.3   The Sokoban Game Application

The *Sokoban* game application illustrates how the various elements of the MIDP APIs can be used to create interactive games. In *Sokoban*, the game player must organize the contents of a "warehouse" by pushing "packages" from their initial locations into a set of designated "storage locations." In this implementation, the pusher is represented as a filled black circle, the storage locations are open rectangles, and the gray squares represent the packages to be stored. The packages can only be pushed so it is important not to move them into a corner or up against a wall where

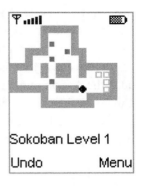

they cannot be moved again. This requires the player to use logic to think ahead—not just speed or fast reflexes. The game can be played to an arbitrary number of levels depending on the creativity of the game designer. The game levels are stored in resource files distributed with the game[1].

The *Sokoban* game implementation is made up of four classes; the Sokoban MIDlet, the SokoCanvas used to display the game board, the Board class used for defining the game logic, and the Score class that handles the scoring. The game uses the Canvas and Graphics classes (low-level user interface API) to draw the game board. The source code illustrates how the action events are handled to move the pieces on the board.

13.3.1   Class Sokoban

The Sokoban class is a MIDlet that initializes and coordinates all of the various screens and transitions of the *Sokoban* game application.

The constructor of the Sokoban class caches the reference to the Display. It creates the Score instance used to save the level and scores for each level. It also creates the SokoCanvas object that displays the game Board.

The startApp method is called each time the game is started or restarted from the paused state. This method opens the record store (represented by the Score object) that contains the scores. It initializes the SokoCanvas display and adds commands to it. The Sokoban object is set as the CommandListener for the Soko-Canvas so it can handle the commands.

The pauseApp and destroyApp methods close the Score store so that the application does not use resources when the application is inactive.

---

[1] An interesting extension of the current implementation would be to load the game levels from the network.

The commandAction method handles all of the Command invocations, depending on the source of the Command and the Command instance. The commands for *Undo*, *Start Over*, *Next Level*, and *Previous Level* are handled by the SokoCanvas itself. The *Show Scores* command opens the Form that is used to display the scores, and adds the *OK* command needed for returning back to Soko-Canvas. When the SokoCanvas reports a *selected* event, the game level has been solved. Then, score information is displayed, and the game advances to the next level.

```
package examples.sokoban;

import javax.microedition.lcdui.*;
import javax.microedition.midlet.*;
import java.io.*;

/**
 * Sokoban implements the command handling and initialization
 * needed to be a MIDlet. It creates and initializes the commands,
 * scores, and Sokoban canvas that displays the game board.
 */
public class Sokoban extends MIDlet implements CommandListener {
    Display display;
    SokoCanvas canvas;
    Score score;
    Screen scoreScreen;

    Command undoCommand = new Command("Undo", Command.BACK, 1);
    Command restartCommand = new Command("Start Over",
                                        Command.SCREEN, 21);
    Command exitCommand = new Command("Exit", Command.EXIT, 60);
    Command scoresCommand = new Command("Show Scores",
                                        Command.SCREEN, 25);
    Command okCommand = new Command("OK", Command.OK, 30);
    Command nextCommand = new Command("Next Level",
                                        Command.SCREEN, 22);
    Command prevCommand = new Command("Previous Level",
                                        Command.SCREEN, 23);
```

```java
/**
 * Creates a new Sokoban instance and caches the Display,
 * Score, and SokoCanvas objects.
 */
public Sokoban() {
    display = Display.getDisplay(this);
    score = new Score();
    canvas = new SokoCanvas(this, score);
}


/**
 * The startApp method opens the score file and retrieves
 * the last level. This method initializes the canvas and
 * adds the commands to it and makes itself the listener
 * for the commands. It should return immediately to keep
 * the dispatcher from hanging.
 */
public void startApp() {
    score.open();
    canvas.addCommand(undoCommand);
    canvas.addCommand(scoresCommand);
    canvas.addCommand(restartCommand);
    canvas.addCommand(exitCommand);
    canvas.addCommand(nextCommand);
    canvas.addCommand(prevCommand);
    canvas.setCommandListener(this);
    display.setCurrent(canvas);
    canvas.init();
}


/**
 * The pauseApp method is used to close the store of Scores.
 */
public void pauseApp() {
    score.close();
}


/**
 * Destroy must clean up.
 * Close the store of scores.
 */
```

```java
    public void destroyApp(boolean unconditional) {
        score.close();
    }


    /*
     * Respond to a commands issued on any Screen
     */
    public void commandAction(Command c, Displayable s) {
        if (c == undoCommand) {
            canvas.undoMove();
        } else if (c == restartCommand) {
            canvas.restartLevel();
        } else if (c == scoresCommand) {
            scoreScreen = canvas.getScoreScreen();
            scoreScreen.addCommand(okCommand);
            scoreScreen.setCommandListener(this);
            display.setCurrent(scoreScreen);
        } else if (c == okCommand && s == scoreScreen) {
            display.setCurrent(canvas);
        } else if (c == exitCommand) {
            destroyApp(false);
            notifyDestroyed();
        } else if (c == List.SELECT_COMMAND && s == canvas) {
            // Solved the level
            scoreScreen = canvas.getScoreScreen();
            scoreScreen.addCommand(okCommand);
            scoreScreen.setCommandListener(this);
            display.setCurrent(scoreScreen);
            canvas.nextLevel(1);
        } else if (c == nextCommand) {
            canvas.nextLevel(1);
            display.setCurrent(canvas);
        } else if (c == prevCommand) {
            canvas.nextLevel(-1);
            display.setCurrent(canvas);
        }
    }
}
```

13.3.2 Class SokoCanvas

Class SokoCanvas handles all the functions that are related to event input and the displaying of the game Board. The logic for playing the game is handled separately in the class Board.

The constructor of class SokoCanvas caches several values for later use, including the width and height of the Canvas, the Display, and the default Font and its height. All this information is used for making layout decisions. The colors to be used are chosen by calling the method initColors. The Score object is saved for later use, and a new game Board object is created.

The init method reads the game board layout for the current level. If the level information cannot be read, an Alert is displayed to notify the user, and the game defaults to level 0.

The initColors and setColors methods compute the colors that are used for various game pieces, based on whether the device is capable of supporting multiple colors or multiple levels of gray.

The undoMove method delegates to the SokoCanvas to reverse the effects of the most recent move. For this game, undo is a very useful function!

The restartLevel method rereads the layout of the game pieces and causes them to be repainted.

The nextLevel method is used when advancing the game to another level. This method updates the scores for the current level and then reads and triggers a repaint for the next level. The *offset* parameter makes it possible to go both forward and back through the *Sokoban* game levels.

The readScreen method handles the location of the input for the requested level from resource files. It uses the method Class.getResourceAsStream to fetch the levels from named files in the application's JAR file. When a level is loaded, the method computes how to map the width and height of the level to the width and height of the screen, and sets the appropriate cell size.

The getScoreScreen method creates a Form object that contains the current and previous scores. If the new scores are better than the old, this method sets the title string of the score display to "Congratulations" instead of just "Scores."

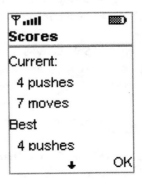

The keyPressed and keyRepeated methods handle the user input events. The keyRepeated events are handled similarly as keyPressed events. The keyPressed method figures out which way the pusher needs to be moved, and tries to move the pusher that way. Then, a repaint is requested to show the new positions. If the move resulted in the level being solved, the `List.Selected` event is signaled to the listener.

The `updateScores` method checks to see if the scores are better than before and if they have already been recorded. If not, the new values are passed to the `Score` object so that the application's record store can be updated.

The `setCommandListener` method is a hook to capture and save the command listener set up for the `Canvas`. This method is used to deliver an event when the current level is solved.

The `paint` method does quite a bit of work to determine which parts of the board are within the clipping region, and to draw the game pieces into the appropriate cells on the screen. This method uses the colors set by method `initColors`, and draws each cell based on the contents of the game board and the current location of the pusher. The current level information is drawn at the bottom of the screen.

```
package examples.sokoban;
import java.io.*;
import javax.microedition.lcdui.*;
import javax.microedition.midlet.*;


/**
 * SokoCanvas displays the game board and handles key events.
 * The Sokoban game logic and algorithms are separated into
 * class Board.
 * SokoCanvas does not set up or use any Commands. Commands for
 * each screen and listener should be set up outside this class.
 * SokoCanvas generates a SELECT_COMMAND when the current level
 * is solved. Sequencing through screens is done in the Sokoban
 * MIDlet.
 * SokoCanvas handles the reading, initialization, and
 * sequencing of individual puzzle screens.
 *
 * SokoCanvas uses the Score class to restore and save game
 * levels and scores for each level. To display the scores use
 * getScoreScreen. It is initialized with the current scores.
 * To select a new level, use the getLevelScreen and gotoLevel
 * methods.
 *
 * SokoCanvas handled key events for LEFT, RIGHT, UP, and DOWN
 * to move the pusher in the game board.
 *
```

```
 * SokoCanvas selects color and grayscale values for the
 * different parts of the board.
 */
class SokoCanvas extends Canvas {
    private int level = 1;
    private boolean solved;
    private int cell = 1;        // number of pixels per cell
    private int width, height;   // dimensions of this canvas

    private Board board;         // Board makes the moves
    private Sokoban sokoban;     // Sokoban MIDlet
    private Display display;      // Display showing this Canvas
    private CommandListener listener; // Listener for notices

    private Score score;         // Score object
    private Form scoreForm;      // Form to show scores
    private Font font;           // Font for text
    private int fh;              // Font height for text lines

    // 2 Bit color/grayscale defaults
    private int wallColor =   0x7f7f7f;
    private int groundColor = 0xffffff;
    private int packetColor = 0x000000;
    private int storeColor =  0x000000;
    private int pusherColor = 0x000000;

    /**
     * Construct a new canvas
     */
    public SokoCanvas(Sokoban sokoban, Score s) {
        height = getHeight();
        width = getWidth();
        font = Font.getDefaultFont();
        fh = font.getHeight();

        this.sokoban = sokoban;
        display = Display.getDisplay(sokoban);
        score = s;
        board = new Board();
        initColors();
    }
```

```java
/**
 * Read the previous level number from the score file.
 * Read in the level data.
 */
public void init() {
    /*
     * Read the last level
     * if it can't be found, revert to level 0
     */
    level = score.level;
    if (!readScreen(level)) {
        level = 0;
        readScreen(level);
    }
    repaint();
}


/*
 * Read the colors to use from the descriptor.
 */
private void initColors() {
    boolean isColor = display.isColor();
    int numColors = display.numColors();

    if (isColor) {
        if (numColors > 2) {
            setColors(0x006D55, 0xffffff,
                      0xff6d00, 0xb60055, 0x6d6dff);
        }
    } else {
        if (numColors > 2) {
            setColors(0x999999, 0xffffff,
                      0x666666, 0xbbbbbb, 0x000000);
        } else {
            setColors(0x6a6a6a, 0xffffff,
                      0x6a6a6a, 0xbbbbbb, 0x000000);
        }
    }
}
```

```
/*
 * Set the colors.
 */
private void setColors(int w, int g, int pa, int s, int pu) {
    wallColor = w;
    groundColor = g;
    packetColor = pa;
    storeColor = s;
    pusherColor = pu;
}

/**
 * Undo the last move if possible.
 * Here so undo can be triggered by a command.
 */
public void undoMove() {
    board.undoMove();
    solved = board.solved();
    repaint();
}

/**
 * Restart the current level.
 */
public void restartLevel() {
    readScreen(level);
    repaint();
    solved = false;
}

/**
 * Start the next level.
 */
public void nextLevel(int offset) {
    updateScores(); // save best scores
    if (readScreen(level+offset)) {
        level += offset;
        score.setLevel(level);
        solved = false;
        repaint();
    }
}
```

```java
/**
 * Read and set up the next level.
 * Opens the resource file with the name "/Screen.<lev>"
 * and tells the board to read from the stream.
 * Must be called only with the board locked.
 *
 *  lev     the level number to read.
 *  return true  if the reading of the level worked,
 *          false otherwise.
 */
private boolean readScreen(int lev) {
    if (lev <= 0) {
        // Initialize the default zero screen
        board.screen0();
    } else {
        InputStream is;
        try {
            String base = "/examples/sokoban/data/screen.";
            is = getClass().getResourceAsStream(base + lev);
            if (is != null) {
                board.read(is, lev);
                is.close();
            } else {
                Alert alert = new Alert(
                    "Could not find level " + level);
                display.setCurrent(alert);
                return false;
            }
        } catch (java.io.IOException ex) {
            try {
                is.close();
            } catch (IOException x) {
            }
            return false;
        }
    }
    cell = ((height-fh)/board.height < width/board.width)
         ? (height-fh)/board.height : width/board.width;
    return true;
}
```

```java
/**
 * Return the Screen to display scores.
 * It returns a screen initialized with the current
 * scores information.
 */
public Screen getScoreScreen() {

    boolean newbest = solved &&
        (score.npushes == 0 ||
         board.npushes < score.npushes);

    Form scoreForm = new Form(null);

    scoreForm.append(newbest ?
                    "New Best:\n" : "Current:\n");
    scoreForm.append("  ");
    scoreForm.append(Integer.toString(board.npushes));
    scoreForm.append(" pushes\n");

    scoreForm.append("  ");
    scoreForm.append(Integer.toString(board.nmoves));
    scoreForm.append(" moves\n");

    scoreForm.append(newbest ? "Old Best:\n" : "Best\n");
    scoreForm.append("  ");
    scoreForm.append(Integer.toString(score.npushes));
    scoreForm.append(" pushes\n");

    scoreForm.append("  ");
    scoreForm.append(Integer.toString(score.nmoves));
    scoreForm.append(" moves\n ");

    String title = "Scores";
    if (newbest) {
        title = "Congratulations";
    }

    scoreForm.setTitle(title);
    return scoreForm;
}
```

```
/*
 * Handle a repeated arrow keys as though it were another
 * press. keyCode the key pressed.
 */
protected void keyRepeated(int keyCode) {
    int action = getGameAction(keyCode);
    switch (action) {
    case Canvas.LEFT:
    case Canvas.RIGHT:
    case Canvas.UP:
    case Canvas.DOWN:
        keyPressed(keyCode);
    break;
    default:
        break;
    }
}


/**
 * Handle a single key event.
 * The LEFT, RIGHT, UP, and DOWN keys are used to
 * move the pusher within the Board.
 * Other keys are ignored and have no effect.
 * Repaint the screen on every action key.
 */
protected void keyPressed(int keyCode) {
    // Protect the data from changing during painting.
    synchronized (board) {

        int action = getGameAction(keyCode);
        int move = 0;
        switch (action) {
        case Canvas.LEFT:
            move = Board.LEFT;
            break;
        case Canvas.RIGHT:
            move = Board.RIGHT;
            break;
        case Canvas.DOWN:
            move = Board.DOWN;
            break;
```

```
            case Canvas.UP:
                move = Board.UP;
                break;

            // Ignore keycodes that don't map to actions.
            default:
                return;
        }

        // Tell the board to move the piece
        // and queue a repaint
        board.move(move);
        repaint();

        if (!solved && board.solved()) {
            solved = true;
            if (listener != null) {
                listener.commandAction(
                    List.SELECT_COMMAND, this);
            }
        }
    } // End of synchronization on the Board.
}


/**
 * Update the scores for the current level if it has
 * been solved and the scores are better than before.
 */
private void updateScores() {
    if (!solved)
        return;

    /*
     * Update the scores. If the score for this level is lower
     * than the last recorded score save the lower scores.
     */
    if (score.npushes == 0 || board.npushes < score.npushes) {
        score.setLevelScore(board.npushes, board.nmoves);
    }
}
```

```java
/**
 * Add a listener to notify when the level is solved.
 * The listener is send a List.SELECT_COMMAND when the
 * level is solved.
 * l the object implementing interface CommandListener
 */
public void setCommandListener(CommandListener l) {
    super.setCommandListener(l);
    listener = l;
}


/*
 * Paint the contents of the Canvas.
 * The clip rectangle of the canvas is retrieved and used
 * to determine which cells of the board should be repainted.
 * g Graphics context to paint to.
 */
protected void paint(Graphics g) {

    // Lock the board to keep it from changing during paint
    synchronized (board) {

        int x = 0, y = 0, x2 = board.width, y2 = board.height;

        // Figure what part needs to be repainted.
        int clipx = g.getClipX();
        int clipy = g.getClipY();
        int clipw = g.getClipWidth();
        int cliph = g.getClipHeight();
        x = clipx / cell;
        y = clipy / cell;
        x2 = (x + (clipx + clipw + cell-1)) / cell;
        y2 = (y + (clipy + cliph + cell-1)) / cell;
        if (x2 > board.width)
            x2 = board.width;
        if (y2 > board.height)
            y2 = board.height;

        // Fill entire area with ground color
        g.setColor(groundColor);
        g.fillRect(clipx, clipy, clipw, cliph);
```

```
        for (y = 0; y < y2; y++) {
            for (x = 0; x < x2; x++) {
                byte v = board.get(x, y);
                switch (v & ~Board.PUSHER) {
                case Board.WALL:
                    g.setColor(wallColor);
                    g.fillRect(x*cell, y*cell,
                            cell, cell);
                    break;

                case Board.PACKET:
                case Board.PACKET | Board.STORE:
                    g.setColor(packetColor);
                    g.fillRect(x*cell+1, y*cell+1,
                            cell-2, cell-2);
                    break;
                case Board.STORE:
                    g.setColor(storeColor);
                    g.drawRect(x*cell+1, y*cell+1,
                            cell-2, cell-2);
                    break;

                case Board.GROUND:
                default:
                    // Noop since already filled.
                    break;
                }
                if ((v & Board.PUSHER) != 0) {
                    g.setColor(pusherColor);
                    g.fillArc(x*cell, y*cell,
                            cell, cell, 0, 360);
                }
            }
        }
        g.setColor(pusherColor);
        g.drawString("Sokoban Level " + level, 0, height-fh,
                Graphics.TOP|Graphics.LEFT);
    }
  }
}
```

13.3.3 Class Board

Class `Board` defines all of the game logic of the *Sokoban* game. In addition, this class contains the functionality to read and decode level data from an `InputStream` in order to create new game boards.

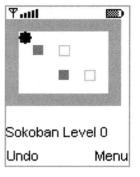

The constructor of the `Board` class initializes the array of *moves* that is needed for the undo operation. The constructor calls the method `screen0`, which initializes the board state to a simple preset level 0.

The `move` and `movePacket` methods handle the basic game piece movement. They determine whether the pusher can be moved in the direction requested by the game player. The `movePacket` method determines if a packet is being pushed and if it can be moved into the adjacent location. If it can, and the packet moves into a location where it can be stored, the packet contributes to the ultimate solution. The number of pushes and moves are counted. If the pusher can be moved, the move is saved in the *moves* array for possible undo later.

The `saveMove` method keeps track of moves, and appends moves to the *moves* array, extending the array as necessary.

The `undoMove` method removes moves from the *moves* array, and reverses the effect of the move by moving the pusher backwards and potentially restoring a packet to its previous location.

The `solved` method checks to see if the number of packets is equal to the number of packets in storage locations.

The `get` and `set` methods retrieve and set the contents of the game board by doing the mapping from (x, y) locations to indices in the array.

The `index` and `indexOffset` methods use the dimensions of the game board level to determine where a given (x, y) offset is within the linear array used to store the game board.

The `read` method reads and decodes new game board configurations from an `InputStream`, and creates the internal array that is used to play the game. This method also decodes the initial location of the pusher.

```
package examples.sokoban;
import java.io.IOException;
/**
 * Board knows how to move the pusher and how the pusher moves
 * the pieces. It also keeps track of the number of moves
 * and pushes and the level.
 */
```

```
public class Board  {

    /*
     * Directly accessible fields of the game board;
     * do not set outside this class.
     */
    int width;              // Width of the board
    int height;             // Height of the board
    int nmoves;             // number of moves executed
    int npushes;            // number of pushes executed

    private byte[] array; // width * height array of game state
    private int pusher;   // pos. of pusher at index into array
    private int packets;  // total number of packets
    private int stored;   // number of packets in Stores
    private byte[] moves; // recorded moves for undo

    // Move directions
    public static final int LEFT = 0;
    public static final int RIGHT = 3;
    public static final int UP = 1;
    public static final int DOWN = 2;
    public static final int MOVEPACKET = 4;

    // Bit definitions for pieces of each board position
    public static final byte GROUND = 0; // If nothing there
    public static final byte STORE = 1;   // Is a storage place
    public static final byte PACKET = 2; // If it has a packet
    public static final byte WALL = 4;    // If it is a wall
    public static final byte PUSHER = 8; // Pusher is there

    /**
     * Creates new Board initialized to a simple puzzle.
     */
    public Board() {
        moves = new byte[200];
        screen0();
    }
```

```java
/*
 * Create the hard coded simple game board.
 */
public void screen0() {
    width = 9;
    height = 7;
    array = new byte[width*height];
    nmoves = 0;
    npushes = 0;
    for (int x = 0; x < width; x++) {
        for (int y = 0; y < height; y++) {
            byte t = (x == 0 || y == 0 ||
            x == width-1 || y == height-1) ? WALL : GROUND;
            set(x, y, t);
        }
    }
    packets = 2; stored = 0;
    set(2, 2, PACKET);
    set(4, 4, PACKET);
    set(4, 2, STORE);
    set(6, 4, STORE);
    pusher = index(1, 1);
}


/**
 * Move the pusher in the direction indicated.
 * If there is a wall, don't move.
 * if there is a packet in that direction, try to move it.
 * move the direction; one of LEFT, RIGHT, UP, DOWN
 */
public void move(int move) {

    int p = pusher + indexOffset(move);

    // Handle the simple cases
    if ((array[p] & WALL) != 0)
        return;

    int m = movePacket(p, move);
    if (m >= 0) {
```

```
        /*
         * Put the pusher in the new index
         * and save the move in case of undo.
         */
        pusher = p;
        saveMove(m);
    }
}


/**
 * Move the packet in the direction indicated relative to
 * the pusher. If it fits into a store position, remember.
 * return -1 if can't be moved or the updated move
 * including the packet flag if there was a packet to move.
 */
private int movePacket(int index, int move) {
    if ((array[index] & PACKET) == 0)
        return move; // no packet to move

    int dest = index + indexOffset(move);
    if (array[dest] > STORE)
        return -1; // can't move packet into next spot.

    // Remove packet from current location
    array[index] &= ~PACKET;
    if ((array[index] & STORE) != 0)
        stored--;

    // Insert packet into new location
    array[dest] |= PACKET;
    if ((array[dest] & STORE) != 0)
        stored++;

    npushes++; // count pushes done
    return move + MOVEPACKET;
}


/*
 * Save a move, extending the array if necessary.
 */
private void saveMove(int move) {
```

```
        if (nmoves >= moves.length) {
            byte[] n = new byte[moves.length+50];
            System.arraycopy(moves, 0, n, 0, moves.length);
            moves = n;
        }
        moves[nmoves++] = (byte)move;
    }


    /*
     * Undo the most recent move
     */
    public void undoMove() {
        if (nmoves <= 0)
            return;
        int move = moves[--nmoves];
        int rev = (move & 3) ^ 3; // reverse the direction
        int back = pusher + indexOffset(rev);

        if ((move & MOVEPACKET) != 0) {
            npushes--; // "unpush"
            movePacket(pusher + indexOffset(move), rev);
        }
        pusher = back;
    }


    /**
     * Determine if the screen has been solved.
     */
    public boolean solved() {
        return packets == stored;
    }


    /*
     * Return the pieces at the location.
     *   x location in the board.
     *   y location in the board.
     * return flags indicating what pieces are in this location.
     * Bit flags; combinations of WALL, PUSHER, STORE, PACKET.
     */
    public byte get(int x, int y) {
        int offset = index(x, y);
```

```
        if (offset == pusher)
            return (byte)(array[offset] | PUSHER);
        else
            return array[offset];
    }

    private void set(int x, int y, byte value) {
        array[index(x, y)] = value;
    }

    private int index(int x, int y) {
        if (x < 0 || x >= width ||
            y < 0 || y >= height) {
            return -1;
        }
        return y * width + x;
    }

    /*
     * Compute the offset in the array of the cell relative
     * to the current pusher location in the direction of
     * the move. NOTE: the walls around the edge always make
     * a +/- guard band. Also, the order of evaluation should
     * never try to get to +/- 2.
     */
    private int indexOffset(int move) {

        switch (move & 3) {
            case LEFT:
                return -1;
            case RIGHT:
                return +1;
            case UP:
                return -width;
            case DOWN:
                return +width;
        }
        return 0;
    }
```

```java
/**
 * Read a board from a stream.
 * Read it into a fixed size array and then shrink to fit.
 */
public void read(java.io.InputStream is, int lev)
    throws IOException
{
    final int W = 20;
    final int H = 20;
    byte[] b = new byte[W*H];

    int c, w = 0;
    int x = 0, y = 0, xn = 0, yn = 0;

    packets = 0;
    stored = 0;
    nmoves = 0;
    npushes = 0;

    while ((c = is.read()) != -1) {
        switch (c) {
            case '\n':
                if (x > w) {
                    w = x;
                }
                y++;
                x = 0;
                break;

            case '$':
                b[y*W + x++] = PACKET;
                packets++;
                break;

            case '#':
                b[y*W + x++] = WALL;
                break;

            case ' ':
                b[y*W + x++] = GROUND;
                break;
```

```
            case '.':
                b[y*W+ x++] = STORE;
                break;

            case '+': // player and store in same place
                b[y*W + x++] = STORE;

            case '@':
                xn = x;
                yn = y;
                x++;
                break;
            }
        }

        /*
         * Copy the board to an array sized to the \
         * width and height of the board.
         */
        width = w;
        height = y;
        array = new byte[width * height];
        for (y = 0; y < height; y++) {
            for (x = 0; x < width; x++) {
                array[y * width + x] = b[y * W + x];
            }
        }
        pusher = index(xn, yn);
    }
}
```

13.3.4 Class Score

Class Score stores the level and high score information in a RecordStore. There are
two types of records in the RecordStore: the current level record, and records that
hold scores for each level. The two types are distinguished by storing a unique tag
value in the first byte of each record.

The constructor of class Score creates a buffer that is used by all reads and
writes to the RecordStore. This makes it unnecessary to create and garbage-col-
lect a new array each time.

The open method opens the RecordStore and enumerates through the records to find the record with the remembered current level.

The setLevel method sets the current level of the Score. It updates the record in the RecordStore that contains the current level and then tries to read the saved scores for that level (if any).

The readScore method enumerates through the records in the RecordStore, looking for a score record for the desired level.

The setLevelScore method updates the record in the RecordStore to contain the level and number of moves and pushes. It sets up a byte array to store the values, and either overwrites the record (if there was a previous record for the level) or creates a new one if necessary.

The getInt and putInt methods are used to decode and encode the integer values into four bytes of an array.

The close method checks if the RecordStore is open, and closes it if necessary.

```
package examples.sokoban;
import javax.microedition.rms.*;


/**
 * Keep track of the last level played.
 * For each level keep track of the number of moves.
 *
 * The scores are kept in a RecordStore named SokoScores.
 * There are two types of records:
 * - Last level record containing the last level played.
 * - Level history consisting of the number of moves and
 *   pushes for that level
 */
class Score {
    // Values from the current records describing the current level
    int level;    // Current level
    int npushes;  // Current number of pushes for level
    int nmoves;   // Current number of moves for level

    private byte[] buffer; // Used for all reading and writing

    // Current level record = {byte LEVEL_TAG; int level;}
    private int levelId; // The record Id of the level record
    private static final int  LEVEL_LEN = 5;
    private static final byte LEVEL_TAG = 1;
```

```
/*
 * Score for level =
 * {byte SCORE_TAG; int level, int pushes; int moves;}
 */
private int scoreId; // Record Id of the current level
private static final int  SCORE_LEN = 13;
private static final byte SCORE_TAG = 2;

private RecordStore store; // Record store, null if not open

/*
 * Construct a new Score handler.
 * Initial values are already set; null for store;
 * level = 0, levelId = 0, scoreId = 0,
 */
Score() {
    buffer = new byte[SCORE_LEN];
}

/**
 * Open the record store and locate
 * the record with the level number in it.
 */
boolean open() {
    try {
        store = RecordStore.openRecordStore("SokobanScores",
                                            true);
    } catch (RecordStoreException ex) {
        return false;
    }

    try {
        // Locate the record containing the current level
        levelId = 0;
        RecordEnumeration enum =
            store.enumerateRecords(null, null, false);
        while (enum.hasNextElement()) {
            int ndx = enum.nextRecordId();
            int len = store.getRecord(ndx, buffer, 0);

            if (len == LEVEL_LEN &&
                buffer[0] == LEVEL_TAG) {
                levelId = ndx;
```

```
                          level = getInt(buffer, 1);
                          break;
                    }
                }
        } catch (RecordStoreException ex) {
            return false;
        }
        return true;
    }


    /**
     * Set the level and update the level record in the RecordStore.
     */
    boolean setLevel(int level) {
        this.level = level;
        buffer[0] = LEVEL_TAG;
        putInt(buffer, 1, level);

        if (store == null)
            return false;
        try {
            if (levelId == 0) {
                levelId = store.addRecord(buffer, 0, LEVEL_LEN);
            } else {
                store.setRecord(levelId, buffer, 0, LEVEL_LEN);
            }
        } catch (RecordStoreException ex) {
            return false;
        }
        return readScore(level); // get the score for the level
    }


    /**
     * Read the score for the current level.  Read through
     * the records looking for the one for this level.
     *    level    the level of which to get the last scores
     */
    boolean readScore(int level) {
        try {
            // Locate the score record for the requested level
            scoreId = 0;
            RecordEnumeration enum =
```

```
                    store.enumerateRecords(null, null, false);
             while (enum.hasNextElement()) {
                 int ndx = enum.nextRecordId();
                 int len = store.getRecord(ndx, buffer, 0);

                 if (len == SCORE_LEN &&
                     buffer[0] == SCORE_TAG &&
                     getInt(buffer, 1) == level) {
                     scoreId = ndx;
                     npushes = getInt(buffer, 5);
                     nmoves = getInt(buffer, 9);
                     return true;
                 }
             }
         } catch (RecordStoreException ex) {
             return false;
         }

         // No record found, start fresh
         npushes = 0;
         nmoves = 0;
         return true;
     }


     /**
      * Set the updated score to the RecordStore.
      */
     boolean setLevelScore(int pushes, int moves) {
         npushes = pushes;
         nmoves = moves;

         // Update the scores in the buffer.
         buffer[0] = SCORE_TAG;
         putInt(buffer, 1, level);
         putInt(buffer, 5, npushes);
         putInt(buffer, 9, nmoves);


         try {
             // Write/Add the record to the store
             if (scoreId == 0) {
                 scoreId = store.addRecord(buffer, 0, SCORE_LEN);
```

```
            } else {
                store.setRecord(scoreId, buffer, 0, SCORE_LEN);
            }
        } catch (RecordStoreException ex) {
            return false;
        }
        return true;
    }


    /**
     * Get an integer from an array.
     */
    private int getInt(byte[] buf, int offset) {
        return (buf[offset+0] & 0xff) << 24 |
               (buf[offset+1] & 0xff) << 16 |
               (buf[offset+2] & 0xff) <<  8 |
               (buf[offset+3] & 0xff);
    }


    /**
     * Put an integer to an array
     */
    private void putInt(byte[] buf, int offset, int value) {
        buf[offset+0] = (byte)(value >> 24);
        buf[offset+1] = (byte)(value >> 16);
        buf[offset+2] = (byte)(value >>  8);
        buf[offset+3] = (byte)(value >>  0);
    }


    /**
     * Close the store.
     */
    void close() {
        try {
            if (store != null) {
                store.closeRecordStore();
            }
        } catch (RecordStoreException ex) {
        }
    }
}
```

13.4   Development Environments for J2ME

Development tools and environments for Java 2 Platform, Micro Edition are currently emerging. The *AddressBook* application discussed in this chapter was developed using the *Metrowerks CodeWarrior* environment (see Figure 13.10). The *PhotoAlbum* and *Sokoban* applications were developed using the *J2ME Wireless Toolkit* and *Forte* environments from Sun Microsystems (`http://java.sun.com/products/j2mewtoolkit`). CLDC- and MIDP-compliant development and debugging environments are also available from other vendors such as Borland.

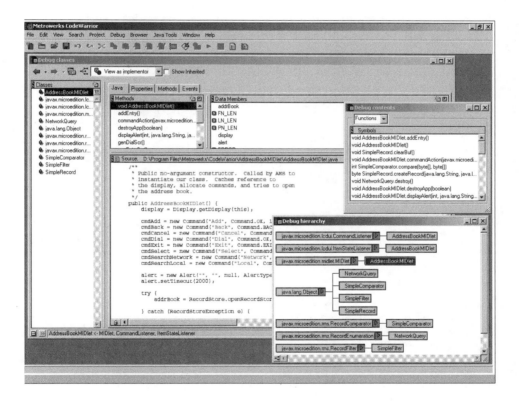

Figure 13.10   Developing MIDlets with an integrated development environment

CHAPTER 14

Summary

In the past few years, we have witnessed the beginning of an exciting new era in the history of computing. Wireless, handheld computing and communication devices, or *mobile information devices* (MIDs), have taken the role that desktop computers had earlier as the forefront of computing technology. As a result of this transition, computing and communication devices are becoming more and more mobile, personal and ubiquitous. The number of mobile information devices has already surpassed the number of conventional personal computers, and this trend is likely to continue and even strengthen in the future. The vast majority of people in the world will probably never use a traditional desktop computer. However, it is very likely that a very large percentage of them will eventually be using some kind of a mobile information device.

At the same time, the rapid emergence of the Internet is playing an increasingly visible role in the development and evolution of mobile information devices. People have become dependent on the information that is available on the Internet, and they will also want access to that information from mobile information devices. This will place much more emphasis on the ability to customize and personalize mobile information devices according to the needs of individual users. Unlike in the past, when wireless devices typically came from the factory with a hard-coded feature set, the devices will become much more dependent on dynamically downloaded software. Consequently, there is a need for technologies that open up the mobile information devices for third party software development, and make it possible to extend and customize the features of mobile information devices for Internet access and Internet-based services in a dynamic, secure fashion.

As discussed in this book, we believe that the Java™ programming language is ideally suited to become the standard application development language for wireless devices. After all, Java technology provides an unsurpassed combination of benefits for device manufacturers, wireless network operators, content providers and individual application developers. These benefits include the dynamic delivery of interactive content, security, cross-platform compatibility, enhanced user experience, and the power of a modern object-oriented programming language with a very large established developer base.

In this book, we have summarized the recent advances in creating a portable, secure, small-footprint Java application development environment for small, connected devices. The initial work in this area started in early 1998 at Sun Microsystems Laboratories (Sun Labs) with the creation of a small new Java execution engine, the *K Virtual Machine* (KVM). This work led to a number of collaborative research and development efforts with major consumer device manufacturers and other companies. Eventually, a number of standardization efforts were started out to harmonize the key features and libraries across a wide variety of possible target devices.

This book has presented the overall architecture of Java™ 2 Platform, Micro Edition (J2ME™), focusing specifically on two key J2ME standards: *Connected, Limited Device Configuration* (CLDC) and *Mobile Information Device Profile* (MIDP). Connected, Limited Device Configuration is intended to serve as a generic, "lowest common denominator" platform or building block that targets all kinds of small, connected devices that have at least 160 kilobytes of memory available for the Java environment and applications. Mobile Information Device Profile builds on top of CLDC and adds valuable application programming interfaces for a specific category of devices: wireless, mobile, two-way communication devices such as cellular telephones and two-way pagers.

A key characteristics of the CLDC and MIDP standards is the incremental and complementary nature of the platforms that they define. A central goal in creating the CLDC and MIDP standards was to avoid any conflicts with existing wireless application technologies such as i-Mode or Wireless Application Protocol (WAP), so that they complement the existing technologies rather than compete with them. In general, the application development environments defined by CLDC and MIDP can be added flexibly on top of the existing software and hardware solutions, regardless of the target architecture or specific networking technology. Typically, the changes required to the existing system software stack are very small. This means that device manufacturers and network operators can continue taking advantage of their investments in the existing software, hardware and networking infrastructure.

Both CLDC and MIDP standards were developed using Java Community Process (JCP), a process that encourages active and open collaboration among industry participants who share the same interests in developing new APIs for the Java platform. The total number of companies who directly participated in the CLDC and MIDP standardization efforts was twenty-four, and more than five hundred companies and individuals participated in these efforts indirectly by sending us feedback and comments on the various versions of the *CLDC Specification* and *MIDP Specification*. In that sense, these standards represent a truly collaborative effort among the key players in the wireless communication and device industry. They also reflect how much general interest there is in the mobile information device area today.

So far, both the CLDC and MIDP standards have been received extremely well by the device manufacturers, network operators, content providers and individual application developers. The first commercially available, CLDC-compliant, Java Powered™ devices arrived in the market in the end of year 2000, and many more commercial devices are scheduled for release all over the world in 2001. Development tools for the Java 2 Platform, Micro Edition are also emerging from major tool vendors such as Borland and Metrowerks.

In summary, we believe that the transition to Internet-enabled, wireless, mobile information devices will fundamentally alter the landscape of computing and communication devices and services. This book has presented the J2ME CLDC and MIDP standards that define powerful, portable, secure, small-footprint application development environments in order to bring Java technology to mobile information devices. We hope that this book, for its part, encourages people to use these technologies and continue the work in this exciting new area.

APPENDIX **A**

CLDC Application Programming Interface

THIS appendix contains the application programming interface documentation in Almanac format for the CLDC. For a description of this format, refer to "Almanac Legend" on page 274.

Full CLDC javadocs with detailed comments are available in the *CLDC Specification* (see "Related Literature and Helpful Web Pages" on page xxii) or as part of the CLDC reference implementation software that can be downloaded from Sun's web site (`http://www.sun.com/software/communitysource/j2me/cldc/`).

Almanac Legend

The Almanac format presents all classes and interfaces in alphabetic order. Each class displays a list of its members in alphabetic order, mixing fields, methods and constructors together.

The Almanac format used in this book is modeled after the style introduced by Patrick Chan in his excellent book *Java Developers Almanac*.

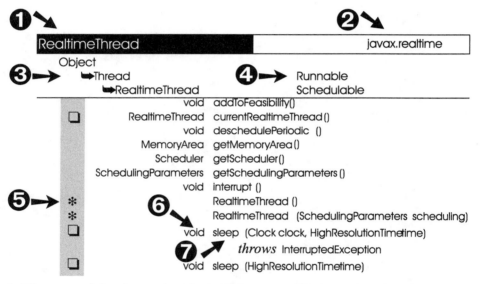

1. The name of the class or interface. If the name refers to an interface, its name is printed in *italics*.

2. The name of the package containing the class or interface.

3. The inheritance chain of superclasses. A class is a subclass of the one above it. Inheritance hierarchies for interfaces are not displayed, because interfaces can potentially inherit multiple superinterfaces.

4. The names of the interfaces implemented by the class to its left on the same line.

5. Icons that indicate modifiers or members. If the "protected" symbol does not appear, the member is public. Private and package-private members have no symbols and are not shown.

  ○ abstract
  ● final
  ❑ static
  ■ static final
  ◆ protected
  ✳ constructor
  ✍ field

6. The return type of a method or the declared type of a field. It is blank for constructors.

7. The name of the member. Members are sorted alphabetically. If it is a method, the parameter list and optional throws clause follows.

java.lang

ArithmeticException   java.lang

```
Object
  ➥Throwable
     ➥Exception
        ➥RuntimeException
           ➥ArithmeticException
```

❋	**ArithmeticException**()
❋	**ArithmeticException**(String s)

ArrayIndexOutOfBoundsException   java.lang

```
Object
  ➥Throwable
     ➥Exception
        ➥RuntimeException
           ➥IndexOutOfBoundsException
              ➥ArrayIndexOutOfBoundsException
```

❋	**ArrayIndexOutOfBoundsException**()
❋	**ArrayIndexOutOfBoundsException**(int index)
❋	**ArrayIndexOutOfBoundsException**(String s)

ArrayStoreException   java.lang

```
Object
  ➥Throwable
     ➥Exception
        ➥RuntimeException
           ➥ArrayStoreException
```

❋	**ArrayStoreException**()
❋	**ArrayStoreException**(String s)

Boolean   java.lang

```
Object
  ➡Boolean
```

✳	**Boolean**(boolean value)
boolean	**booleanValue**()
boolean	**equals**(Object obj)
int	**hashCode**()
String	**toString**()

Byte   java.lang

```
Object
  ➡Byte
```

✳	**Byte**(byte value)
byte	**byteValue**()
boolean	**equals**(Object obj)
int	**hashCode**()
byte	**MAX_VALUE**
byte	**MIN_VALUE**
byte	**parseByte**(String s)
	throws NumberFormatException
byte	**parseByte**(String s, int radix)
	throws NumberFormatException
String	**toString**()

Character   java.lang

```
Object
  ➡Character
```

✳	**Character**(char value)
char	**charValue**()
int	**digit**(char ch, int radix)
boolean	**equals**(Object obj)
int	**hashCode**()
boolean	**isDigit**(char ch)
boolean	**isLowerCase**(char ch)
boolean	**isUpperCase**(char ch)
int	**MAX_RADIX**
char	**MAX_VALUE**
int	**MIN_RADIX**
char	**MIN_VALUE**

	char **toLowerCase**(char ch)
	String **toString**()
	char **toUpperCase**(char ch)

Class   java.lang

Object
  ➥Class

	Class **forName**(String className)
	throws ClassNotFoundException
	String **getName**()
	java.io.Input-Stream **getResourceAsStream**(String name)
	boolean **isArray**()
	boolean **isAssignableFrom**(Class cls)
	boolean **isInstance**(Object obj)
	boolean **isInterface**()
	Object **newInstance**()
	throws InstantiationException, IllegalAccessException
	String **toString**()

ClassCastException   java.lang

Object
  ➥Throwable
    ➥Exception
      ➥RuntimeException
        ➥ClassCastException

	ClassCastException()
✳	**ClassCastException**(String s)

ClassNotFoundException   java.lang

Object
  ➥Throwable
    ➥Exception
      ➥ClassNotFoundException

	ClassNotFoundException()
✳	**ClassNotFoundException**(String s)

Error   java.lang

Object
  ➡Throwable
    ➡Error

✳	**Error**()
✳	**Error**(String s)

Exception   java.lang

Object
  ➡Throwable
    ➡Exception

✳	**Exception**()
✳	**Exception**(String s)

IllegalAccessException   java.lang

Object
  ➡Throwable
    ➡Exception
      ➡IllegalAccessException

✳	**IllegalAccessException**()
✳	**IllegalAccessException**(String s)

IllegalArgumentException   java.lang

Object
  ➡Throwable
    ➡Exception
      ➡RuntimeException
        ➡IllegalArgumentException

✳	**IllegalArgumentException**()
✳	**IllegalArgumentException**(String s)

IllegalMonitorStateEx-   java.lang
ception

Object
  ➡Throwable

➥Exception
   ➥RuntimeException
      ➥IllegalMonitorStateException

✳	**IllegalMonitorStateException**()
✳	**IllegalMonitorStateException**(String s)

IllegalThreadStateException   java.lang

Object
  ➥Throwable
    ➥Exception
      ➥RuntimeException
        ➥IllegalArgumentException
          ➥IllegalThreadStateException

✳	**IllegalThreadStateException**()
✳	**IllegalThreadStateException**(String s)

IndexOutOfBoundsException   java.lang

Object
  ➥Throwable
    ➥Exception
      ➥RuntimeException
        ➥IndexOutOfBoundsException

✳	**IndexOutOfBoundsException**()
✳	**IndexOutOfBoundsException**(String s)

InstantiationException   java.lang

Object
  ➥Throwable
    ➥Exception
      ➥InstantiationException

✳	**InstantiationException**()
✳	**InstantiationException**(String s)

Integer   java.lang

Object
   →Integer

	byte	**byteValue**()
	boolean	**equals**(Object obj)
	int	**hashCode**()
❋		**Integer**(int value)
	int	**intValue**()
	long	**longValue**()
✐■	int	**MAX_VALUE**
✐■	int	**MIN_VALUE**
❑	int	**parseInt**(String s)
		throws NumberFormatException
❑	int	**parseInt**(String s, int radix)
		throws NumberFormatException
	short	**shortValue**()
❑	String	**toBinaryString**(int i)
❑	String	**toHexString**(int i)
❑	String	**toOctalString**(int i)
	String	**toString**()
❑	String	**toString**(int i)
❑	String	**toString**(int i, int radix)
❑	Integer	**valueOf**(String s)
		throws NumberFormatException
❑	Integer	**valueOf**(String s, int radix)
		throws NumberFormatException

InterruptedException   java.lang

Object
   →Throwable
     →Exception
       →InterruptedException

❋	**InterruptedException**()
❋	**InterruptedException**(String s)

Long   java.lang

Object
   →Long

	boolean	**equals**(Object obj)
	int	**hashCode**()
❋		**Long**(long value)

```
          long longValue()
✎■        long MAX_VALUE
✎■        long MIN_VALUE
❑         long parseLong(String s)
                    throws NumberFormatException
❑         long parseLong(String s, int radix)
                    throws NumberFormatException
        String toString()
❑       String toString(long i)
❑       String toString(long i, int radix)
```

Math   java.lang

```
Object
  ➥Math
```

```
❑          int abs(int a)
❑         long abs(long a)
❑          int max(int a, int b)
❑         long max(long a, long b)
❑          int min(int a, int b)
❑         long min(long a, long b)
```

NegativeArraySizeException   java.lang

```
Object
  ➥Throwable
    ➥Exception
      ➥RuntimeException
        ➥NegativeArraySizeException
```

```
✳          NegativeArraySizeException()
✳          NegativeArraySizeException(String s)
```

NullPointerException   java.lang

```
Object
  ➥Throwable
    ➥Exception
      ➥RuntimeException
        ➥NullPointerException
```

```
✳          NullPointerException()
✳          NullPointerException(String s)
```

NumberFormatException   java.lang

```
Object
   ➡Throwable
      ➡Exception
         ➡RuntimeException
            ➡IllegalArgumentException
               ➡NumberFormatException
```

❈	**NumberFormatException**()
❈	**NumberFormatException**(String s)

Object   java.lang

```
Object
```

	boolean **equals**(Object obj)
●	Class **getClass**()
	int **hashCode**()
●	void **notify**()
●	void **notifyAll**()
❈	**Object**()
	String **toString**()
●	void **wait**() throws InterruptedException
●	void **wait**(long timeout)
	throws InterruptedException
●	void **wait**(long timeout, int nanos)
	throws InterruptedException

OutOfMemoryError   java.lang

```
Object
   ➡Throwable
      ➡Error
         ➡VirtualMachineError
            ➡OutOfMemoryError
```

❈	**OutOfMemoryError**()
❈	**OutOfMemoryError**(String s)

Runnable   java.lang

```
Runnable
```

	void **run**()

Runtime · java.lang

Object
　➡Runtime

	void	**exit**(int status)
	long	**freeMemory**()
	void	**gc**()
❏	Runtime	**getRuntime**()
	long	**totalMemory**()

RuntimeException · java.lang

Object
　➡Throwable
　　➡Exception
　　　➡RuntimeException

✳	**RuntimeException**()
✳	**RuntimeException**(String s)

SecurityException · java.lang

Object
　➡Throwable
　　➡Exception
　　　➡RuntimeException
　　　　➡SecurityException

✳	**SecurityException**()
✳	**SecurityException**(String s)

Short · java.lang

Object
　➡Short

	boolean	**equals**(Object obj)
	int	**hashCode**()
✐■	short	**MAX_VALUE**
✐■	short	**MIN_VALUE**
❏	short	**parseShort**(String s) throws NumberFormatException
❏	short	**parseShort**(String s, int radix) throws NumberFormatException
✳		**Short**(short value)
	short	**shortValue**()
	String	**toString**()

String	java.lang

Object
 ➡String

```
            char charAt(int index)
             int compareTo(String anotherString)
          String concat(String str)
         boolean endsWith(String suffix)
         boolean equals(Object anObject)
          byte[] getBytes()
          byte[] getBytes(String enc)
                    throws java.io.UnsupportedEncoding-
                    Exception
            void getChars(int srcBegin, int srcEnd,
                    char[] dst, int dstBegin)
             int hashCode()
             int indexOf(int ch)
             int indexOf(int ch, int fromIndex)
             int indexOf(String str)
             int indexOf(String str, int fromIndex)
             int lastIndexOf(int ch)
             int lastIndexOf(int ch, int fromIndex)
             int length()
         boolean regionMatches(boolean ignoreCase,
                    int toffset, String other,
                    int ooffset, int len)
          String replace(char oldChar, char newChar)
         boolean startsWith(String prefix)
         boolean startsWith(String prefix,
                    int toffset)
     *          String()
     *          String(byte[] bytes)
     *          String(byte[] bytes, int off, int len)
     *          String(byte[] bytes, int off, int len,
                    String enc)
                    throws java.io.UnsupportedEncoding-
                    Exception
     *          String(byte[] bytes, String enc)
                    throws java.io.UnsupportedEncoding-
                    Exception
     *          String(char[] value)
     *          String(char[] value, int offset,
                    int count)
     *          String(String value)
```

✳	**String**(StringBuffer buffer)
	String **substring**(int beginIndex)
	String **substring**(int beginIndex, int endIndex)
	char[] **toCharArray**()
	String **toLowerCase**()
	String **toString**()
	String **toUpperCase**()
	String **trim**()
❏	String **valueOf**(boolean b)
❏	String **valueOf**(char c)
❏	String **valueOf**(char[] data)
❏	String **valueOf**(char[] data, int offset, int count)
❏	String **valueOf**(int i)
❏	String **valueOf**(long l)
❏	String **valueOf**(Object obj)

StringBuffer   java.lang

```
Object
  ➥StringBuffer
```

StringBuffer	**append**(boolean b)
StringBuffer	**append**(char c)
StringBuffer	**append**(char[] str)
StringBuffer	**append**(char[] str, int offset, int len)
StringBuffer	**append**(int i)
StringBuffer	**append**(long l)
StringBuffer	**append**(Object obj)
StringBuffer	**append**(String str)
int	**capacity**()
char	**charAt**(int index)
StringBuffer	**delete**(int start, int end)
StringBuffer	**deleteCharAt**(int index)
void	**ensureCapacity**(int minimumCapacity)
void	**getChars**(int srcBegin, int srcEnd, char[] dst, int dstBegin)
StringBuffer	**insert**(int offset, boolean b)
StringBuffer	**insert**(int offset, char c)
StringBuffer	**insert**(int offset, char[] str)
StringBuffer	**insert**(int offset, int i)
StringBuffer	**insert**(int offset, long l)

	StringBuffer	**insert**(int offset, Object obj)
	StringBuffer	**insert**(int offset, String str)
	int	**length**()
	StringBuffer	**reverse**()
	void	**setCharAt**(int index, char ch)
	void	**setLength**(int newLength)
❊		**StringBuffer**()
❊		**StringBuffer**(int length)
❊		**StringBuffer**(String str)
	String	**toString**()

StringIndexOutOfBoundsException   java.lang

```
Object
  ➡Throwable
    ➡Exception
      ➡RuntimeException
        ➡IndexOutOfBoundsException
          ➡StringIndexOutOfBoundsException
```

❊	**StringIndexOutOfBoundsException**()
❊	**StringIndexOutOfBoundsException**(int index)
❊	**StringIndexOutOfBoundsException**(String s)

System   java.lang

```
Object
  ➡System
```

☐	void	**arraycopy**(Object src, int src_position, Object dst, int dst_position, int length)
☐	long	**currentTimeMillis**()
✍■	java.io.PrintStream	**err**
☐	void	**exit**(int status)
☐	void	**gc**()
☐	String	**getProperty**(String key)
☐	int	**identityHashCode**(Object x)
✍■	java.io.PrintStream	**out**

Thread · java.lang

```
Object
    ➥Thread                              Runnable
```

❏	int **activeCount**()
❏	Thread **currentThread**()
●	int **getPriority**()
●	boolean **isAlive**()
●	void **join**() throws InterruptedException
✎■	int **MAX_PRIORITY**
✎■	int **MIN_PRIORITY**
✎■	int **NORM_PRIORITY**
	void **run**()
●	void **setPriority**(int newPriority)
❏	void **sleep**(long millis) throws InterruptedException
	void **start**()
✳	**Thread**()
✳	**Thread**(Runnable target)
	String **toString**()
❏	void **yield**()

Throwable · java.lang

```
Object
    ➥Throwable
```

	String **getMessage**()
	void **printStackTrace**()
✳	**Throwable**()
✳	**Throwable**(String message)
	String **toString**()

VirtualMachineError · java.lang

```
Object
    ➥Throwable
        ➥Error
            ➥VirtualMachineError
```

✳	**VirtualMachineError**()
✳	**VirtualMachineError**(String s)

ByteArrayInputStream   java.io

```
Object
   ➥InputStream
      ➥ByteArrayInputStream
```

	int	**available**()
✍◆	byte[]	**buf**
✳		**ByteArrayInputStream**(byte[] buf)
✳		**ByteArrayInputStream**(byte[] buf, int offset, int length)
	void	**close**() throws IOException
✍◆	int	**count**
✍◆	int	**mark**
	void	**mark**(int readAheadLimit)
	boolean	**markSupported**()
✍◆	int	**pos**
	int	**read**()
	int	**read**(byte[] b, int off, int len)
	void	**reset**()
	long	**skip**(long n)

ByteArrayOutputStream   java.io

```
Object
   ➥OutputStream
      ➥ByteArrayOutputStream
```

✍◆	byte[]	**buf**
✳		**ByteArrayOutputStream**()
✳		**ByteArrayOutputStream**(int size)
	void	**close**() throws IOException
✍◆	int	**count**
	void	**reset**()
	int	**size**()
	byte[]	**toByteArray**()
	String	**toString**()
	void	**write**(byte[] b, int off, int len)
	void	**write**(int b)

DataInput   java.io

DataInput

```
   boolean readBoolean() throws IOException
      byte readByte() throws IOException
      char readChar() throws IOException
      void readFully(byte[] b)
               throws IOException
      void readFully(byte[] b, int off, int len)
               throws IOException
       int readInt() throws IOException
      long readLong() throws IOException
     short readShort() throws IOException
       int readUnsignedByte()
               throws IOException
       int readUnsignedShort()
               throws IOException
    String readUTF() throws IOException
       int skipBytes(int n) throws IOException
```

DataInputStream   java.io

Object
 →InputStream
    →DataInputStream   DataInput

```
         int available() throws IOException
        void close() throws IOException
※            DataInputStream(InputStream in)
✍◆ InputStream in
        void mark(int readlimit)
     boolean markSupported()
         int read() throws IOException
●       int read(byte[] b) throws IOException
●       int read(byte[] b, int off, int len)
               throws IOException
●    boolean readBoolean() throws IOException
●       byte readByte() throws IOException
●       char readChar() throws IOException
●       void readFully(byte[] b)
               throws IOException
●       void readFully(byte[] b, int off, int len)
               throws IOException
●        int readInt() throws IOException
```

●   long **readLong**() throws IOException
●   short **readShort**() throws IOException
●   int **readUnsignedByte**()
            throws IOException
●   int **readUnsignedShort**()
            throws IOException
● String **readUTF**() throws IOException
■ String **readUTF**(DataInput in)
            throws IOException
   void **reset**() throws IOException
   long **skip**(long n) throws IOException
●   int **skipBytes**(int n) throws IOException

DataOutput   java.io

DataOutput

   void **write**(byte[] b) throws IOException
   void **write**(byte[] b, int off, int len)
        throws IOException
   void **write**(int b) throws IOException
   void **writeBoolean**(boolean v)
        throws IOException
   void **writeByte**(int v) throws IOException
   void **writeChar**(int v) throws IOException
   void **writeChars**(String s) throws IOException
   void **writeInt**(int v) throws IOException
   void **writeLong**(long v) throws IOException
   void **writeShort**(int v) throws IOException
   void **writeUTF**(String str) throws IOException

DataOutputStream   java.io

Object
  ➥OutputStream
    ➥DataOutputStream   DataOutput

          void **close**() throws IOException
❋   **DataOutputStream**(OutputStream out)
          void **flush**() throws IOException
⚐◆   OutputStream **out**
          void **write**(byte[] b, int off, int len)
             throws IOException
          void **write**(int b) throws IOException
●   void **writeBoolean**(boolean v)
             throws IOException

●	void **writeByte**(int v) throws IOException
●	void **writeChar**(int v) throws IOException
●	void **writeChars**(String s) throws IOException
●	void **writeInt**(int v) throws IOException
●	void **writeLong**(long v) throws IOException
●	void **writeShort**(int v) throws IOException
●	void **writeUTF**(String str) throws IOException

EOFException   java.io

Object
   ➡Throwable
      ➡Exception
         ➡IOException
            ➡EOFException

✳	**EOFException**()
✳	**EOFException**(String s)

InputStream   java.io

Object
   ➡InputStream

	int **available**() throws IOException
	void **close**() throws IOException
✳	**InputStream**()
	void **mark**(int readlimit)
	boolean **markSupported**()
○	int **read**() throws IOException
	int **read**(byte[] b) throws IOException
	int **read**(byte[] b, int off, int len) throws IOException
	void **reset**() throws IOException
	long **skip**(long n) throws IOException

InputStreamReader   java.io

Object
   ➡Reader
      ➡InputStreamReader

	void **close**() throws IOException
✳	**InputStreamReader**(InputStream is)
✳	**InputStreamReader**(InputStream is, String enc) throws UnsupportedEncodingException

```
         void mark(int readAheadLimit)
              throws IOException
      boolean markSupported()
          int read() throws IOException
          int read(char[] cbuf, int off, int len)
              throws IOException
      boolean ready() throws IOException
         void reset() throws IOException
         long skip(long n) throws IOException
```

InterruptedIOException   java.io

```
Object
  ➥Throwable
     ➥Exception
        ➥IOException
           ➥InterruptedIOException
```

	int **bytesTransferred**
✳	**InterruptedIOException**()
✳	**InterruptedIOException**(String s)

IOException   java.io

```
Object
  ➥Throwable
     ➥Exception
        ➥IOException
```

✳	**IOException**()
✳	**IOException**(String s)

OutputStream   java.io

```
Object
  ➥OutputStream
```

	void **close**() throws IOException
	void **flush**() throws IOException
✳	**OutputStream**()
	void **write**(byte[] b) throws IOException
	void **write**(byte[] b, int off, int len)
	throws IOException
○	void **write**(int b) throws IOException

OutputStreamWriter   java.io

```
Object
  ➡Writer
     ➡OutputStreamWriter
```

	void	**close**() throws IOException
	void	**flush**() throws IOException
*		**OutputStreamWriter**(OutputStream os)
*		**OutputStreamWriter**(OutputStream os, String enc) throws UnsupportedEncodingException
	void	**write**(char[] cbuf, int off, int len) throws IOException
	void	**write**(int c) throws IOException
	void	**write**(String str, int off, int len) throws IOException

PrintStream   java.io

```
Object
  ➡OutputStream
     ➡PrintStream
```

	boolean	**checkError**()
	void	**close**()
	void	**flush**()
	void	**print**(boolean b)
	void	**print**(char c)
	void	**print**(char[] s)
	void	**print**(int i)
	void	**print**(long l)
	void	**print**(Object obj)
	void	**print**(String s)
	void	**println**()
	void	**println**(boolean x)
	void	**println**(char x)
	void	**println**(char[] x)
	void	**println**(int x)
	void	**println**(long x)
	void	**println**(Object x)
	void	**println**(String x)
*		**PrintStream**(OutputStream out)

♦	void **setError**()
	void **write**(byte[] buf, int off, int len)
	void **write**(int b)

Reader   java.io

Object
　→Reader

○	void **close**() throws IOException
⚒♦	Object **lock**
	void **mark**(int readAheadLimit)　throws IOException
	boolean **markSupported**()
	int **read**() throws IOException
	int **read**(char[] cbuf) throws IOException
○	int **read**(char[] cbuf, int off, int len)　throws IOException
✳♦	**Reader**()
✳♦	**Reader**(Object lock)
	boolean **ready**() throws IOException
	void **reset**() throws IOException
	long **skip**(long n) throws IOException

UnsupportedEncodingException   java.io

Object
　→Throwable
　　→Exception
　　　→IOException
　　　　→UnsupportedEncodingException

✳	**UnsupportedEncodingException**()
✳	**UnsupportedEncodingException**(String s)

UTFDataFormatException   java.io

Object
　→Throwable
　　→Exception
　　　→IOException
　　　　→UTFDataFormatException

✳	**UTFDataFormatException**()
✳	**UTFDataFormatException**(String s)

Writer	java.io

Object
   ➡Writer

○	void **close**() throws IOException
○	void **flush**() throws IOException
✍◆	Object **lock**
	void **write**(char[] cbuf) throws IOException
○	void **write**(char[] cbuf, int off, int len) throws IOException
	void **write**(int c) throws IOException
	void **write**(String str) throws IOException
	void **write**(String str, int off, int len) throws IOException
❊◆	**Writer**()
❊◆	**Writer**(Object lock)

Calendar   java.util

```
Object
    ➡Calendar
```

	boolean	**after**(Object when)
✍■	int	**AM**
✍■	int	**AM_PM**
✍■	int	**APRIL**
✍■	int	**AUGUST**
	boolean	**before**(Object when)
✳◆		**Calendar**()
✍■	int	**DATE**
✍■	int	**DAY_OF_MONTH**
✍■	int	**DAY_OF_WEEK**
✍■	int	**DECEMBER**
	boolean	**equals**(Object obj)
✍■	int	**FEBRUARY**
✍■	int	**FRIDAY**
●	int	**get**(int field)
❑	Calendar	**getInstance**()
❑	Calendar	**getInstance**(TimeZone zone)
●	Date	**getTime**()
◆	long	**getTimeInMillis**()
	TimeZone	**getTimeZone**()
✍■	int	**HOUR**
✍■	int	**HOUR_OF_DAY**
✍■	int	**JANUARY**
✍■	int	**JULY**
✍■	int	**JUNE**
✍■	int	**MARCH**
✍■	int	**MAY**
✍■	int	**MILLISECOND**
✍■	int	**MINUTE**
✍■	int	**MONDAY**
✍■	int	**MONTH**
✍■	int	**NOVEMBER**

🔖⬛	int	**OCTOBER**
🔖⬛	int	**PM**
🔖⬛	int	**SATURDAY**
🔖⬛	int	**SECOND**
🔖⬛	int	**SEPTEMBER**
●	void	**set**(int field, int value)
●	void	**setTime**(Date date)
◆	void	**setTimeInMillis**(long millis)
	void	**setTimeZone**(TimeZone value)
🔖⬛	int	**SUNDAY**
🔖⬛	int	**THURSDAY**
🔖⬛	int	**TUESDAY**
🔖⬛	int	**WEDNESDAY**
🔖⬛	int	**YEAR**

Date   java.util

Object
   ➡Date

❋		**Date**()
❋		**Date**(long date)
	boolean	**equals**(Object obj)
	long	**getTime**()
	int	**hashCode**()
	void	**setTime**(long time)

EmptyStackException   java.util

Object
   ➡Throwable
      ➡Exception
         ➡RuntimeException
            ➡EmptyStackException

❋	**EmptyStackException**()

Enumeration   java.util

Enumeration

boolean	**hasMoreElements**()
Object	**nextElement**()

Hashtable   `java.util`

```
Object
  ➥Hashtable
```

	void	**clear**()
	boolean	**contains**(Object value)
	boolean	**containsKey**(Object key)
	Enumeration	**elements**()
	Object	**get**(Object key)
✳		**Hashtable**()
✳		**Hashtable**(int initialCapacity)
	boolean	**isEmpty**()
	Enumeration	**keys**()
	Object	**put**(Object key, Object value)
◆	void	**rehash**()
	Object	**remove**(Object key)
	int	**size**()
	String	**toString**()

NoSuchElementException   `java.util`

```
Object
  ➥Throwable
    ➥Exception
      ➥RuntimeException
        ➥NoSuchElementException
```

✳	**NoSuchElementException**()
✳	**NoSuchElementException**(String s)

Random   `java.util`

```
Object
  ➥Random
```

◆	int	**next**(int bits)
	int	**nextInt**()
	long	**nextLong**()
✳		**Random**()
✳		**Random**(long seed)
	void	**setSeed**(long seed)

Stack   java.util

```
Object
  ➡Vector
     ➡Stack
```
	boolean **empty**()
	Object **peek**()
	Object **pop**()
	Object **push**(Object item)
	int **search**(Object o)
✳	**Stack**()

TimeZone   java.util

```
Object
  ➡TimeZone
```
❑	String[] **getAvailableIDs**()
❑	TimeZone **getDefault**()
	String **getID**()
○	int **getOffset**(int era, int year, int month, int day, int dayOfWeek, int millis)
○	int **getRawOffset**()
❑	TimeZone **getTimeZone**(String ID)
✳	**TimeZone**()
○	boolean **useDaylightTime**()

Vector   java.util

```
Object
  ➡Vector
```
	void **addElement**(Object obj)
	int **capacity**()
✍♦	int **capacityIncrement**
	boolean **contains**(Object elem)
	void **copyInto**(Object[] anArray)
	Object **elementAt**(int index)
✍♦	int **elementCount**
✍♦	Object[] **elementData**
	Enumeration **elements**()
	void **ensureCapacity**(int minCapacity)
	Object **firstElement**()
	int **indexOf**(Object elem)

```
      int indexOf(Object elem, int index)
     void insertElementAt(Object obj, int index)
  boolean isEmpty()
   Object lastElement()
      int lastIndexOf(Object elem)
      int lastIndexOf(Object elem, int index)
     void removeAllElements()
  boolean removeElement(Object obj)
     void removeElementAt(int index)
     void setElementAt(Object obj, int index)
     void setSize(int newSize)
      int size()
   String toString()
     void trimToSize()
*         Vector()
*         Vector(int initialCapacity)
*         Vector(int initialCapacity,
               int capacityIncrement)
```

javax.microedition.io

Connection	javax.microedition.io

Connection

void **close**() throws java.io.IOException

ConnectionNotFoundException	javax.microedition.io

Object
  ➡Throwable
    ➡Exception
      ➡java.io.IOException
        ➡ConnectionNotFoundException

✳	**ConnectionNotFoundException**()
✳	**ConnectionNotFoundException**(String s)

Connector	javax.microedition.io

Object
  ➡Connector

❏	Connection	**open**(String name)
		throws java.io.IOException
❏	Connection	**open**(String name, int mode)
		throws java.io.IOException
❏	Connection	**open**(String name, int mode,
		boolean timeouts)
		throws java.io.IOException
❏	java.io.Data-InputStream	**openDataInputStream**(String name)
		throws java.io.IOException
❏	java.io.Data-OutputStream	**openDataOutputStream**(String name)
		throws java.io.IOException
❏	java.io.Input-Stream	**openInputStream**(String name)
		throws java.io.IOException
❏	java.io.Output-Stream	**openOutputStream**(String name)
		throws java.io.IOException
✍▪	int	**READ**
✍▪	int	**READ_WRITE**
✍▪	int	**WRITE**

ContentConnection	**javax.microedition.io**
ContentConnection	StreamConnection

String **getEncoding**()
long **getLength**()
String **getType**()

Datagram	**javax.microedition.io**
Datagram	java.io.DataInput, java.io.DataOutput

String **getAddress**()
byte[] **getData**()
int **getLength**()
int **getOffset**()
void **reset**()
void **setAddress**(Datagram reference)
void **setAddress**(String addr)
        throws java.io.IOException
void **setData**(byte[] buffer, int offset, int len)
void **setLength**(int len)

DatagramConnection	**javax.microedition.io**
DatagramConnection	Connection

int **getMaximumLength**()
        throws java.io.IOException
int **getNominalLength**()
        throws java.io.IOException
Datagram **newDatagram**(byte[] buf, int size)
        throws java.io.IOException
Datagram **newDatagram**(byte[] buf, int size,
        String addr)
        throws java.io.IOException
Datagram **newDatagram**(int size)
        throws java.io.IOException
Datagram **newDatagram**(int size, String addr)
        throws java.io.IOException
void **receive**(Datagram dgram)
        throws java.io.IOException
void **send**(Datagram dgram)
        throws java.io.IOException

InputConnection	`javax.microedition.io`
InputConnection	Connection

java.io.DataInputStream	**openDataInputStream**()
	throws java.io.IOException
java.io.InputStream	**openInputStream**()
	throws java.io.IOException

OutputConnection	`javax.microedition.io`
OutputConnection	Connection

java.io.DataOutputStream	**openDataOutputStream**()
	throws java.io.IOException
java.io.OutputStream	**openOutputStream**()
	throws java.io.IOException

StreamConnection	`javax.microedition.io`
StreamConnection	InputConnection, OutputConnection

StreamConnectionNotifier	`javax.microedition.io`
StreamConnectionNotifier	Connection

StreamConnection	**acceptAndOpen**()
	throws java.io.IOException

MIDP Application Programming Interface

THIS appendix contains the application programming interface documentation in Almanac format for the MIDP. For a description of this format, refer to "Almanac Legend" on page 274.

Full MIDP javadocs with detailed comments are available in the *MIDP Specification* (see "Related Literature and Helpful Web Pages" on page xxii) or as part of the MIDP reference implementation software that can be downloaded from Sun's web site (`http://www.sun.com/software/communitysource/j2me/midp/`).

java.lang

IllegalStateException	java.lang

```
Object
  ➡Throwable
     ➡Exception
        ➡RuntimeException
           ➡IllegalStateException
```

✳	**IllegalStateException**()
✳	**IllegalStateException**(String s)

java.util

Timer — java.util

Object
  ➡Timer

void **cancel**()	
void **schedule**(TimerTask task, Date time)	
void **schedule**(TimerTask task, Date firstTime, long period)	
void **schedule**(TimerTask task, long delay)	
void **schedule**(TimerTask task, long delay, long period)	
void **scheduleAtFixedRate**(TimerTask task, Date firstTime, long period)	
void **scheduleAtFixedRate**(TimerTask task, long delay, long period)	
✳	**Timer**()

TimerTask — java.util

Object
  ➡TimerTask   Runnable

boolean **cancel**()	
○	void **run**()
long **scheduledExecutionTime**()	
✳◆	**TimerTask**()

313

javax.microedition.io

ContentConnection
   ➥HttpConnection

        String **GET**
          long **getDate**() throws java.io.IOException
          long **getExpiration**() throws java.io.IOException
        String **getFile**()
        String **getHeaderField**(int n)
              throws java.io.IOException
        String **getHeaderField**(String name)
              throws java.io.IOException
          long **getHeaderFieldDate**(String name, long def)
              throws java.io.IOException
          int **getHeaderFieldInt**(String name, int def)
              throws java.io.IOException
        String **getHeaderFieldKey**(int n)
              throws java.io.IOException
        String **getHost**()
          long **getLastModified**()
              throws java.io.IOException
          int **getPort**()
        String **getProtocol**()
        String **getQuery**()
        String **getRef**()
        String **getRequestMethod**()
        String **getRequestProperty**(String key)
          int **getResponseCode**()
              throws java.io.IOException
        String **getResponseMessage**()
              throws java.io.IOException
        String **getURL**()
        String **HEAD**
          int **HTTP_ACCEPTED**
          int **HTTP_BAD_GATEWAY**
          int **HTTP_BAD_METHOD**
          int **HTTP_BAD_REQUEST**
          int **HTTP_CLIENT_TIMEOUT**

```
        int HTTP_CONFLICT
        int HTTP_CREATED
        int HTTP_ENTITY_TOO_LARGE
        int HTTP_EXPECT_FAILED
        int HTTP_FORBIDDEN
        int HTTP_GATEWAY_TIMEOUT
        int HTTP_GONE
        int HTTP_INTERNAL_ERROR
        int HTTP_LENGTH_REQUIRED
        int HTTP_MOVED_PERM
        int HTTP_MOVED_TEMP
        int HTTP_MULT_CHOICE
        int HTTP_NO_CONTENT
        int HTTP_NOT_ACCEPTABLE
        int HTTP_NOT_AUTHORITATIVE
        int HTTP_NOT_FOUND
        int HTTP_NOT_IMPLEMENTED
        int HTTP_NOT_MODIFIED
        int HTTP_OK
        int HTTP_PARTIAL
        int HTTP_PAYMENT_REQUIRED
        int HTTP_PRECON_FAILED
        int HTTP_PROXY_AUTH
        int HTTP_REQ_TOO_LONG
        int HTTP_RESET
        int HTTP_SEE_OTHER
        int HTTP_TEMP_REDIRECT
        int HTTP_UNAUTHORIZED
        int HTTP_UNAVAILABLE
        int HTTP_UNSUPPORTED_RANGE
        int HTTP_UNSUPPORTED_TYPE
        int HTTP_USE_PROXY
        int HTTP_VERSION
     String POST
       void setRequestMethod(String method)
            throws java.io.IOException
       void setRequestProperty(String key,
            String value) throws java.io.IOException
```

javax.microedition.lcdui

Alert — javax.microedition.lcdui

```
Object
  ➭Displayable
      ➭Screen
          ➭Alert
```

	void **addCommand**(Command cmd)
❋	**Alert**(String title)
❋	**Alert**(String title, String alertText, Image alertImage, AlertType alertType)
✍■	int **FOREVER**
	int **getDefaultTimeout**()
	Image **getImage**()
	String **getString**()
	int **getTimeout**()
	AlertType **getType**()
	void **setCommandListener**(CommandListener l)
	void **setImage**(Image img)
	void **setString**(String str)
	void **setTimeout**(int time)
	void **setType**(AlertType type)

AlertType — javax.microedition.lcdui

```
Object
  ➭AlertType
```

✍■	AlertType **ALARM**
❋◆	**AlertType**()
✍■	AlertType **CONFIRMATION**
✍■	AlertType **ERROR**
✍■	AlertType **INFO**
	boolean **playSound**(Display display)
✍■	AlertType **WARNING**

317

Canvas   `javax.microedition.lcdui`

```
Object
    ➡Displayable
        ➡Canvas
```

✳◆		**Canvas**()
✍■	int	**DOWN**
✍■	int	**FIRE**
✍■	int	**GAME_A**
✍■	int	**GAME_B**
✍■	int	**GAME_C**
✍■	int	**GAME_D**
	int	**getGameAction**(int keyCode)
	int	**getHeight**()
	int	**getKeyCode**(int gameAction)
	String	**getKeyName**(int keyCode)
	int	**getWidth**()
	boolean	**hasPointerEvents**()
	boolean	**hasPointerMotionEvents**()
	boolean	**hasRepeatEvents**()
◆	void	**hideNotify**()
	boolean	**isDoubleBuffered**()
✍■	int	**KEY_NUM0**
✍■	int	**KEY_NUM1**
✍■	int	**KEY_NUM2**
✍■	int	**KEY_NUM3**
✍■	int	**KEY_NUM4**
✍■	int	**KEY_NUM5**
✍■	int	**KEY_NUM6**
✍■	int	**KEY_NUM7**
✍■	int	**KEY_NUM8**
✍■	int	**KEY_NUM9**
✍■	int	**KEY_POUND**
✍■	int	**KEY_STAR**
◆	void	**keyPressed**(int keyCode)
◆	void	**keyReleased**(int keyCode)
◆	void	**keyRepeated**(int keyCode)
✍■	int	**LEFT**
○◆	void	**paint**(Graphics g)
◆	void	**pointerDragged**(int x, int y)
◆	void	**pointerPressed**(int x, int y)
◆	void	**pointerReleased**(int x, int y)

●	void	**repaint**()
●	void	**repaint**(int x, int y, int width, int height)
✍■	int	**RIGHT**
●	void	**serviceRepaints**()
◆	void	**showNotify**()
✍■	int	**UP**

Choice   `javax.microedition.lcdui`

Choice

	int	**append**(String stringPart, Image imagePart)
	void	**delete**(int elementNum)
✍■	int	**EXCLUSIVE**
	Image	**getImage**(int elementNum)
	int	**getSelectedFlags**(boolean[] selected Array_return)
	int	**getSelectedIndex**()
	String	**getString**(int elementNum)
✍■	int	**IMPLICIT**
	void	**insert**(int elementNum, String stringPart, Image imagePart)
	boolean	**isSelected**(int elementNum)
✍■	int	**MULTIPLE**
	void	**set**(int elementNum, String stringPart, Image imagePart)
	void	**setSelectedFlags**(boolean[] selected Array)
	void	**setSelectedIndex**(int elementNum, boolean selected)
	int	**size**()

ChoiceGroup — javax.microedition.lcdui

```
Object
  ➥Item
    ➥ChoiceGroup                 Choice
```

	int	**append**(String stringPart, Image imagePart)
✻		**ChoiceGroup**(String label, int choiceType)
✻		**ChoiceGroup**(String label, int choiceType, String[] stringElements, Image[] imageElements)
	void	**delete**(int elementNum)
	Image	**getImage**(int elementNum)
	int	**getSelectedFlags**(boolean[] selected Array_return)
	int	**getSelectedIndex**()
	String	**getString**(int elementNum)
	void	**insert**(int elementNum, String stringElement, Image imageElement)
	boolean	**isSelected**(int elementNum)
	void	**set**(int elementNum, String stringPart, Image imagePart)
	void	**setSelectedFlags**(boolean[] selected Array)
	void	**setSelectedIndex**(int elementNum, boolean selected)
	int	**size**()

Command — javax.microedition.lcdui

```
Object
  ➥Command
```

✍■	int	**BACK**
✍■	int	**CANCEL**
✻		**Command**(String label, int commandType, int priority)
✍■	int	**EXIT**
	int	**getCommandType**()
	String	**getLabel**()
	int	**getPriority**()
✍■	int	**HELP**

```
✍■               int ITEM
✍■               int OK
✍■               int SCREEN
✍■               int STOP
```

CommandListener — javax.microedition.lcdui

```
CommandListener
                void commandAction(Command c,
                        Displayable d)
```

DateField — javax.microedition.lcdui

```
Object
   ➥Item
      ➥DateField
✍■                    int DATE
✍■                    int DATE_TIME
❊                         DateField(String label, int mode)
❊                         DateField(String label, int mode,
                              java.util.TimeZone timeZone)
           java.util.Date getDate()
                      int getInputMode()
                     void setDate(java.util.Date date)
                     void setInputMode(int mode)
✍■                    int TIME
```

Display — javax.microedition.lcdui

```
Object
   ➥Display
                   void callSerially(Runnable r)
            Displayable getCurrent()
❑               Display getDisplay(
                            javax.microedition.midlet.MIDlet m)
                boolean isColor()
                    int numColors()
                   void setCurrent(Alert alert,
                            Displayable nextDisplayable)
                   void setCurrent(Displayable nextDisplayable)
```

Displayable   javax.microedition.lcdui

```
Object
  ➥Displayable
```

void	**addCommand**(Command cmd)
boolean	**isShown**()
void	**removeCommand**(Command cmd)
void	**setCommandListener**(CommandListener l)

Font   javax.microedition.lcdui

```
Object
  ➥Font
```

int	**charsWidth**(char[] ch, int offset, int length)
int	**charWidth**(char ch)
int	**FACE_MONOSPACE**
int	**FACE_PROPORTIONAL**
int	**FACE_SYSTEM**
int	**getBaselinePosition**()
Font	**getDefaultFont**()
int	**getFace**()
Font	**getFont**(int face, int style, int size)
int	**getHeight**()
int	**getSize**()
int	**getStyle**()
boolean	**isBold**()
boolean	**isItalic**()
boolean	**isPlain**()
boolean	**isUnderlined**()
int	**SIZE_LARGE**
int	**SIZE_MEDIUM**
int	**SIZE_SMALL**
int	**stringWidth**(String str)
int	**STYLE_BOLD**
int	**STYLE_ITALIC**
int	**STYLE_PLAIN**
int	**STYLE_UNDERLINED**
int	**substringWidth**(String str, int offset, int len)

Form
javax.microedition.lcdui

```
Object
  ➥Displayable
    ➥Screen
      ➥Form
```

int	**append**(Image img)
int	**append**(Item item)
int	**append**(String str)
void	**delete**(int itemNum)
✳	**Form**(String title)
✳	**Form**(String title, Item[] items)
Item	**get**(int itemNum)
void	**insert**(int itemNum, Item item)
void	**set**(int itemNum, Item item)
void	**setItemStateListener**(ItemStateListener iListener)
int	**size**()

Gauge
javax.microedition.lcdui

```
Object
  ➥Item
    ➥Gauge
```

✳	**Gauge**(String label, boolean interactive, int maxValue, int initialValue)
int	**getMaxValue**()
int	**getValue**()
boolean	**isInteractive**()
void	**setMaxValue**(int maxValue)
void	**setValue**(int value)

Graphics
javax.microedition.lcdui

```
Object
  ➥Graphics
```

int	**BASELINE**
int	**BOTTOM**
void	**clipRect**(int x, int y, int width, int height)
int	**DOTTED**

```
       void drawArc(int x, int y, int width,
                int height, int startAngle,
                int arcAngle)
       void drawChar(char character, int x,
                int y, int anchor)
       void drawChars(char[] data, int offset,
                int length, int x, int y,
                int anchor)
       void drawImage(Image img, int x, int y,
                int anchor)
       void drawLine(int x1, int y1, int x2,
                int y2)
       void drawRect(int x, int y, int width,
                int height)
       void drawRoundRect(int x, int y,
                int width, int height,
                int arcWidth, int arcHeight)
       void drawString(String str, int x, int y,
                int anchor)
       void drawSubstring(String str,
                int offset, int len, int x, int y,
                int anchor)
       void fillArc(int x, int y, int width,
                int height, int startAngle,
                int arcAngle)
       void fillRect(int x, int y, int width,
                int height)
       void fillRoundRect(int x, int y,
                int width, int height,
                int arcWidth, int arcHeight)
        int getBlueComponent()
        int getClipHeight()
        int getClipWidth()
        int getClipX()
        int getClipY()
        int getColor()
       Font getFont()
        int getGrayScale()
        int getGreenComponent()
        int getRedComponent()
        int getStrokeStyle()
        int getTranslateX()
        int getTranslateY()
        int HCENTER
        int LEFT
```

✍■	int	**RIGHT**
	void	**setClip**(int x, int y, int width, int height)
	void	**setColor**(int RGB)
	void	**setColor**(int red, int green, int blue)
	void	**setFont**(Font font)
	void	**setGrayScale**(int value)
	void	**setStrokeStyle**(int style)
✍■	int	**SOLID**
✍■	int	**TOP**
	void	**translate**(int x, int y)
✍■	int	**VCENTER**

Image   javax.microedition.lcdui

Object
   ➡Image

❑	Image	**createImage**(byte[] imageData, int imageOffset, int imageLength)
❑	Image	**createImage**(Image source)
❑	Image	**createImage**(int width, int height)
❑	Image	**createImage**(String name) throws java.io.IOException
	Graphics	**getGraphics**()
	int	**getHeight**()
	int	**getWidth**()
	boolean	**isMutable**()

ImageItem   javax.microedition.lcdui

Object
   ➡Item
      ➡ImageItem

	String	**getAltText**()
	Image	**getImage**()
	int	**getLayout**()
✳		**ImageItem**(String label, Image img, int layout, String altText)
✍■	int	**LAYOUT_CENTER**
✍■	int	**LAYOUT_DEFAULT**
✍■	int	**LAYOUT_LEFT**
✍■	int	**LAYOUT_NEWLINE_AFTER**
✍■	int	**LAYOUT_NEWLINE_BEFORE**

```
                          int LAYOUT_RIGHT
                         void setAltText(String text)
                         void setImage(Image img)
                         void setLayout(int layout)
```

Item   javax.microedition.lcdui

```
Object
   ➥Item
```

```
                       String getLabel()
                         void setLabel(String label)
```

ItemStateListener   javax.microedition.lcdui

```
ItemStateListener
```

```
                         void itemStateChanged(Item item)
```

List   javax.microedition.lcdui

```
Object
   ➥Displayable
      ➥Screen
         ➥List                          Choice
```

```
                          int append(String stringPart,
                                  Image imagePart)
                         void delete(int elementNum)
                        Image getImage(int elementNum)
                          int getSelectedFlags(
                                  boolean[] selectedArray_return)
                          int getSelectedIndex()
                       String getString(int elementNum)
                         void insert(int elementNum,
                                  String stringPart, Image imagePart)
                      boolean isSelected(int elementNum)
                              List(String title, int listType)
                              List(String title, int listType,
                                  String[] stringElements,
                                  Image[] imageElements)
                      Command SELECT_COMMAND
                         void set(int elementNum, String stringPart,
                                  Image imagePart)
```

```
            void setSelectedFlags(
                        boolean[] selectedArray)
            void setSelectedIndex(int elementNum,
                        boolean selected)
             int size()
```

Screen   javax.microedition.lcdui

```
Object
  ➥Displayable
      ➥Screen
```

```
         Ticker getTicker()
         String getTitle()
           void setTicker(Ticker ticker)
           void setTitle(String s)
```

StringItem   javax.microedition.lcdui

```
Object
  ➥Item
      ➥StringItem
```

```
         String getText()
           void setText(String text)
    *             StringItem(String label, String text)
```

TextBox   javax.microedition.lcdui

```
Object
  ➥Displayable
      ➥Screen
          ➥TextBox
```

```
           void delete(int offset, int length)
            int getCaretPosition()
            int getChars(char[] data)
            int getConstraints()
            int getMaxSize()
         String getString()
           void insert(char[] data, int offset,
                        int length, int position)
           void insert(String src, int position)
           void setChars(char[] data, int offset,
                        int length)
           void setConstraints(int constraints)
            int setMaxSize(int maxSize)
```

```
      void setString(String text)
       int size()
  *        TextBox(String title, String text,
                     int maxSize, int constraints)
```

TextField   **javax.microedition.lcdui**

```
Object
  ➥Item
     ➥TextField
```

✎■	int **ANY**
✎■	int **CONSTRAINT_MASK**
	void **delete**(int offset, int length)
✎■	int **EMAILADDR**
	int **getCaretPosition**()
	int **getChars**(char[] data)
	int **getConstraints**()
	int **getMaxSize**()
	String **getString**()
	void **insert**(char[] data, int offset, int length, int position)
	void **insert**(String src, int position)
✎■	int **NUMERIC**
✎■	int **PASSWORD**
✎■	int **PHONENUMBER**
	void **setChars**(char[] data, int offset, int length)
	void **setConstraints**(int constraints)
	int **setMaxSize**(int maxSize)
	void **setString**(String text)
	int **size**()
*	**TextField**(String label, String text, int maxSize, int constraints)
✎■	int **URL**

Ticker   **javax.microedition.lcdui**

```
Object
  ➥Ticker
```

```
     String getString()
      void setString(String str)
  *        Ticker(String str)
```

javax.microedition.midlet

MIDlet	javax.microedition.midlet

```
Object
   ➥MIDlet
```

○◆	void **destroyApp**(boolean unconditional)
	throws MIDletStateChangeException
●	String **getAppProperty**(String key)
✳◆	**MIDlet**()
●	void **notifyDestroyed**()
●	void **notifyPaused**()
○◆	void **pauseApp**()
●	void **resumeRequest**()
○◆	void **startApp**()
	throws MIDletStateChangeException

MIDletStateChangeException	javax.microedition.midlet

```
Object
   ➥Throwable
      ➥Exception
         MIDletStateChangeException
```

✳	**MIDletStateChangeException**()
✳	**MIDletStateChangeException**(String s)

javax.microedition.rms

InvalidRecordIDException — javax.microedition.rms

```
Object
  ➥Throwable
    ➥Exception
      ➥RecordStoreException
        ➥InvalidRecordIDException
```

❋	**InvalidRecordIDException**()
❋	**InvalidRecordIDException**(String message)

RecordComparator — javax.microedition.rms

RecordComparator

	int **compare**(byte[] rec1, byte[] rec2)
✎◼	int **EQUIVALENT**
✎◼	int **FOLLOWS**
✎◼	int **PRECEDES**

RecordEnumeration — javax.microedition.rms

RecordEnumeration

void	**destroy**()
boolean	**hasNextElement**()
boolean	**hasPreviousElement**()
boolean	**isKeptUpdated**()
void	**keepUpdated**(boolean keepUpdated)
byte[]	**nextRecord**()
	throws InvalidRecordIDException, RecordStoreNotOpenException, RecordStoreException
int	**nextRecordId**()
	throws InvalidRecordIDException
int	**numRecords**()
byte[]	**previousRecord**()
	throws InvalidRecordIDException, RecordStoreNotOpenException, RecordStoreException

```
                      int previousRecordId()
                              throws InvalidRecordIDException
                     void rebuild()
                     void reset()
```

RecordFilter	**javax.microedition.rms**

RecordFilter

```
        boolean matches(byte[] candidate)
```

RecordListener	**javax.microedition.rms**

RecordListener

```
              void recordAdded(RecordStore recordStore,
                      int recordId)
              void recordChanged(RecordStore recordStore,
                      int recordId)
              void recordDeleted(RecordStore recordStore,
                      int recordId)
```

RecordStore	**javax.microedition.rms**

Object
  ➡RecordStore

```
           int addRecord(byte[] data, int offset,
                      int numBytes)
                      throws RecordStoreNotOpenException, Record-
                      StoreException, RecordStoreFullException
          void addRecordListener(RecordListener listener)
          void closeRecordStore()
                      throws RecordStoreNotOpenException, Record-
                      StoreException
          void deleteRecord(int recordId)
                      throws RecordStoreNotOpenException,
                      InvalidRecordIDException,
                      RecordStoreException
    ❑     void deleteRecordStore(String recordStoreName)
                      throws RecordStoreException,
                      RecordStoreNotFoundException
       Record- enumerateRecords(RecordFilter filter,
       Enum-        RecordComparator comparator,
       eration      boolean keepUpdated)
                      throws RecordStoreNotOpenException
          long getLastModified()
                      throws RecordStoreNotOpenException
        String getName() throws RecordStoreNotOpenException
```

```
          int getNextRecordID()
                  throws RecordStoreNotOpenException,
                  RecordStoreException
          int getNumRecords()
                  throws RecordStoreNotOpenException
       byte[] getRecord(int recordId)
                  throws RecordStoreNotOpenException,
                  InvalidRecordIDException,
                  RecordStoreException
          int getRecord(int recordId, byte[] buffer,
                  int offset)
                  throws RecordStoreNotOpenException,
                  InvalidRecordIDException,
                  RecordStoreException
          int getRecordSize(int recordId)
                  throws RecordStoreNotOpenException,
                  InvalidRecordIDException,
                  RecordStoreException
          int getSize() throws RecordStoreNotOpenException
          int getSizeAvailable()
                  throws RecordStoreNotOpenException
          int getVersion()
                  throws RecordStoreNotOpenException
```
❑   `String[] listRecordStores()`
❑   `Record- openRecordStore(String recordStoreName,`
```
       Store     boolean createIfNecessary)
                  throws RecordStoreException, RecordStore-
                  FullException, RecordStoreNotFoundException
         void removeRecordListener(
                  RecordListener listener)
         void setRecord(int recordId, byte[] newData,
                  int offset, int numBytes)
                  throws RecordStoreNotOpenException,
                  InvalidRecordIDException, RecordStore-
                  Exception, RecordStoreFullException
```

RecordStoreException   javax.microedition.rms

```
Object
    ➡Throwable
       ➡Exception
          ➡RecordStoreException
```
✳   **RecordStoreException**()
✳   **RecordStoreException**(String message)

RecordStoreFullException   javax.microedition.rms

```
Object
  ➥Throwable
    ➥Exception
      ➥RecordStoreException
        ➥RecordStoreFullException
```

✳	**RecordStoreFullException**()
✳	**RecordStoreFullException**(String message)

RecordStoreNotFoundException   javax.microedition.rms

```
Object
  ➥Throwable
    ➥Exception
      ➥RecordStoreException
        ➥RecordStoreNotFoundException
```

✳	**RecordStoreNotFoundException**()
✳	**RecordStoreNotFoundException**(String message)

RecordStoreNotOpenException   javax.microedition.rms

```
Object
  ➥Throwable
    ➥Exception
      ➥RecordStoreException
        ➥RecordStoreNotOpenException
```

✳	**RecordStoreNotOpenException**()
✳	**RecordStoreNotOpenException**(String message)

Index

P

The Java™ Series

ISBN 0-201-70433-1

ISBN 0-201-31005-8

ISBN 0-201-70323-8

ISBN 0-201-70393-9

ISBN 0-201-74622-0

ISBN 0-201-48558-3

ISBN 0-201-43299-4

ISBN 0-201-75282-4

ISBN 0-201-75484-3

ISBN 0-201-71623-2

ISBN 0-201-31002-3

ISBN 0-201-31003-1

ISBN 0-201-48552-4

ISBN 0-201-71102-8

ISBN 0-201-70329-7

ISBN 0-201-30955-6

ISBN 0-201-31000-7

ISBN 0-201-31008-2

ISBN 0-201-63456-2

ISBN 0-201-70277-0

ISBN 0-201-31009-0

ISBN 0-201-70502-8

ISBN 0-201-32577-2

ISBN 0-201-43294-3

ISBN 0-201-70267-3

ISBN 0-201-74627-1

ISBN 0-201-70456-0

ISBN 0-201-71041-2

ISBN 0-201-43321-4

ISBN 0-201-43328-1

ISBN 0-201-70969-4

ISBN 0-201-72617-3

Please see our web site (http://www.awl.com/cseng/javaseries)
for more information on these titles.

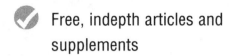
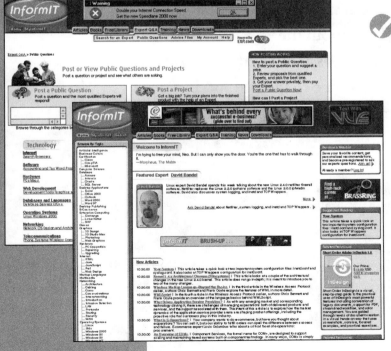
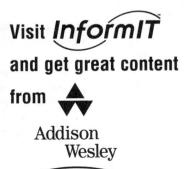